MW01702488

FOR OUR DEAR FRIEND,
HOPE YOU ENJOY!

HUCKSTER

MY LIFE AS AN AD MAN

RON ELGIN

Huckster

Cover & Bio Photos: Michael Nally, michaelnalleyphotography.com
Cover & Interior Design: Fusion Creative Works, fusioncw.com
Primary Editor: Tyler R. Tichelaar

Library of Congress Control Number: 2014907045
ISBN: 978-1-938686-96-2

Published by Aviva Publishing
Lake Placid, NY, USA
Tel: 518-523-1320
www.avivapubs.com

AVIVA PUBLISHING

Printed in the United States of America

DEDICATION

To the hundreds of dedicated employees who made the agency such a wonderful place over our three decade life and the dozens of great clients who enabled its success.

Most of all, I dedicate this book, as I have my life, to Beautiful Bonnie for her endless efforts to make me into a better person. Don't give up on me yet, babe; I'll try even harder during our next 45 years together.

CONTENTS

FOREWORD

The agency world can be brutal. The barrier to entry is low, but the barrier to building a successful, long sustained agency is extremely high.

It's a talent business—dependent entirely on the people who make up the agency. The most successful agencies are made up of the most talented individuals—with egos to match. The only things sold are ideas. And ideas are fleeting—changed daily as the context of culture, the marketplace, and consumers constantly evolve. Agencies, therefore, are in a continual state of innovation and creation, recreating the wheel daily for their clients. Leading an agency while molding a phenomenal culture that fuels it all into a perfect balance is no small feat.

Outside of the agency it's even crazier. Competition among agencies for clients and talent is beyond fierce. Client relations is an art unto itself with the average agency client relationship lasting no longer than three years.

And it's within this dynamic that Ron Elgin thrived—growing his agency to a quarter of a billion dollars in revenue.

Some of the nation's biggest brand names were among Ron's longest tenured clients, many lasting more than two decades.

In an agency world of dynamic personalities, Ron stands alone. There is truly no one like him.

His tailored suits and hundreds of ties. His house and wine cellar. His hair. His Bentley, which cost more than my first house. He does nothing to fit in—everything about him stands out.

That's what people see on the outside. In contrast to the flash is a man of immense insight, kindness, and generosity.

I joined Elgin Syferd in the mid-90s as an account executive. In my fourth month on the job, I was fortunate to bring in a high profile client. My phone rang the afternoon after receiving the news that the client was coming on board. I saw Ron's name on the caller ID. I had only met him on my first day, and I had received the occasional head nod and smile in the hallway. His personality was larger than life, and I was intimidated. When I saw his name, I was nervous to pick up. He was calling to congratulate me on the win and to tell me how important the win was for the agency. I was thrilled with the call, but I told my wife that night, "I think he was just 'PR'ing' me with the importance to the agency thing."

In the latter part of the '90s, I left Elgin-Syferd to take on new opportunities. After a stint managing international PR for The Boeing Company's presence in Europe, and managing a PR division for Intel's new online services initiative, I rejoined what was now DDB. Ron's agency had been acquired by DDB, one of the largest advertising agencies in the world, and he was serving as the CEO in Seattle.

On an afternoon in 2005, I received a call from Ron's assistant saying Ron wanted me to join him for lunch at The Met, a famous steakhouse in Seattle and just a two-block walk from our downtown office on Second and Madison. Even though it had been nearly ten years since I got that first call from Ron, and I was at this point an account director in his firm, I contemplated asking his assistant whether I could meet him at the restaurant so I could avoid the walk. I was fearful I wouldn't be able to hold an insightful conversation with him covering the two-block walk, the lunch, and the walk back. I was still intimidated.

We had a great lunch. Toward the end, Ron told me if the PR group's managing director ever left, he would appoint me the head of the group. I told my wife that night, "It was a really great conversation, but I think he was just 'PR'ing' me with the head of the PR group thing."

In 2007, Tom Phillips, the head of DDB PR and a good friend, left DDB to head up communications for a division within Microsoft. I found out Tom was leaving early in the morning, and I was offered the opportunity to take over Tom's role later that afternoon.

A few months later, I was sitting in Ron's office for my monthly one-on-one meeting with him where we'd go over status. I told him, "You know, I always thought you were just being nice to me when you said you were going to appoint me to head the group if Tom ever left." He said, "You should know two things: I'll never lie to you, and I'm not nice."

The year before I left the agency, we had a leadership team meeting in the main conference room over lunch and people brought in whatever they wanted to eat. I had gone down to the little Mexican food place in the bottom of our building to get a burrito. It was huge. And when I sat down next to Ron, he leaned over and said, "Are you going to eat that?! That fuckin' thing is bigger than my…arm." I laughed and said, "I thought you were going to say something else." He smiled and said, "I told you I'd never lie to you."

He did lie, though. He has been nothing but beyond nice—truly kind—to me ever since. Ron has turned into my most trusted mentor.

In 2010, I started an agency called "Curator." Ron allowed me and my team to have free office space for our first year, and when we moved into our new building, he sent furniture. Just about every month since then, we have lunch at Il Terrazzo Carmine's in Pioneer Square, just a couple of blocks from our office, and we talk about our families and business. I very much look forward to those walks now.

He starts the business portion by saying, "Don't bullshit me. How are you doing? How are your numbers?" The conversations have been invaluable. At our first lunch after I started Curator, he focused solely on the art and importance of delegation. I never knew the story behind why he was so adamant that we start there—you'll be able to read the reason behind that later in the book.

Ron has sent clients Curator's way, and while I've loved partnering with him from time to time, and being in meetings with him to hear how he finesses an issue with a client, it's his mentorship and friendship I covet most. When I'm entering unchartered territory for me at the agency, I call Ron and he shares his advice. When I have a pressing client issue or I need a quick sounding board, I call him. He always makes time.

A few years ago, he was given a Lifetime Achievement Award at the Addy's. All the other heads of agencies who got up to share a story essentially said the same thing: In our hyper-competitive field, Ron stands out for both his success and his desire to make others successful.

Successful multi-decade businesses don't just happen. Being married to a woman far outside your league for forty-five years and building a beautiful family doesn't just happen.

Ron is an anomaly. He's driven, charismatic, flashy, over-the-top, and wildly successful. And, under it all, it's his kindness and humor you fall in love with most.

I love the title of this book. Perhaps Ron could be viewed as a Huckster by those who only know him in passing. From the outside looking in, he concurred an agency world full of the smartest and most dynamic marketers. People probably assume you have to be a bit of a *Huckster* to do that. But, from the inside, and as you'll learn in this book, it's just perception.

Nobody tells a story like Ron Elgin. I'm convinced it's one of the reasons so many business leaders want to spend time with him as clients. If you're someone in the agency business or you work in communications on the client side, you'll love the insights in this book. No matter what field you're in, you'll love the life lessons, and above all else, the way Ron tells the story.

Now, in this book you get to hear the stories and business advice I've been laughing at and soaking in at Carmine's.

Enjoy.

— Scott Battishill, founder, Curator

1.

THE BEGINNING

"I have an idea; let's start our own agency!"

That was Dave Syferd talking to me over beer and chips at a Mexican dive in late 1980.

"You're fucking nuts," I replied. "That's a really stupid idea."

I asked the cute waitress to bring us more beers. "And bring some tequila, too. My friend has lost his mind."

A couple of weeks later, Dave and I were at the same watering hole having beer and chips again.

"Have you given any further thought to my idea?" asked Dave.

"Hell no," I replied. "Why would I even consider such an idiotic, goofball idea? I'm an executive vice president at the biggest advertising agency in the entire Pacific Northwest. I'm also head of all their disciplines other than traditional advertising. And I make a shit-pot of money."

"But—" started Dave.

"But nothing, asshole. We just sold Cole & Weber to Ogilvy, who backed up an armored car and started throwing money at us. The company even gave me a new car—a Cadillac no less. We just bought a big house on the lake, and for the first time in my life, I have a few extra bucks in the bank. And you want me to sacrifice any or all of that to start a new business with you? I'll say it again: You're fucking nuts."

"Besides," I continued before he could interrupt, "you're a PR guy. I have lots of PR guys who work for me. Why in hell would I want to go into business with one?"

Dave simply sat there and smiled at me for a couple of minutes. "If you're done ranting, asshole, I'll tell you. There are plenty of reasons. But I'll start with why I want to start my own company. One, although I like my job, I want to get back to doing agency work. I guess I'm just not cut out for corporate life. I've been talking with some of my peers and a few of them feel the same way." Dave was head of corporate communications for the region's second largest financial institution.

"Then start a PR shop with them," I urged.

"I thought of that, but when I looked into the financial side, it seems that ad agencies make more money. Look, I know you don't give a shit about what I want. But I know you pretty well, and I know what really drives you. You want to do better than just making a shit-pot of money. You want to be rich. Really rich. Come on, Ron; face it—you're never going to be that kind of rich working for the man. You need to help create your own thing, grow the hell out of it, and take it public or sell it to someone for really big money. That's my main pitch, but you'll also care about the second, third, and fourth reasons because they're also about you. You like your job, but not your bosses; you really do want to be an entrepreneur, but you're afraid to get off your ass to do anything about it; and at thirty-nine, you're running out of time. Once you hit forty, your golden handcuffs will be near impossible to remove."

"You forgot to add that I'm arrogant enough to think that I could do it successfully."

"No, I was getting to that, but you interrupted me. Seriously, you bring up a really good point. You couldn't possibly do this on your own."

"Why do you think that?" I asked.

"I'm a really nice guy and you're an asshole. So, you need me."

I hated to admit it, but Dave had made some really good points. I didn't completely agree with his last remark, but I had to agree he was a much nicer guy than I was. What really hit home though was the part about getting rich.

Dave had always dreamed of retiring before age fifty, so he could buy a bookstore on the top of a mountain with no front door. I imagined continuing to work until 100, but with enough money in the bank to say, "Fuck you" to anyone, anytime. Dave was right; we couldn't get there by working for the man all our lives. He had convinced me. If we were going to get rich, we'd have to do it on our own. We weren't sure how long it would take to reach our goal, but from that point on, we were determined to make it happen.

2.

A LITTLE BACKGROUND

For years, friends and associates have said that they've enjoyed hearing stories about my experiences in and around the advertising business and suggested I write a book. I resisted, thinking that if anyone wanted to read about the ad biz, they'd rather read the thoughts and ruminations of someone from one of the ad meccas like New York. But then I was reminded that while Seattle may not be the biggest market, it's definitely one of the coolest. After all, Seattle was the birthplace of the Grunge Movement: Jimi Hendrix, Nirvana, Pearl Jam, and Sound Garden; Microsoft, Starbucks, Nordstrom, and Amazon; the most educated populace in the nation; home to a half-dozen self-made billionaires; and much more. Don't get me wrong; I'm not putting myself in any of those categories, but when I entered the business, I figured, as Frank Sinatra would have said, "If I can make it there, I'll make it anywhere."

The result was that Dave and I did go into business together, and our agency had the most successful thirty-year run of any agency in the history of this ultra-cool city. No agency in modern times had climbed to the top faster or stayed there longer. Perhaps success in Seattle did give me at least a modicum of credibility. Bolstered by that fact, I kicked around the idea of writing a "How To" book to help others succeed in this fascinating business irrespective of where they chose to ply the profession. That is, I kicked around the idea for a few days until I remembered why I had never been a huge fan of "How To" books. Although my experience was limited, those I had read were too much like work. So being a creative guy, I decided to write a textbook that was both helpful and fun to read. After pounding out an outline for the first dozen chapters, I sent it to Jan Edmondson, a close friend. Actually, he's way more than that. He worked with me for about twenty years and retired as vice chairman of our company. He's very smart, a great writer, and not afraid to tell me when I'm being stupid.

"Ron, you're being stupid," he said. "A textbook on advertising written by you would never get off the shelves." He suggested that instead I write a true-life "womb to tomb" story about my career in advertising. "The very idea that Ron Elgin could become a success at anything is not just funny," he said. "It is fucking hilarious." I told you he was smart.

So you won't find chapters in this book promising to teach you the secrets of becoming a great presenter, or showing you the formula for guaranteed financial success, or giving you tips on client retention, or even a diagram showing how to button your fly. Instead, I'm going to share with you stories. True stories—well, at least how I remember them. Anyway, my hope is that perhaps through this collection of bizarre but true stories, you can learn from my mistakes, benefit from when we did get it right, and most of all, just have fun reading about an incredible magic carpet ride.

3.

LET'S DO IT

By the time we opened our doors on June 15, 1981, Dave and I had added another partner and two full-time employees. My wife, the Beautiful Bonnie, agreed to be our part-time bookkeeper in addition to working her full-time job. Oh, and I paid our eight-year-old daughter, Alison, a dollar to art direct and execute a sign for the front door declaring us "Elgin Kirkland Syferd." We opened with no clients and no clue about being the owners of a company. Before calling it quits on December 31, 2011, the agency had soared to 200-plus people with a quarter of a billion dollars in billings and significant national recognition. As Jan pointed out, I became living proof that you don't have to be a genius to be successful.

Well, we definitely weren't "Bill Gates" successful. Maybe not even "Bernie the Plumber" successful. But we did pretty well. Here's a snapshot of some of our successes:

- Before we started, Dave and I counted up every company that could be even remotely considered a competitor: ad agencies, PR firms, design shops, direct companies, literally anyone from whom we might be able to steal a buck or two of revenue. There were 252 in the phone book. That put us at 253rd. Within twenty years, we had kicked, scratched, and clawed our way to the very top of the heap.

- We earned an international reputation for client longevity. Two examples: McDonald's for thirty years and Holland America Line for twenty-eight. The worldwide average is four-and-a-half years.
- We became damn good at making money. We lost a few bucks once, but we more than made up for it every other year. In fact, many knowledgeable money types claimed we were a model for financial management in the agency world. Others said our luck trumped our skills. All we knew or cared was that the steady stream of profit meant a lot in terms of decent salaries, bonuses, and a very generous selling price. Whether we were lucky or good—who gives a shit?
- We won enough creative awards to keep our egos inflated, but we were also smart enough to know our primary goal was to help make our clients' cash registers ring. That meant the awards most people in the company coveted were the American Marketing Association's Effies. In 2005, we won more Effies than any other agency in America. Our other years were pretty productive, too.
- In 1984, *Washington CEO Magazine* ranked us as the best small company (less than 100 employees) in the state. The following year, our employee count put us in

the mid-sized company category (more than 100, but less than 1,000). It took us three more years to top that poll. A key component of the ranking was the opinion of current and former employees.

4.

IDEA CENTRIC: CHANNEL AGNOSTIC

The best way to start an agency is to have one or more accounts willing to roll the dice with you. An even better way is to have a very rich uncle who needs a big tax write-off. Unfortunately, we had neither. So we had to start the old-fashioned way by networking and dialing for dollars.

When we weren't on the phone chasing leads or trying to make appointments, we found ourselves trying to justify the decision of having given up our salaries. We told each other how cool it was to be our own bosses; how exciting it was to be building a company from the ground up; how neat it was to be in a place where we looked forward to showing up in the morning and dreaded leaving at night. We actually became so good at justifying that we started to trivialize things like: How are we going to pay our mortgages? Feed our families? Buy beer? So putting those concerns aside, we began addressing serious issues.

One of the first was for us to figure out what kind of agency we wanted to be. Seriously, did we want to build a creative powerhouse, or become research/strategy/account management driven, or be an ad shop with PR, or a PR shop that could do ads, or one of those "We can do everything and anything" places? At the same time, we knew it would take more than just wanting to be something; we had to pick one and then put some meat on the bone. We needed a differentiator that was true to our core; that we could emotionally embrace and physically create and live with for the long-haul. The great twentieth century Spanish philosopher José Ortega y Gasset counseled that "The first act of any society is the selection of a point of view." It was with that in mind that we set out to find our primary differentiator.

In the late 1970s, Ed Ney, Chairman Emeritus of the venerable Young & Rubicam marketing and communications company, introduced what was called the "whole egg theory." Basically, it was the idea of integrating solutions to marketing communications challenges. At the time, the notion commonly inspired outsider comments ranging from "No kidding" to "They've got to be kidding." While this may not have been a perfect or even workable concept on a macro level, we felt that because of our ownership structure, we might be able to make it work in our market.

I grew up in an age where most advertising agencies didn't just claim to do everything—they really did do everything. Advertising? That's us! Direct marketing? Of, course! Graphic design? Sure! Public relations? While you wait! With this model, the agency's client contact person accepted the job and simply assigned the "non-advertising" task either to someone who had a working knowledge of the discipline or the least skilled ad person. The latter were people who could afford to be spared from the more important "advertising-only" assignments. A slightly more sophisticated model was to create separate internal groups or outside affiliates to represent the various disciplines. In those cases, the brief was simply to execute the advertising idea in a different discipline. The third model was to create relationships with firms highly regarded within their own disciplines. Of the three, the latter usually yielded the best results for the clients, but it was far and away the most difficult for the typical advertising agency to digest. Not only would the good firms not "do as they were told," but the agency was usually conflicted because of: 1) concern the "outside" firm might embarrass the agency and hurt the client relationship; 2) worry that the work wouldn't look like the agency's and the campaign would become fragmented and disjointed; and 3) fear the "outside" firm would perform too well and the agency would become superfluous.

Although Dave and I came from different disciplines, we both believed that the idea is paramount, and therefore, agreed our agency would be idea centric and channel agnostic—the idea would always determine the discipline or media to be used. The manner in which we would arrive at the idea would break from tradition. We would bring together the best and the brightest from different disciplines as equal partners. Not until the idea materialized would the channel or channels be selected. Although we anticipated more than one channel would be selected, we'd never initially decide which discipline would play the major role, initiate the campaign, or have the payoff role. The other major difference would be that we'd not only allow but encourage each discipline to interpret the idea in a manner most appropriate to its medium.

In our situation, even though in my heart of hearts I believed advertising was the cure to all the world's ills, I could not dictate an ad-only solution because Dave had an equal voice. Nor could he shove a PR-only solution up my ass.

Sounded good. Even looked good on paper. We were ready to find out whether it actually worked.

5.

ONLY ONE ASSHOLE ALLOWED

Dave truly is and always has been a really nice person. I was never as nice, even before I became an asshole at an early age.

"Wouldn't it be great if we could have a company that was always as nice as I am and you try to be?" pondered Dave. He knew that because I had worked in a hostile environment for so many years, I had such a deep appreciation for nice that sometimes I tried to be like him—not often, but sometimes.

That was the point at which we began talking seriously about the culture we wanted to create. We knew that a company's culture could be one of its main differentiators. Not that we would in any way abandon the Idea Centric: Channel Agnostic philosophy, but that philosophy was what we'd do; our culture was what we'd be.

Our first conversations about culture centered on the idea of family. Fortunately, we both had great ones to use as models. We decided to try to create an office environment that fostered that same family atmosphere; a place where people could feel comfortable expressing themselves without fear of reprisal; a place where people scorned politics in favor of helping team members. It may sound corny, but we wanted a place where people loved and respected one another. A place where we would not tolerate people, irrespective of their talent or experience, who were bullies, office politicians, empire builders, connivers, or who treated others without the respect or dignity every person rightfully deserves. A nice family place where it would be okay to shoot anyone who acted like an asshole. I saw that as an incentive to try more often to be like Dave.

We also talked about the effect bad clients had on the mental state and overall morale of employees. We'd both worked at places that had clients you'd kill for and clients you'd pay to kill. At minimum, a bad client always results in a few sour attitudes in the shop. Left unchecked, the inevitable result was an unhappy place, the loss of good people, and the probable loss of the asshole client anyway.

We sat around one night trying to think of the best way to communicate this epiphany. We remembered a dinner conversation we'd had with Bob Truex, CEO of Rainier Bank, who was Dave's former boss, my client, and a great friend to both of us. During dinner, we broke the news to him that we were starting our own company. After a few congratulatory toasts, he told us that of all the things we were going to have to monitor closely, including income, expenses, profit, and unprofitable and late-paying clients, the most important was our "asshole ratio." He said he was sure we would start off by hiring some really good A-type people. A's tend to attract and hire other A's—smart, talented people who can perpetuate your culture. But eventually, a B will slip in under the radar.

B's will tend to hire C's and D's (Duds) because they are non-threatening to themselves. He said the larger we became, the further removed we could become in the process. "You can never allow the hiring of your people to be out of your control. If you do, before you know it, your asshole ratio may become too high to remain successful. Look at it this way: You're starting with two people and already your asshole ratio is at 50 percent."

Then it hit us like the proverbial light from a train in a tunnel, our mantra would be: We will not work with or for assholes!

The highly respected Robert Sutton published a book in 2007 titled *The No Asshole Rule.* It became a huge bestseller. He says in the book that he first heard the title's term fifteen years earlier, which led him to publish an article about it in the *Harvard Business Review.* Let's see; that would make his amazing discovery date to about 1992. In other words, we coined the No Asshole Rule. I still have the 1981 Seattle newspaper story that quoted "Elgin Syferd's No A#####e Rule." No disrespect Bob, but that makes you an asshole. *We coined the term years before you even heard of it!*

No matter how diligently we tried, over the years, a few assholes slipped into our place—both as clients and employees. Shit happens.

You can't always spot a bad client right off. Some are sneaky and able to hide their true selves—for a while, at least. And, to be fair, occasionally we'd convince ourselves that even though Client X had a reputation for being an asshole, we could somehow turn him around. We learned, though, that if a client had a reputation for being an asshole, it was probably because he was an asshole. If you're ever in this situation, don't spend time trying to change these people. They were probably born with the disease. Believe me, *it's virtually impossible to change a bad client into a good one.*

My first agency boss used to preach that you can pay too much for your money.

Think about the incredible wisdom contained in those few words for everything you do in life: *You can pay too much for your money.*

Dave and I agreed that we weren't perfect and each of us had some personal limitations. Actually, I remember thinking that was only true for Dave, but I didn't argue the point. Partnerships are all about compromise. So our plan was to screen out the assholes, hire only the best people, and then allow them to use their unfettered talents to make us better than we could possibly be by ourselves. Allowing people the freedom to be while maintaining a single culture is difficult, but it became one of our hallmarks and principle reasons for success.

David Ogilvy, advertising legend and one of my early heroes, famously said, "Hire people who are better than you; then leave them to get on with it. Look for people who will aim for the remarkable, who will not settle for the routine." We were smart enough to understand that David's wise counsel could be a key factor in our success. Indeed, this became an important part of our company's foundation. I have to add that many of our employees over the years told us that hiring people smarter than the two of us was a great policy, but they suggested that the company might be better off if we set the bar significantly higher.

Looking back, it was good that we had the luxury of those few weeks of not having to worry about doing actual work. The lax time enabled us to be thoughtful about the vision, direction, culture, personality, policies, and all the other necessities needed for creating and launching a successful company. That was essential since we knew we couldn't get rich selling an unsuccessful one.

6.

IS IT TIME YET?

Our company became real mid-June, 1981. Oh, in case you weren't around back then, let me tell you what was going on in the world around us.

Top officials at the Federal Reserve Board, including its chairman, Paul A. Volcker, said that its policy of reducing the expansion of money and credit would mean little or no economic growth in 1981 and continuing high interest rates. In a series of interviews, the officials said that the lack of improvement in the prospects for curbing inflation had renewed their conviction that the Federal Reserve should maintain a tight monetary policy in the absence of a dramatic shift in the economic outlook. They went on to say the depth of the recession would be in July of 1981, and there were no accurate predictions for recovery.

Why should you care about the economic condition way back then? You may not. But if you're reading this book with even the inkling of ever starting your own company, here's some advice: If a person has a dream and the passion to make that dream a reality, ignore the bullshit about waiting until the time is right. Just fucking do it.

7.

BEFORE THE BEGINNING

You may have seen the cartoon with two guys in a bar, one face down and the other staring at his own image in the mirror saying, "Well, enough about me. What do you think of me?"

I'll try to keep your head off the bar, but there are a few things I want to tell you about my early years that I believe prepared me for and allowed me to start my own business. Hopefully, you'll run across a helpful hint or two along the way. As they say, the past is prologue to the future. And besides, some of it is pretty funny.

I grew up living in a low-income housing project in Seattle that probably played a big part in my lifelong thirst to be rich. As a kid, I helped out our family where I could by collecting and selling beer bottles from the neighbors' yards, and eventually, I graduated to killing rats at the Fisher Flour Mill for fifty cents each. I got my first hourly jobs while in high school. The two longest lasting were the graveyard shift at the railroad as a yard clerk (also aptly named "mudhoppers") and after school at a service station pumping gas and changing oil. Between being constantly sleep deprived and being an asshole, I was kicked out of two high schools and lost a bunch of credits along the way. After finally being accepted by and receiving a diploma from Edison Technical Training School, I switched to a different but better paying graveyard-shift job. I was hired at Boeing to install wire-bundles in the cockpit of its new 727s. Interesting at first, but I ended up hating the endless monotony of screwing screws in the same holes on different airplanes. I knew there had to be a better way. So a year later with a slightly altered school transcript in hand (this was years before SATs were required), I headed over to the University of Washington at age nineteen.

After stumbling around campus for an hour, I finally found the Admissions Office where I was sent to this crotchety old guy sitting behind a sign that read "Career Guidance Counselor." The guy studied my amateurishly altered transcript for a few minutes through his Coke-bottle bifocals and then asked whether I had given thought to a career choice.

"Yes, sir," I answered eagerly. "I want to be an engineer!"

"What kind?" he grunted.

"Ah, I didn't know there were different kinds," I admitted.

"What *do* you know about engineers?"

"I know they live in big houses and drive fancy cars. That's why I want to be an engineer."

Looking at me as though I was from another planet and then again at my transcript, he took off his glasses and said,

"You didn't bother upgrading your math scores. Or were they even lower than what I see?"

"No, those are my real scores. I don't really like math," I admitted.

"You honestly don't know what engineers do, do you?"

"No, sir," I answered. "I just know they live in big houses and drive fancy cars."

After a not-too-subtle shaking of his head and staring at me for a couple of more minutes, he asked, "Were there any subjects you did like and got okay grades in? Honest grades?"

That question honestly stumped me. I had always thought of school as an unpleasant obligation. I finally answered after a couple of minutes of torturous contemplation.

"Well, I did like working on the school newspaper. I wrote a cool car column and was the editor during my senior year."

"I'm going to do you a favor and put you in the journalism sequence," he said.

My world was rocked.

"Do you know where journalists live and what they drive?" I dejectedly inquired.

"No, and I really don't care. I'm just trying to give you a reasonable chance to get out of here with a degree and the remote possibility of a career. Now please leave while I look for some aspirin."

As it turned out, the crotchety old guy did me a huge favor. I not only made it through the first two years of classes, but for the first time in my life, I enjoyed school. I especially loved my journalism classes and writing for the University of Washington's *The Daily*. It was a grind working full-time and carrying a full load, but I was able to maintain a fair GPA. Well, for me anything above the minimally required 2.0 was fair.

One afternoon on the way to *The Daily*, I was stopped in the hallway of the communications building by a short, wiry guy sporting a gray military buzz cut. "I'm Dan Warner, head of the advertising sequence. I've been reading your by-line articles. You're a damn good writer. I think you should consider switching majors to advertising and becoming a copywriter."

"Sorry, sir. I know very little about the advertising profession and nothing about what a copywriter does."

"Copywriting is kind of like being a journalist, but you make about ten times as much."

Was this guy sent to me from heaven? "Sign me up, sir. I do believe I am a fucking copywriter!" Big house, fancy car, here I come!

Dan Warner was a maverick in many ways: retired Marine colonel; successful Madison Avenue advertising executive; feisty as hell and prone to do things his way irrespective of "the rules." For example, in his somewhat twisted evaluation process for the advertising internship program, he didn't give much consideration to the students' GPAs. In fact, no one could quite figure out his ranking for students, but rank them he did.

With everyone in the junior class placed in ranked order, he would send the top three for interviews with the number one agency in the market. After the number one agency made its selection, the remaining two students were paired with his number four pick, and that group was then sent to the number two agency. As you know, this process is the exact opposite of professional sports teams' drafts, which are designed to help weaker teams become stronger by getting a shot at the best athletes. Dan didn't give a shit about fairness. Dan wanted what he thought was best for his students and his beloved advertising industry.

During my junior year, I was fortunate to be in the top three, which meant I got to interview with Cole & Weber, far and away the most dominant agency in the Pacific Northwest with offices in Seattle, Tacoma, and Portland. Its client list was the envy of every competitor in the region. Back then, the company and its people were virtually without peer.

The interview—the first *professional* interview of my life—was scheduled with Lee Jacobi, President and CEO of the company. Jacobi was the most highly regarded head honcho of all the agencies in the Northwest. I was scared shitless.

Lee was a handsome man's man. Not huge in stature, he still looked like he could whip guys half his age. He flashed a devilish smile and scared me nearly into paralysis. So there I was, nervous as hell, trembling before this very important guy as I gave my well-rehearsed pat answers to the expected questions until he blurted out, "What the fuck do you have on your hands?"

I stopped mid-sentence and looked at my frozen-in-space, grease-stained hands. I didn't know what to do or say. It was obviously too late to hide them. I told myself, "Fuck it; this is no time to be a wimp; I am what I am."

"I work in a gas station at night and have for the last six years. Sorry; this is as clean as they get."

"No shit! I hauled ice all through college in San Francisco. Up and down thousands of stairs with a fucking fifty-pound block on my back. I like your grit kid; you get the internship."

Over the years, I've told some people that I earned the internship because of my intelligence. To people who knew that couldn't have been the case, I said it was my personality and charm. When that didn't work either, I had to admit it was the dirty hands.

Dan Warner may have had the most unique draft system, but Lee Jacobi and his management team had crafted the best internship program. The average college junior doesn't know shit about the specifics of his chosen career path. Understanding that, Cole & Weber scheduled its intern for two weeks in each of the major departments: account management, creative, media, and production. And when I say "in," that doesn't mean the intern reports to the department for duties like fetching coffee or filing papers. Interns were given actual assignments. No life-threatening work, mind you, but actual work for real clients. Then, after completion of the first eight weeks and consultation with the department heads and intern, Jacobi decided where they would spend their final two weeks. Everyone, including the interns, knew they weren't "real" employees, but everyone at the agency also knew the interns were grownups (or, almost) and were given the opportunity to learn while actually contributing. I adopted this very model years later at our own agency. It worked for us, too. Our program was considered one of the best in the nation. And year after year, it yielded great employees for us from all over the country. Over time, we had many who went from intern to valued employee to some of the top leadership positions in our company.

8.

MY FIRST "MAD MEN" EXPERIENCE

At the conclusion of my first eight weeks at Cole & Weber, Lee and his partner Sid Copeland, an extraordinary man who paradoxically was creative director while at the same time head of both Public Relations and Advertising Account Management, decided that I should extend my internship and spend most of the four weeks in the creative department as a copywriter. Needless to say, I was ecstatic.

I had a great experience working with a variety of art directors primarily on magazine ads for Western International Hotels (now Westin Hotels). My final assignment had been to create a small newspaper ad and brochure for Seattle Transit (the bus company). Sid told me he was so pleased with my work that he wanted me to present it to the client. If the client approved the work, I would become an honest-to-God published copywriter with work that could be seen right in my own hometown!

You may know from watching the television show *Mad Men* that back then, all men in the advertising agency business wore suits and ties, especially when meeting with a client. "All men" meant interns, too.

"You do have a suit, don't you?" Sid asked me.

I didn't have to answer. Sid could tell by the look on my face and what I was wearing that neither suit nor tie had yet found their way to my closet. Without another word, he walked me around the office, grabbed a sports jacket from one guy, and took the tie off another. With an almost white shirt and a pair of relatively clean chinos back at my apartment, I was ready for the big day.

The presentation was set for lunch at Rosellini's 410, which at the time was Seattle's most famous and elegant restaurant. At least that's what my agency coworkers told me. A fancy meal for me was eating in the University of Washington's cafeteria.

Although I didn't quite trip over my feet on the way to our table, I was absolutely in awe of everything around me: the elegance of the décor, the staff in black tie, the beautiful people; just being in a place like that was enough to make my head spin. I had never felt so damn important.

Shortly after being seated, Sid shouted, "Hey, you wop, what the hell does a person have to do to get a fucking drink around here?"

What the hell?

"We don't serve drinks to fat, ugly Jews," bellowed a very large man heading toward our table. Should I bravely jump between these two or take a cowardly dive under the table? Halfway to the floor, I saw them embrace. But as friends!

What the hell?

"Ron, I want you to meet my dear friend, Vic Rosellini. He runs this poor excuse of a restaurant."

"Nice to meet you, Ron. Any friend of this fat, ugly Jew is a friend of mine. The usual for you, Sid? And what can I bring you, my new young friend?"

Surreal. This is how important people talk with one another? I very nervously replied, "I'll just have water, please."

"Do not fucking embarrass me in front of my overweight friend, kid. He'll have the same as me, Vic."

"Two of our special martinis, coming right up!"

Martinis? Martinis! At lunch? Are you fucking shitting me? I'm a college kid. When I can afford to drink, I drink beer, not martinis! And nothing during the day. Especially on this day. This is nuts.

"Here are your extra dry martinis over ice in buckets, just like you like them, Mr. Copeland," said the smiling waiter. Holy shit! I could barely get both hands around the glass. It must have been at least a quadruple.

I wasn't too many sips into my very first martini before my mouth was numb up to my freaking eyebrows. Which was very scary considering that's about the time Sid was introducing me to Bob, the managing director of the Seattle Transit Authority.

"Hey, bring Bob here a martini, and while you're at it, bring us two more!"

Whoa, was he kidding? My eyebrows were now completely paralyzed. I figured I better make my presentation while I was still somewhat coherent. I damn near fell out of my chair reaching for the presentation materials.

"There you go, embarrassing me again. You need to start practicing being a professional. Professionals don't talk business until after socializing a bit. Leave that for later." So we socialized. Or at least they did. I was busy trying to stay upright.

"Okay, what do you say we order and have a couple more with our meal?" At that point, I was beyond rational thought. I used the old closing-one-eye trick to try to read the menu. Then I realized that even getting the words in focus didn't help much. This was definitely not the cafeteria's menu board. I had never seen some of the words. Unfortunately, the menu items I did recognize were way too heavy and rich for my current condition. My stomach was telling me I had better go light or I might suffer the consequences.

When it was my turn, I ordered "The sweetbreads, please."

"Finally you did something that didn't embarrass me! Good choice," said Sid.

"So can I present now?" I asked.

"No. We talk business after we eat."

Thank God, the waiter finally arrived with our food. "I'm sorry; this isn't mine," I slurred. "I ordered the sweetbreads; you know, those fluffy little light things…er, pastries." The stuff he put in front of me was definitely not fluffy little light things.

"Yes, sir, these are the sweetbreads—a specialty of the house. We prepare the finest thymus and pancreas glands in the city. Our master chef sautés these particular glands to perfection, sir."

Oh, my God! I didn't know a thymus from a pancreas, but my stomach was screaming, "You ain't putting no fucking glands in here, you asshole!" I jumped up, bounced off a couple of people and one wall, but made it to the men's room just in time to throw up all the way from my heels. I puked everything I had even smelled in the previous week. I'm positive all the hurling was probably the only thing that kept the vodka from permanently damaging my liver. By the time I was able to let go of the toilet and get upright, I felt almost human. When I splashed cold water on my face and looked in the mirror, I realized the almost human feeling had not manifested itself into my body. I looked like death, only slightly warmed over.

By the time I returned to the table, all the plates had been removed. Thank God. Without missing a beat, Sid told me it was time to make the presentation. I wish I could tell you that I sucked it up and blew them away. Not even close. I did learn, however, that sometimes it's wisest to let the work speak for itself. Apparently it did because before I realized it, Bob was shaking my hand outside the restaurant. I kind of remember Sid guiding me back to the office where I slept in the supply room until time to go home.

Years later, I found out that Sid had set up the whole thing with his friends Vic and Bob to introduce me to the glamorous world of advertising. It was a forever memorable introduction to the world of Mad Men.

9.

AND I GET PAID, TOO?

As my internship drew to a close, Lee called me into his office. "You've done a good job here, kid. You work hard. And the work has been pretty good. You've made a lot of friends and supporters. So this is the deal: Quit the gas station and work here while you finish your senior year."

"Really? Wow! That's incredible! I don't mean to be brash, but what would be my job?"

"Copywriter, of course."

By this time, for a variety of reasons, I had my sights set on being on the business side of the business, but this was not the time to press the issue. Still, I had to ask.

"Lee, I've been wondering: Do you think it would be possible for me to work on the account side?"

"Don't be fucking stupid, Ron. There's no such thing as a part-time account person. Good account people spend every hour of their lives finding ways to make their clients more successful. Even our bad ones spend more time than you have available. You can't be an account guy and go to school, too.

Sid says you're really good at putting words together. You can do that between classes and come to the office and work with the team after school. What do you say?"

"When do I start?"

10.

BACK TO SCHOOL

Senior year was awesome. The experience gained working at the agency definitely gave me a leg up on most of my classmates. In fact, those of us who had been fortunate enough to work at the more progressive agencies around town became unofficial mentors. I was doubly fortunate to be awarded the Seattle Ad Club Inspirational Scholarship Award. To prove to my classmates that I was still an immature college kid at heart, over the next week, I blew most of the money getting all of us hammered on cheap beer at the Duchess Tavern. My award was turned into a pretty cool win for everyone.

I graduated in the spring of 1965. With graduation came a full-time job offer from Cole & Weber. Even though I thought I was finally ready to be an account person, Lee didn't. So I started as a copywriter at the nearly unbelievable salary (to me) of $10,000 a year! I was convinced I was finally on my way to that big house and fancy car.

My first purchase was a car, which may not have been fancy, but at least it started when I wanted. My transportation during school had been an ancient piece of shit that had an undiscoverable short in the electrical system. After going through two batteries in as many weeks, for two years I had to push the damn thing every time to start it on compression. I wasted way too much gas in constant search of level or (Thank God!) downhill parking spaces.

For the next year, I learned to drink martinis at lunch and still be able to find my way to the agency. As far as work went, I wrote some good ads and even won a few awards. I was learning and getting better every day.

A very talented guy by the name of Doug Sandland was the creative director by then and my ultimate boss. Since I was the new kid on the block, he had me filling in with all the teams on a mix of accounts such as Western International Hotels, Heisdorf-Nelson (a national company that raised and sold baby chicks), National Bank of Commerce, and *The Seattle Times*. I had the opportunity to work with and learn from some local industry greats like Jerry Requa, Gus Swanson, Dick Rugwell, and Martin Banke. After accepting me as one of their own, I also learned why account people wanted to keep the creative people in cages. One small example was an ad for the baby chick company that required a photo of the chicks exiting a box in a prescribed, artful manner. The chicks apparently didn't agree with the art direction because they scattered faster than the photographer's shutter speed. The solution was to send the chicks to their maker, stuff them, prop them, and shoot them before lights made them smell too bad. And the art director who conceived the plan and executed the chicks was the sanest of the bunch. I loved my coworkers but learned quickly that the really gifted creatives were the nuttiest.

My main account was the bank, which was the second largest in the region. The way it worked back then was the account person would meet with the client and help determine the size and scope of the advertising assignment. The account person would then come back and set up three or more individual meetings. Usually, that meant meeting with the Print Creative Team, the Radio/TV Creative Team, and the Media Team. Not together as a whole team, but separately as individual teams. Hard to believe, I know. But this was how the big time agencies in Seattle were still operating in the mid-1960s.

I was the writer part of the Print Creative Team. Although this was several years before writers and art directors were fully functional as a team, at C & W, we at least talked with one another—just not with other departments. After a couple of assignments and seeing the only correlation between the print and electronic executions was the logo, I decided to wander down the hall to the Radio/TV Department.

The Radio/TV Department was headed by Larry Fields, one of the nicest and most talented people in the agency. He had a great staff, too. In my few months at the agency, we had become really good friends.

"Bill just gave me the new assignment for the bank," I said to Larry's staff, "and I know he's talked with you guys as well. I thought it might be cool if we could work together and collaborate on this one."

From the looks on their faces, you would have thought an alien had entered their domain and started muttering gibberish. After a long and uncomfortable silence, Larry said, "I don't mean any disrespect, Ron, but you're just a print person. We're radio and television specialists. We deliver our messages in a completely different way than you do. We take flat words and bring them to life with sound and motion. We live in a completely different professional world. We're simply not comfortable collaborating with outsiders."

I remember being embarrassed at my naivety.

Fortunately for Seattle, a new philosophy was spreading westward from New York, and over the next few years, that separatism faded and advertising became better because of it.

Don't get me wrong; I was extremely grateful to be a copywriter of any kind. It's just that looking around the agency, I could see that the competition for my future advancement was the people in the creative department. For example, there was another young writer in the Tacoma office by the name of John Brown. This is the same John Brown who earned international acclaim as one of the world's best and had the awards to prove it. His "There Is No Finish Line" work for Nike virtually launched the brand and is still considered iconic. It wasn't too hard to see that if I stayed in the creative department, I'd never be better than someone's number two. Or three. Or worse. I could string words together as well as anyone, but guys like John Brown always seemed to have a creative idea that was a little bigger than any of mine. On the other hand, although there were a few pretty sharp people on the account side, there was no one I felt inferior to—less experienced, yes, but inferior to, no. I was determined eventually to move to the business side of the business. Know your weaknesses as well as your strengths.

It was about that time that I saw an ad for After Six Tuxedos in *The New Yorker*. The copy read: "People may love me or hate me but no one will ever be indifferent to me." I needed to be that man.

11.

UNCLE SAM BECKONS

Just when everything in my life couldn't have been more perfect, Uncle Sam told me how much he loved me by sending a fucking draft notice. It was 1965, the war in Viet Nam was going strong, and the United States Army said it wasn't indifferent to me.

I reluctantly reported to the Army Induction Center in a state of semi-disbelief. There I was, standing in line with a dozen guys, half of whom seemed gung-ho and eager to go shoot someone while the rest of us looked ready to cry.

This big guy, a sergeant I learned, had us line up and then yelled, "Drop your pants, bend over, and spread them!" Obeying his order while looking skyward, I whispered, "Why me, Lord? Why me?" The Lord didn't answer, but the sergeant did. "Okay, pull 'em up and get your asses into the next room!"

As far as I could tell, everyone, even the lamest of us, passed his physical exam. When it was my turn to report my success to the sergeant at the desk, he took my paperwork and said, "So you're a college grad, huh? Do you know about the College Op Program?"

“Sir, I know nothing about nothing when it comes to the Army.”

“Don’t you dare call me ‘sir’ again, you fucking ignoramus! I’m not an officer; I work for a living! Now, the College Op Program means if you can make it through ten ball-busting months of Basic Training, Advanced Infantry Training (AIT), and Officer Candidate School (OCS), you get commissioned and proudly get to serve your country for two more years as an officer.”

“I’m sorry; I don’t understand. Even if officers don’t work, the draft is only two years. That program is almost three. What’s the advantage in that?”

“Simple. Nowadays everyone’s going to Viet Nam. As a regular two-year draftee, you’ll probably go immediately to the front line as a rifleman. Probably get killed right off. But if you make it through all the training, you’ll become an officer. Officers just sit around over there in their tents jacking off.”

“Sign me up, Sergeant. I’m positive I could be good at that.”

“Smart choice. What’s your degree in?” he asked.

“Advertising.”

He opened the Military Occupation Specialty (MOS) Manual and searched for Advertising. Nope. Shit. I told him to try Journalism. Damn! Ten minutes earlier, I was considering becoming a draft dodger, and now I was panicking because they wouldn’t let me in the tent!

I thought for a moment. Let’s see; I was in the School of Communications. “How about Communications?”

"This is your lucky day, son. The MOS is right there. You're on your way to becoming an officer in the United States Army!"

It may have been a lucky day, but it was a shitty next few weeks. Lee was devastated. He even called his close friend, Senator Henry "Scoop" Jackson, to ask whether he could use his influence to declare my job used as a deferment. Scoop thanked Lee for the best laugh he'd had in ages. Lee shook my hand and said that if I lived through the war, my job would be there waiting for me. I'm sure he thought the tears in my eyes were out of gratitude. I was actually reacting to the first part.

The part that really made me tear-up on several occasions over the following days was the thought of maybe never again seeing Bonnie Kay Visintainer. I had been dating Beautiful Bonnie for several months, and I was beginning to believe I was in love. I never felt that more strongly than when she kissed me farewell at the airport when I boarded the plane for Fort Dix, New Jersey.

Both the Basic Training at Fort Dix and Advanced Infantry Training at Fort Rucker in Anniston, Alabama were pretty stupid. So were most of my classmates. Together, we learned to run, jump, roll in the dirt, shoot guns, live in tents, and tolerate shitty food. Remarkably, a few guys couldn't even make it through Basic, let alone AIT. As trite and cliché as it may be, most of the Southern boys reveled in the experience and said they had never had it as easy or so good. They were lifers from their first day. Those boys may have been country, but they sure made great soldiers.

I have to say, though, as stupid as those six months were, the experiences I encountered along the way ranged from interesting to life-changing.

Fort Dix is a bus ride away from New York. I had never been to New York. After my first trip, I wasn't sure I ever wanted to return. For example, the bus let me off at the Port Authority near Times Square. Times Square then was nothing like Times Square now. Gritty, grimy, dirty, hookers, pimps, sex shops, and theaters. I thought I was in heaven. Just kidding. I was intimidated—a new soldier in his Class A's bewildered at his surroundings. After checking into a fleabag hotel, I went out to find a cheap meal. I found myself at a stoplight next to a crippled up, grizzled old guy who looked to be at least one hundred. He was bent over a cane, trying to shuffle across the street. I asked whether I could help and he smiled and offered his arm. As we slowly crossed the street to the sound of impatient drivers, he told me that he had lost his only son in the Korean War and thanked me for my service. He said he was afraid I would lose my life too and wanted to repay my kindness for helping him cross the street. I told him that wasn't necessary.

"Son, I insist. I owe it to my country. In the memory of my fallen son, let me give you a blow job."

I didn't know whether to hit him, cry, or run away. I chose the latter. I checked out of the hotel and took a late bus back to Fort Dix.

I don't know whether training bases are intentionally designed as shitholes or whether they mature into them, but

Fort Dix was a prime example of a place where you didn't want to spend a lot of time.

We were out in the woods on something the sergeant said was a bivouac. I learned very quickly that was a fancy way of saying that you lived in a tent for a week, on the ground, with creepy crawly things in 100-degree temperatures and equal humidity with strenuous "maneuvers" during the day. On the fifth night, it rained. Being from Seattle, I thought I knew rain. Not this kind of rain. This rain had drops like golf balls, and all the drops were joined together. I jumped up, tore off my skivvies, grabbed a bar of soap, and headed out when my tent mate yelled, "What are you doing?" I told him I was tired of being filthy and was going to take a shower in the rain. "I wouldn't do that if I were you," he replied, but I ignored him.

I was happily lathering my entire body when God shut off the water. I now knew a little more about rain on the other coast.

Next up was Fort Rucker in Alabama where I became an expert marksman on every weapon from a .45 automatic to a .50 caliber machine gun. I even became proficient at shooting shoulder-fired rockets and throwing grenades. I also became friends with a bunch of Southern boys. I was fascinated with one guy who collected scorpions and kept them in his foot-locker as pets until an inspecting sergeant was nearly stung. My new buddies asked whether I'd like to spend our first weekend pass with them watching the stock car races. Twelve of us headed to Anniston where we bought a couple of cases of beer and rented a motel room—not at a track but in the middle of town. The race was on the little black and white television. About a half-dozen guys jumped on the bed, and two others grabbed the only chairs, leaving the rest of us to stand or sit on the floor. A great time was had smoking, chewing, drinking, yelling, swearing, spitting, and watching the crashes. I sneaked out after about four hours, having decided even the shithole base was better than that. I don't think the others ever knew I left. I learned that not all soldiers enjoyed the same activities.

Signal Officer Candidate School was a different animal. Fort Gordon, Georgia was a paradise compared to the other two bases. But whereby the non-comm's (corporals and low-level sergeants) gave valiant efforts to intimidate and run their charges into the ground, the officers-in-charge at OCS were absolutely capable of both. They let us know from the outset that they were there to identify the weak "sick pukes" and send "those pathetic weaklings" to Viet Nam as cannon fodder. They informed us that their job was to sort the wheat from the chaff. These guys prided themselves on being assholes. For the next six months, I took pride in my determination to be a solid grain of wheat.

Nietzsche said, "That which does not kill us makes us stronger." I remember seeing G. Gordon Liddy say that on TV while burning his own hand with a cigarette lighter. OCS was something like that.

The instructors hated everyone equally and tried their best to have everyone fail. The logic was: Better to have someone fall apart during training than on the battlefield. Even with that in mind, as well as the knowledge that dropouts were sent immediately to Viet Nam as front-line riflemen, we lost about 20 percent of the class in the first few weeks.

I never liked to run and, consequently, I didn't do it very well. Before OCS, that is. I had never heard of one handed push-ups until I was doing them. I like to sleep. I learned it wasn't necessary. I learned to take and then give orders. I dropped twenty-five pounds, then put it back on as muscle. Great for waging war, but I wasn't sure it would help me write better ads for the Army. My non-combat training classes seemed even less helpful. We even had a bunch of silly training where you hooked wires together.

We had goofy rules with consequences, such as not being fast enough saying, "Sir, Officer Candidate Elgin reporting for duty, sir!" or maybe too fast. Either way, the response would be, "Drop and give me fifty, Officer Candidate Elgin, you sick puke!" In the mess hall, you had to sit ramrod straight and stare directly ahead with your arms and hands down at your sides. In precise movement, you raised your hands, picked up the knife and fork, and cut a portion to be chewed three times before swallowing. No more, never less. And heaven forbid you looked anywhere but straight ahead. One night, for whatever reason, it was my turn to be excessively harassed. By the time we were dismissed from the table, I had consumed less food than what would have satisfied a gerbil. On the quick march to the dumpster to rid the tray of my dinner, with no one the wiser, I grabbed a handful of food and stuffed it in my face.

"Officer Candidate Elgin, you fucking pig!" screamed a previously unnoticed TAC Officer. "Dump the rest of your tray in the dumpster and then climb in after it, you fucking animal. Go ahead and root around in there; eat as much as you want. No hurry; you're going to be in there all fucking night, you fucking pig!"

I didn't root. I no longer had an appetite. I simply sat in humiliation as the soldiers of Bravo Company dumped the remains of their dinners on me. The misery was ended after only about three hours when another TAC Officer opened the dumpster lid and screamed that I was dangerously close to being AWOL from lights out at my barracks. In a relatively short time, I had learned there were times in life when it was essential to follow orders.

Even though there were moments and days when it seemed like the pain of OCS would never end, six months had passed. I was commissioned as a Signal Corps Officer who still didn't know shit about hooking wires together. I had figured out, however, the Army's definition of communications was different than mine.

Each graduating class was divided into thirds. One third was sent directly to Viet Nam, presumably to jack off in their tents for a year. One third stayed stateside for a twelve-month tour to be immediately followed by an automatic year of jacking off in Viet Nam. And a third of us were sent to Europe for two years. A person gets so gung-ho in OCS that I was disappointed with my deployment to Germany—until I learned that the extremely high mortality rates for lieutenants in Viet

Nam were not from excessive masturbation but being fragged by their own men while in their tents. Actually, most new lieutenants were killed in combat while leading their patrols.

I was assigned to the Command and Control Battalion for USASTRATCOM-EUROPE just outside Heidelberg, Germany. On my first day, I reported to the commanding officer, a hard-ass infantry major whose first words were that he didn't like me even before meeting me. Stunned, I stood there at attention as he went on to say he hated the Signal Corps and all its pussy officers. His ravings included the fact that he had the Signal Corps Crossed Flags Insignia (waving diapers, as he put it) painted on the bottom of his toilet so he could shit on the Signal Corps every morning before work. He said this terrible assignment to a Signal Corps unit was punishment for trying to extend his fourth tour in Viet Nam. He said the nut doctors thought there was something wrong with him. I felt as though I had just become a character in the novel *Catch-22*.

Anyway, after his ranting ceased, he asked why I signed up to be a pussy signal guy. I explained that because of my ignorance of the military, I thought being a "communications officer" would lead me to sitting in the Pentagon writing ads or PR releases instead of being in Germany not knowing jack shit about hooking wires together.

He cracked a smile for the first time since meeting him. Then he chuckled. Then he roared with laughter. When he recovered, wiping tears from his eyes, he told me he loved that the Army had fucked me, too. He went on to say that he was going to make up for the Army fucking me by giving me the opportunity to be a writer. He was going to make me his new S1 Adjutant. My primary job, he said, was never to question him, and on whatever it was that he handed me, just write "For the Commander, Ronald A. Elgin, 2nd Lieutenant, United States Army." It wasn't exactly what I had in mind to further my writing career, but it seemed infinitely better than hooking wires together for the next two years.

"Lieutenant Elgin, I want you to call a battalion formation at 0700 tomorrow," he bellowed. "I want to make sure everyone is performing at their peak. I want you to find out from Captain Davis the name of our best trooper, call him to the front and center of the formation, and I'll shoot him."

After several months working for the man, I was starting to understand him. "Sir, I don't think killing one of the troops is permissible," I replied.

"I told you never to question my orders, Lieutenant. Besides, I was just planning on winging him."

"With all due respect, sir, even if you're going to wound someone, wouldn't it make more sense to shoot one of our worst performing soldiers?"

"No, you dumb shit! If I shoot the worst grunt, the rest of the troops would think it understandable. If I shoot the best, they'll know they better be better than the best or their asses will be toast, too."

After a minute of me standing there with a stupid look on my face, he started laughing. "I don't really want you to call a formation; I'm just trying to teach you a lesson, dumb shit. *In this man's army, good is never good enough. When lives and country depend on performance, every soldier, every action must be better than good. Remember that.*"

I immediately understood how this applied to combat situations. Since then, I've learned that his philosophy could and should be applied to every endeavor—even advertising. I found that to be pretty incredible wisdom from a guy who enjoyed killing people for a living.

My primary duty as adjutant was the oversight of all personnel matters for the one thousand soldiers in the battalion. With the stroke of a pen, I had the power to make people's lives better or worse—promotions, transfers, duty assignments, even court-martials. I took that responsibility very seriously and quickly learned that valuable lessons can come from anywhere—even from the Army.

The Battalion Headquarters was allowed to employ two local nationals (non-U.S. civilian employees—LNs) to assist with administrative duties. Since both positions were currently vacant, my top (an E7 sergeant) scheduled interviews with two local nationals for me. The first was a drop-dead gorgeous Finnish girl; the second was an even better-looking Norwegian. My troops were lined up ten-deep just to get a look at them. The first one couldn't type, and the other had such an accent I could barely understand her.

I viewed this as an opportunity to make a meaningful management decision and teach a lesson to my junior officers. Being pretty sure of the outcome, I called a headquarters staff meeting of everyone from Specialist 4 and above. Everyone at the meeting was acutely aware of the applicants' physical attributes so I explained the two candidates' shortcomings. My question to the staff was simple: "Would you be willing to spend extra hours doing the work of the LNs, and would this adversely or positively affect your morale?" Their response was unanimous: "Enhance our workplace environment and we'll respond with better work from happier workers!"

Over the next eighteen months, I hired several more beautiful LNs. Most of whom, by the way, turned out to be highly skilled workers once they learned "the Army way." Not that it mattered, though. My troops whistled while they worked, and we had the highest morale in the European command. High morale led to high proficiency. Not necessarily a politically correct management decision, but a highly effective one. I penned the Battalion Motto: Excellence Exceeded Only by Efforts. Thank God for the LNs who gave the motto credibility.

Years later at Cole & Weber, I asked the office manager why he hired mean, ugly people. He said because they were mean and ugly, they had no other lives so they didn't mind working longer than regular people. Bullshit. Beautiful people can perform as well or better than ugly ones. Anyone even vaguely familiar with the reputation of our agency can attest to that. And when I say beautiful, I mean on the outside as well.

Perhaps the most important management lesson of my life was also a product of my time in the military. It went like this:

Like any professional organization, the military has a formal system to evaluate its employees. The Army's system is called an Officer Evaluation Report (OER). I'll generalize the details so as not to bore you. Let's say there are forty areas where a soldier is rated with an A through F score for attributes and skills such as command presence, punctuality, physical capabilities, marksmanship, interpersonal skills, and so on. Their report card concludes with "Promote or Do Not Promote."

My first OER was not from the nut job, but from a very tough, smart career officer. It was a life-changer for me. In civilian terms, I received thirty-nine A's and one F. I was riding high. Until he got to the Promote/Do Not Promote part, that is. This asshole looked me straight in the eye and said that based on this OER, he was recommending that I not be promoted. Not be promoted? Was he shitting me? Then he drove it in deeper by saying he was putting me in the Below Center Mass—Do Not Retain category. Mind you, I was drafted. The Army was not my choice. Until that moment, I couldn't wait to get the fuck out, but now I was humiliated. Major league pissed, I asked him what was so important about getting an F in "Delegation."

"The reason you aced everything else on the review was because you're a micromanager. If you hadn't personally done it, you had a strong hand in it." I was thinking, that's a good thing, isn't it? He went on to say that as I attempted intimately and personally to control the work of more people, my overall performance would deteriorate. At that point, I'd start an inevitable slide into mediocrity and probably failure. He suggested that with my inability to grasp the concept of delegation, perhaps I should consider a career as a men's room attendant in the civilian world. I can be awfully thick sometimes, but even I began to understand. I thanked him and walked out, determined to become the best damn delegator known to man.

The ability to delegate successfully is the most valuable skill a manager can possess.

The art and science of delegation became a lifelong passion. I consider it the most important single skill for anyone wanting to manage people. And after fifty years as a manager and an observer of managers, I can tell you it is the hardest to teach and definitely the most difficult to master.

After I had lived alone in the Bachelor Officer Quarters for a year, my fiancée, the Beautiful Bonnie, joined me, and a few months later, we were married in Basel, Switzerland. A year after being promoted to first lieutenant, I received my discharge papers. Bonnie and I took off on a once-in-a-lifetime honeymoon traveling through Europe. After a year on the road, we ran out of money in Madrid and headed home to resume our civilian careers.

12.

BACK TO BEING AN AD GUY

Four years older and with considerably more life experience, I headed back to Cole & Weber to meet with my old boss, Lee Jacobi. The reunion was terrific, and he told me my old position as a copywriter was there waiting for me.

"Thanks, Lee, but I think I'm ready now to be an account executive."

"No, you're not. Let me show you around the agency; a lot of your old friends are excited to say, 'Hi'!" Lee then toured me through the agency's new building with great enthusiasm. With each stop, he'd say, "Look who's back in our creative department!" When we reached the office of the creative director, he made the same comment. I decided it was time for me to take a stand.

"Good to see you again, Hal," I said, "but I'm not rejoining the creative team. I've decided to find out whether I can be of value on the account side." Lee ushered me out as Hal's face began turning crimson.

"Ron, he'll never let you back in his department again after that stupid comment."

"Lee, I appreciate everything you and the agency have done for me. I know I can be an okay writer, but I want to be a great leader on the account side. If I don't try, I'll never know if I can do it." I left Lee with a smile and a handshake in pursuit of an account executive position elsewhere.

On the advice of a college buddy, Jim Johnson, I met with his friend Ken Hatch, who at that time was the general sales manager for the local CBS television and radio affiliate, KIRO. Ken was a very friendly, dynamic guy whom I immediately liked. We had a great conversation about our backgrounds and his station.

"Would you like to work here, Ron?"

"Jeez, Ken, I really don't know."

"Okay, let me ask you this. It's 4:55 on a Friday night and you still have some inventory to sell. What would you do?"

"Punt?"

"No, no! You'd run to the top of our building and shout at the top of your lungs that you have the best availabilities in town and you're going to allow some deserving clients to buy them at unbelievable rates! You'd shout that message until you had buyers lined up around the block."

To this day, I don't know whether my now dear friend was serious, joking, or making a point. In any event, he helped me realize that I would never be a great salesman. Maybe not even a good one. I became even more resolute in becoming simply an honest ad guy—or is that an oxymoron?

After interviewing at a few other places around town for about a week, I got a call from Lee. He said he had mulled it over and wanted to talk with me about a possible account position. He forewarned me there was a catch to the offer. I headed over to find out the size and shape of the catch.

One of the agency's key accounts was the very same large financial institution for which I had written copy years earlier. I barely remembered the guy running the business, but I was told that he knew banking inside and out; however, he had three pretty serious problems: He was a terrible ad guy; he was a drunk; and he was a complete asshole.

Part of the catch was that the guy had the account in his pocket. Agency management believed that if it fired the jerk, it might lose the business. However, with this guy in control, the staff would never be able to do really good work, and management feared that someday the client might wake up to that fact. The account had become one of those that no one wanted to work on, so people had to be forced to do so. Agency management compounded the situation by allowing the guy to hire weak "yes men" because whenever one of his underlings attempted to grow a pair, this asshole would undermine the person's credibility with the client. Management wanted to get rid of him, but it also desperately wanted to keep the business and do better work for the client. My instinct was to tell the agency to grow a pair and can his ass, but it wasn't my company, so I asked how I could help.

Lee said that my role in the "catch" was to become an expert in the financial business, to earn the respect of the very same creative department I had just spurned in favor of becoming a suit, and not get undermined before the client by the asshole. I thought this might be similar to getting fragged in a tent in Viet Nam while jacking off, but I accepted the challenge.

I found out quickly the guy's daily routine included showing up at the client's reception area to greet all the important people as they came to work. He would then tour the executive floor, telling everyone about all the good things he was personally doing for them. I followed him around like a pet dog wanting to puke. After about an hour of that, we'd head back to the agency in time for him to walk around telling everyone how much the client loved him, how he saved their work with his brilliant changes, and a bunch of other bullshit. Then we'd head out for lunch at one of his favorite watering holes where he'd proceed to get absolutely hammered. Returning to the agency around 2 p.m., he'd stagger around, living up to his reputation as an obnoxious asshole. His routine also included leaving about 4 p.m. or earlier, depending on his sobriety. Or lack of same.

It's never easy to go drink for drink with a professional drunk, but my career was on the line so I learned to become pretty good at it. After a while, I found that I could work myself sober by the late afternoons. Evenings became my productive time. Over the next eighteen grueling months, I helped improve the agency's product and win the client's trust without incurring the asshole's wrath.

The day came that Jacobi was finally able to tell the jerk that he was voluntarily going to retire, effective immediately. The asshole actually laughed and said that he would determine when he retired, and it wouldn't be any time soon. Jacobi laughed back and said he'd met with the top people at the bank and they were okay with "Bill's decision to retire" now that they had me there as his replacement. Lee went on to say that if he tried to derail any part of his retirement, they'd sue his sorry ass. Very reluctantly, the jerk agreed to take the money and run. Happily, I lost my drinking buddy that day and never saw him again. My liver began its recovery.

I was rewarded with a title change, a few more bucks, and some great advice. Lee told me never to let an account become tied too closely to any single individual. And for the long-term sake of an agency, not even to the head of the firm. It's a temptation that must be considered and tempered carefully. *Clients love stability, consistency, and attention from the top dogs. However, in order to grow both personally and professionally, effective delegation must be employed.*

Most clients can accept the fact that one person can't do everything. But they also know it's much easier for them to deal with just one person. Those clients must be trained. The easiest way is to put the fear of the unknown to them by asking them to consider what would happen if their lead person got hit by a bus. Of course, their counter is usually, "That's your problem," but instinctually, they know it would be a problem for everyone. That's not to say there shouldn't be a lead person on every piece of business, but no one benefits long-term if any single person is allowed to become indispensable.

The "I, I, me, me," strategy is a flawed one for any agency. Unless you really want to be a small shop forever, that is. That is definitely not what we wanted, so I grew very comfortable and even brazen telling clients that the top two or three people on their business were all being trained to take over the lead spot. This policy also enables the lead on the business to grow in other areas or on to other accounts. *If an employee shows reluctance to be replaced on any piece of agency business, perhaps it's time for that person's future with the company to be reevaluated.*

In my case, getting away from the day-to-day bullshit allowed me time to concentrate on the client's overall business at the highest levels. It shouldn't surprise anyone to learn that the top executives of most companies are there for some damn good reasons. Almost inevitably, they are not only skilled managers but also decent, interesting, fascinating people. One of my goals in life has always been to become friends with as many decent, interesting, fascinating people as possible. I've been fortunate to find these friends in business, politics, the arts, and charitable institutions. However, there's no more rewarding way than to find these friends at the two places where one spends most of the day: the agency and its clients.

Friendships with the top people at the client are not created by telling them why their recent production job was 10 percent over or under budget, but by contributing in strategic discussions and initiatives to help move their business forward. It's also important to remember these leaders are on top for more reasons than their business acumen; they are some of the best and brightest in the affairs of the world and life. Being friends with such people has truly enriched my life.

One of the most valuable pieces of advice Jacobi gave me was: *Never forget that it is always more difficult for a client to fire a friend than someone he or she hardly knows or, worse, doesn't particularly like.* Not impossible, of course, but more difficult. This fact can never be the basis for a friendship, but once a true friendship is formed, it's definitely a cool by-product of an agency relationship.

13.

TO REHEARSE OR NOT TO REHEARSE: THAT CAN'T BE THE QUESTION

"I don't need to rehearse; I have it down pat. No sweat, I'll ace the pitch. Trust me."

There was a time, early in my career, when I actually uttered those words. It didn't take too many fuck ups before I saw the benefit in solo rehearsing, and not too many more before I discovered the incredible power of team rehearsals.

"Do you have your presentation to the bank ready for our meeting tomorrow?" Jacobi asked me. "Absolutely," I answered.

The truth was, I had read and reread my solo presentation so many times I had it memorized, but I was so nervous that my mind would wander while spouting the words and I'd be forced back to my notes. Actually, my "notes" was the entire one-hour script. This was my first solo presentation to the top executives at my largest client and the CEO of our company. I kept telling myself, "As soon as I get in front of the group and start the presentation, I'll calm myself down and sail through it." The problem right now was that I was being distracted by several things, including the thought of someone overhearing me practicing, the question of whether I should be walking around at this point of the speech, how long should the pauses be before starting the next part, and a dozen others. I finally convinced myself that I'd be fine during the presentation.

I wasn't better, though; I was worse. I stumbled at the outset and never recovered. I got so flustered about ten minutes into it that for the next forty minutes I hardly took my eyes off the script. When it came time for questions, there were virtually none. Undoubtedly, I tried to tell myself, there were no questions because the presentation's substance was sound and those in the room had been subjected to that substance, word by word. As the client's team members filed out, they left us with words like "Good plan" and "Very well thought-out and documented." Then I started to think that it hadn't gone as badly as I feared.

Until Lee told me otherwise.

"That was the worst fucking presentation I've ever seen! You fucking embarrassed me. Hell, I hope you embarrassed yourself! You said you were prepared. Bullshit! You read the whole fucking thing. It was obvious you didn't care enough even to rehearse!"

"That's not true, Lee," I meekly protested. "I must have read the script two dozen times."

"That's not a rehearsal! Didn't you practice in front of anyone without that fucking script in your hands?"

"No."

"Oh, for God's sake. If I didn't feel partially responsible for this incredible fiasco by not forcing you to give me a run-through, I'd fire your sorry ass right now or at the very least send you to a Dale Carnegie presentation course. I'll tell you what I'm going to do, though; you have one week to develop this material into a *real* presentation that you are going to deliver to me and the rest of the executive committee. Got it?"

I did get it. I was embarrassed, humbled but determined. The first thing I did was to confess the failure to my closest friend in the agency. Well, confess may have been too strong a statement. I lied and told him that Lee had suggested that I polish the presentation because he wanted the executive committee to hear our plans for the bank. I asked whether he would be willing to act as my audience the following night. I also offered beer, so he agreed.

I knew the basics of a good presentation and also some of the fundamentals of rehearsing—I just hadn't bothered to execute any of them. I immediately began transcribing the key element of each section onto 3 x 5 note cards, being careful not to write sentences, just thoughts. That night, I confessed to my wife that I hadn't done as well as I'd liked, and so "for the next time," I was going to practice to see how good I really could have been. Obviously, I was still embarrassed. Anyway, for a good part of that night, I stood in front of a mirror with my notes and practiced eye contact and body movements while trying to remember what I was speaking about. The next night, I practiced in front of my friend. That was much tougher than the mirror. It wasn't really good according to my friend, but I got through it. The following night, I practiced in front of my wife. She said I was terrible. "Believe it or not, you actually have a nice personality. Not a shred of that came through in your presentation. I can't believe I'm saying this, but be yourself!"

The next day, I asked three of my fellow account managers whether they would do me a big favor and critique the content of a presentation I was going to be making the following week. They agreed. I stumbled through it and they did give some helpful comments about the content. No word about my delivery, but that was not what I had asked of them. What their listening did do was give me more practice and confidence.

The week was up and I was on. Back in the same room with the same material, but in front of an even scarier audience. Lee Jacobi times five. I was petrified. I actually considered just walking out and never coming back. Then Lee said for me to get on with it. And I did. I know I wasn't great, but compared to a week earlier, I had vastly improved. Not only did I feel better about my performance, but Lee said in front of the group, "You didn't embarrass me this time, Ron. Get back to work." I considered it to be high praise.

PRACTICE, PRACTICE, THEN PRACTICE MORE

Even with all the experience gained over the years, I don't consider myself to be a Zig Ziglar by any stretch of the imagination, but since that early experience, I can deliver a good speech as long as I remember to adhere to the basics.

It's human nature for most people to fear speaking in front of a group. The way to overcome that fear is practice, practice, practice. There's also a little trick you should know. The trick is to use the nervousness to trigger the same adrenaline that causes the physiological change in your body during either excitement or fear. There's a story about President John F. Kennedy told by his press secretary, Pierre Salinger. It seems that just before an important speech by the world acclaimed orator, a cable connection came loose and Pierre climbed under the table to tighten it. When he looked over to where the President was sitting, he was amazed to see Kennedy's hands trembling. By the time Salinger had climbed out from under the table, the President had started his speech and transferred his nervousness into one of his patented vibrant performances. He had channeled his adrenaline.

A tip I've never mastered is being able to picture the audience naked, which is probably a good thing. Who would ever want to look at a bunch of hairy old, fat men? I do have a few other tips, though.

Try to make each speech a personal dialogue between yourself and a few audience members. Single out some friendly faces in various parts of the room. Talk to them. Don't look at it as an obligation to present a set of facts or a point of view. View it as an opportunity to communicate your message to a number of people. Better yet, a chat with a friend.

Always remember to be your authentic self. If you have faults in communicating, work on correcting or overcoming them off-stage. Once you're up there, it's too late to be anything other than who you are. If you try to be anything else, chances are you'll fail and it will make it just that much harder the next time.

There are sayings in the advertising agency business like "Poisoned by PowerPoint" and "Death by Deck." Reading words from a screen may get you through the presentation, but rarely will it get your message through to your audience. Use your voice and memory to deliver the words and the screen to communicate your points with visuals. Words can make powerful statements on the screen as visuals, but never as scripts to be read by the presenter.

14.

A MILLION WAYS TO SOLVE A PROBLEM

When the agency started working for Alaska Airlines in the '70s, it was strictly a regional carrier serving ten cities in the Great Land with one daily "outside" flight to Seattle. The airline was pretty fucked up back then. For example, the company was so close to financial collapse that its marketing decisions were based almost entirely on cash flow. This meant that it advertised in the summer when its flights were full and cash was plentiful, but it went dark during the winter months when it desperately needed revenue. Other things like the famous fistfight at one of its board meetings also made for interesting speculation as to its long-term viability.

Although usually budget-constrained, the airline's marketing people were smart, crafty, and savvy. They understood that without the money for adequate media support, their ads had to work twice or three times as hard. Cole & Weber jumped at the challenge. They had been doing some good, solid work for a number of clients, but this was the agency's opportunity of a lifetime.

The majority of the airline's flights were inside Alaska, but everyone knew the real opportunity for growth lay outside the state. This insight led to the iconic position: "Nobody Knows Alaska Like Alaska Knows Alaska." This bold claim made it abundantly clear that since the airline's pilots and crew had conquered the icy, mountainous terrain of the Great Land, to fly anywhere in the lower forty-eight was a piece of cake for them. The ads and commercials spawned by that position swept the awards shows for several years. A particularly memorable tourism ad featured a plane flying over the majestic mountains of Alaska with a headline: "After Seeing Alaska, Everything Else Looks Like Kansas." In addition to a Best of Show award at the Addy Awards, the ad earned a Cease and Desist Letter from the Governor of Kansas.

Speaking of the Addys, one year I ended up representing both the client and agency. I was called to the stage to accept an award so frequently the emcee finally said, "Ron, it will save us a lot of time if you just stay up here with me." Needless to say, I left New York City thinking we were pretty hot shits.

I must add that we were not the only arrogant agency in the country. Far from it. The tide of arrogance was sweeping the country. And it spread quickly. The economy was brisk and agencies were taking full credit for the increased sales. We started to believe that we knew more about what was right for our clients than they did. Agencies began living the philosophy "We know what's best" and "If you don't like it, fuck off." It didn't matter whether the advertising was off strategy. Hell, it didn't matter if the advertising had no strategy. This was the era when if the creatives deemed the work to be right, it was right.

My bank client had been an English major and was very particular about grammar. I presented an inconsequential newspaper ad to him one day and he corrected a simple grammatical error that the proofreader should have caught back at the agency. It was such a nothing ad that I hadn't even bothered to read it. Once pointed out, I agreed to change it.

When I returned to the office, I told the copywriter, "Dave, the client loved your ad but found a grammatical error that we corrected. Other than that, it's ready to go."

Dave took the copy from my hand, studied it for a couple of minutes, then tore it in half, folded it, and tore it again. He kept tearing it until it was confetti. Then he tossed it in his wastebasket.

"What the fuck are you doing?" I asked.

"You allowed that illiterate asshole to ruin my ad. Now I'll have to start all over. It will be a couple of weeks."

"Are you fucking crazy? You wrote 'effect' when it should have been 'affect.' Lou is not illiterate; he has a Master's in English. Even I can see it's wrong. You're wrong! And the ad is due at the paper next week. Just fix it."

"Get out of my office."

Guess who won that battle. The fucking copywriter.

Not all clients were swayed by awards and bullying. And it wasn't just the traditional Consumer Packaged Goods (CPG) clients who shouted, "Bullshit!" But the battle raged. Account people were ordered to sell or die. I knew account types who would hide the bad news of not cramming a bad ad down the throat of a client for days on end. Better to be home faking an illness than facing the music. I heard of one guy who actually resigned by registered letter rather than living up to his failure.

The former head of marketing for Alaska Airlines reminded me the other day of one of our unique experiences. This particular incident was born strictly out of our agency's arrogance. In 1974, the airline had created a business relationship with Braniff International which they jointly named "The Pipeline Express." Braniff used its Boeing 727-200s to carry pipeline workers from Houston and Dallas to Seattle. Alaska Airlines crews flew the aircraft to the northern terminus. The reverse took place with Alaska planes being staffed in Seattle by Braniff crews and flown south. The ad our creatives proposed for the north to south route had a pipe connecting the two states with a plane flying from the top of the ad to the bottom. The client objected, saying that showing a plane heading straight down was a big industry taboo. We argued. They argued back. We refused to show another option or to back down. It was that era I referred to when our people felt that because they worked at an agency, by birthright and occupation, they were smarter than the client. We absolutely knew consumers would agree with us. We pushed it just shy of being fired and then retreated to the agency. The client probably thought we had finally seen the light and were going back to create new work. Instead, agency management decided I should fly to Anchorage and show the ad to travelers at the airport to prove that we were right. I was on the first flight the next morning.

To say things did not go the agency's way would be a huge understatement. People were horrified at the visual. One guy even threatened to kick my ass if I didn't stop walking around scaring people. I went to another part of the terminal and kept showing the ad, hoping to be able to report that "Some people liked it" or even "Not everyone hated it." That was not the case. Not only did everyone hate the ad, but I got arrested by airport security!

I can usually talk my way into or out of most situations. Not this time. Security saw me as an honest threat and put me behind bars. I'm exaggerating about the bars, but it was a secured room and I was under arrest. I used my one allotted call to the agency and listened to a recorded answering service telling me to call back in the morning.

For whatever administrative or security reason, the airport officials called the President of Alaska Airlines to report the incident. Thankfully, the president knew who I was and had heard about the controversial ad. He must have told them I wasn't a security threat, just a dumb fucking ad guy, because they released me with an admonition never to return to Anchorage International.

The airline's marketing folks were understandably pissed, but I think they were also secretly pleased that they were right about the ad. I was severely criticized by the creatives for conducting a flawed focus group. The compromise ad had a large pipe running at an angle across two pages with "Anchorage/

Fairbanks" at one end and "Dallas/Houston" at the other. The big difference was that because of the angle, one plane appeared to be taking off while the other was landing—not crashing. The creatives forgave me once we started winning awards for the ad.

I remember a time after that incident when I failed to sell some work to the Alaska Airlines client. Remember, this was the client that constantly pushed the agency for edgier work. This particular campaign had been created by a new hotshot team hired from a global agency out of New York City. In addition to their credentials, these people had the accents and airs about them. In keeping with the client's desire for fame and the agency's arrogance, the ads were edgy and bold. None of the ads made much sense, but they were creative as hell. No matter how I tried, I couldn't convince the client to buy the work. Nervous as hell, I returned to the agency and presented the bad news to the new creative guy. Did I mention that he was also a foot taller than me, thirty pounds heavier, and scared the shit out of me?

"I'm really sorry, Bill. I gave it my best shot, but the client wouldn't buy the work. If you want, I could wait a couple of days and try again."

"No, no, that's fine. I have some time right now. I'll get started on another approach," he said. "If the brief is still okay, it must mean they just didn't like the work, right?"

"You're not pissed at me? You're not going to yell or throw something?"

"Come on; don't be a jerk. There are a million ways to solve any particular problem. Get the fuck out of here; you're wasting my time." *Throughout the rest of my career, I reflected on those words: "A million ways to solve a particular problem." Not, "It's my way or the highway." Or, "Don't offer options; this is the only solution that will work."*

It's true that some clients don't want to be presented with options. I guess it makes some jerks' lives easier when they don't have to make a decision. Or that it's a timesaver for them to have to nitpick only one campaign. I've even had some clients say that the agency was hired to give them the right answer, period. Even with those clients, years later our agency almost always insisted on taking them through multiple approaches before showing our recommendation. I found that even with clients who say, "I know you went through a lengthy process before arriving at the solution, you don't have to prove it to me," they learn to appreciate the process. Occasionally, we admitted that the agency was divided on two solutions. The client's hostility to our "ambivalence" was usually won over by our honesty. Most clients, however, preferred to see multiple options. In these cases, we never argued the point but instead displayed confidence in our solution, our salesmanship, or our alternate campaigns.

• • • •

Cole & Weber and Alaska Airlines had a phenomenal run together, but in the agency business, even great relationships come to an end. A year after the business moved to Chiat Day, we received a Request for Proposal (RFP) from the second largest airline in Alaska and second oldest in the U.S., Wien Air Alaska. Hal Dixon, I, and a couple of others put together some spec ads featuring, of all things, a goose in a tiny leather pilot's cap and headed to the pitch in Anchorage. Fortunately, none of the security people at the airport recognized me.

The president of Wien was a guy by the name of Jim Flood. The only other guy in the room where we were to present was his chief operating officer. During the presentation, I referred to him as Mr. Flood. I did this not just out of respect for his position but also from fear of the man. He was very somber and had this way of turning his whole body toward you rather than just his head—he came off as very stiff.

About three quarters into our presentation, Mr. Flood interrupted me, turned to his COO, and asked how many more agencies were scheduled. The reply was that two more were scheduled for the following day.

"Call them right now," said Mr. Flood, "and tell them we're cancelling because we just hired these guys."

My life has been filled with a lot of firsts, but this was one of the onlys.

I left Cole & Weber a year or so after we won Wien Air Alaska, but my relationship with Mr. Flood continued and flourished. He became Jim shortly after I found out the reason he appeared stiff was that he had broken his neck surfing in Hawaii. I quickly learned that in addition to being a shrewd businessman, he was a hell of a great guy. He went on to buy the airline, sell it, and then buy it back and sell it again two or three different times, making a huge fortune in the process. We attended many Super Bowls together and an annual lunch with two mutual friends over the last fifteen years. Jim recently passed away and the world lost a wonderful human being.

15.

NUTTY CLIENTS AND NUTTIER COWORKERS

During my years at Cole & Weber as an account person, I had the opportunity to work and become friends with some wonderfully talented people, some assholes, and a whole bunch of absolute whackos. I learned a lot from all of them. As I've said before, just about any experience can help shape your life—if you are willing to learn from it. Some immediately; others, years later.

At one point while I worked there, Cole & Weber consolidated its Seattle and Tacoma operations into one office across the highway from the Sea-Tac Airport. After years of bitching by the Seattle-based clients, the company agreed to open a satellite office in the downtown area. Since most of my clients were Seattle-based, including Rainier Bank, which was my largest client, I was directed to move myself and support staff to the new office.

There's an old saying that there's a fine line between genius and insanity. After Jacobi retired, Hal Dixon moved from executive creative director to CEO. Hal epitomized that old saying. He was a genius when it came to all things creative, but an absolute fruitcake when it came to most everything else. Especially in dealing with people.

"Where the fuck is he?" screamed Dixon as he stormed past the receptionist.

"Elgin, where the fuck are you?"

The Seattle office was pretty small; twenty offices in an open floor plan separated by dividers. My office was way in the back.

He was two-thirds of the way through the office before he spotted me. Before I could say a word, he pointed to the only enclosed room in the building and screamed, "Get in there!"

I was completely flummoxed. I had no idea why he was so screaming mad. I wasn't exactly scared; I just didn't know why this nutcase was being even nuttier than normal. Okay, I may have been a bit scared too.

He led me into the room, then turned and slammed the sliding glass door so hard it came out of its track. Paying no attention to the damage, he yelled, "Who the fuck put you in charge of this office?"

By this time, he was right in my face. "No one put me in charge. I saw a void and filled it," I replied.

"Well, you can't fucking do that without a title, goddamnit!" he screamed. "You're now the managing director of this office, goddamnit!"

With that, he tried to slide open the damaged door and yelled, "You're letting this fucking place go to shit already."

I helped move the door out of his way and watched as he stormed out of the office. I often wonder whether my answer changed his mind about firing me or whether that was a normal way for a crazy person to give a promotion.

Speaking of strange, one time I saw Hal tell a senior art director to fire Carl, an old paste-up artist. The guy was probably in his sixties but looked to be a hundred. Hal didn't give a reason, just wanted him gone.

Several weeks later, Hal saw Carl in the hallway. He rushed to Dan's office and screamed at him for not getting rid of the old guy.

"I tried, Hal. I told him we were very sorry, but we had to let him go," Dan said. "But he told me he wasn't leaving because he needed the job."

Carl worked there for another three-and-a-half years and retired when he was damn well ready.

Still in the strange category, Jacobi told me that years before, he sent one of his older, most senior accounting guys to an American Association of Advertising Agencies finance seminar in Los Angeles. The guy was about sixty, shy, quiet, and pretty wimpy. He had never been on a business trip, but being an accountant, he did know about expense reports. His expense report, however, made Jacobi explode. He ordered the guy to his office and closed the door.

"What the hell are you doing submitting a request to reimburse for payment to three different prostitutes?" Lee inquired harshly.

"It's kind of embarrassing, Lee."

"Out with it!"

"Well, I'm used to having sex with my wife at least twice a day," he nervously replied, "and after the first day, I just couldn't concentrate on the seminar. My wife wasn't there and I had to do something." He was almost in tears.

"Jesus Christ. Now I've heard them all. Redo the fucking report and claim the expense as dinner and booze with a bunch of associates." It was the guy's last business trip on Cole & Weber, but Lee admitted a newfound respect for the old stud.

Lee told me another strange expense report story. One of the senior art directors, Bob, was given the opportunity to go solo to L.A. for a two-day photoshoot. Lee found out from accounting that the art director had returned nearly half the $200 advance and hadn't asked for any other reimbursement. Curious, he asked Bob what the hell was going on.

"I'm sorry if I asked for too much money," he said, "but everyone told me the trip would be really expensive."

"It is really expensive," replied Lee. "How the fuck did you make the trip for only a hundred bucks?"

"I took the Greyhound bus that made lots of stops because it was the cheapest, and I found a small room at the YMCA. Everyone said the food was going to be really expensive, but the McDonald's is the same price as up here," confessed Bob.

Lee loved that story, but the creatives voted never to allow Bob to go on another shoot by himself.

Then there was the time when one of the wackier creatives stole one of the janitors' keys to the mechanical room. On a day when he knew George Weber, principal owner of the agency, was going to be in the office, he sneaked into the mechanical room and smoked about a dozen joints. At 9 a.m. when the air conditioner came on, it emptied the clouded room's smoke throughout the two floors of the office. For about two hours, George walked around the office muttering, "Why, what's the meaning of this?"

Before leaving the Cole & Weber nuthouse for the one we created, I must share this story of parsimony. It's pretty common in the agency business for people to carry around pens, pencils, markers, paper clips, memo pads, and what-have-you from meeting to meeting. It's also common to leave aforementioned implements in chalk trays, on the tables and chairs, or even on the floor. Cole & Weber had an extremely anal executive who finished each day going from room to room collecting the forgotten and returning them to the supply room. I can't confirm this, but I was told he lobbied each year for management to devote an area where he could lock up all supplies. When a person needed a new pen or pencil, he would be required to bring in his dry pens or worn-to-a-stub pencils in order to exchange them for new ones. The executive was also fanatical about never having to buy paper clips—since they come free on most documents. "Just save them for your own use," he would say. I laughed along with my coworkers at his weird obsessions—until I started my own company, that is. *Watch your pennies and the dollars will be well cared for.*

I went to a Mariners ball game the other night with the CEO of Ivar's restaurant chain, and it reminded me of a couple of stories that happened while I was still at Cole & Weber.

First, I have to tell you a little about Ivar's just in case you've never been to Seattle. Ivar's Acres of Clams restaurants are iconic in this area, and so was the restaurant's founder, Ivar Haglund. He was known as an entertainer, folksinger, restaurateur, and ultimately, the "King," "Mayor," or "Patriarch" of Seattle's waterfront. The story of Ivar's seafood restaurants began in 1938 when thirty-three-year old Ivar opened Seattle's first aquarium on Pier 54. Droves of people lined up and paid a nickel to view the sea life that Ivar had collected from Puget Sound. Noticing his patrons had worked up an appetite, he started preparing and selling clam chowder and fish 'n chips at the site. The food was an instant success. Over the years, Ivar became extremely successful through the combination of great food and his brilliant marketing mind (he was constantly engineering infamous pranks such as octopus wrestling and clam eating contests, and strolling through the downtown department stores with Patsy, his pet seal). His financial success was the reason he came into my life.

One of our most talented creative directors, John Brown, conceived a brilliant campaign for National Bank of Commerce (which became Rainier Bank, which was eventually purchased by Bank of America). The basic premise was that even Washington's most famous and wealthy people started with a simple savings account at NBofC. Historic records revealed that Ivar Haglund was one of those people.

As the account guy, I sold the campaign to the advertising manager who loved the idea. My next job was to convince Ivar to star in radio, TV, newspaper, and outdoor ads. Knowing that he was a natural born promoter and ham, I figured it would be a slam dunk.

"No."

"Perhaps you didn't understand, Mr. Haglund; the bank is putting a lot of media weight behind this campaign. Everyone will be exposed to it!"

"That's the problem. If people think I'm rich, they'll steal my knives and forks, not to mention the salt and pepper shakers!"

"You must be kidding."

"No. They already steal from me. If my customers think I'm rich, everyone will steal from me! I won't do it!"

I was so stunned I had no retort; I simply thanked him for his time and hung up the phone. When I broke the bad news to John, he was devastated.

"Ivar is so perfect for this campaign. The other people we have lined up will be good, but Ivar is so well-known and loved he's perfect. He's already an accomplished actor—I see him as the cornerstone of the entire campaign. Isn't there something you can do to convince him?"

I agreed with John, got in my car, and headed down to the waterfront to do some research, beginning with the first person I met at one of Ivar's restaurants.

"Excuse me, sir; I see you're having a cup of Ivar's clam chowder."

"Yes, it's the best I've ever had. We try to get down here for a meal at least once a week."

"Would it surprise you to know that Ivar has become very wealthy because of his restaurants?"

"It wouldn't surprise me at all, and I'm happy for him. This is one restaurant I hope never goes out of business!"

And so went my hip-pocket research. Everyone knew that our Seattle icon was wealthy, and they were all happy for him.

"Mr. Haglund, we've just conducted a fairly extensive research study of your customers that I think may interest you. May we come talk with you about our findings?"

Of course, he agreed. Free research? Why wouldn't he? We set the meeting for the next morning—8 a.m. at his waterfront restaurant office. John was ecstatic.

When I explained the situation to the ad manager, he insisted on coming along. The three of us met outside the restaurant a few minutes before eight o'clock. We found a janitor who led us to a narrow staircase and then said we'd find Ivar's office at the top.

I knocked at the small door at the top of the staircase and was rewarded with Ivar's deep baritone voice instructing us to come in. I opened the door to a tiny office that contained a fair-sized desk, a single visitor's chair, and Ivar, resplendent in his usual nautical attire. We crowded in, gave our client the chair, and started in with our pitch.

"Before you tell me too much about my free research, would anyone like a cup of coffee?" We all said yes, so he picked up his phone and placed the order. Then he said, "Go ahead." So I did.

"Really? Everyone knows I'm rich? Is that why they're already stealing from me?"

"I don't think that's the reason, Ivar," I said. "Everyone is happy you're rich. It assures them that their favorite restaurant isn't going away. I think people are taking your cutlery and other items as mementoes of their experience with you. I think if you set up a souvenir stand with branded mementoes, the theft will stop and be replaced with additional revenue."

The coffee arrived, and because of the crowded situation, it was passed from the server to me and on to the others. Ivar's cup had his name on it, and when I passed it to him, I noticed it was only half-full. He opened a desk drawer, took out a bottle of whiskey, and filled the rest of his cup. "Would anyone else like a little wake-me-up?" We all declined and continued with our presentation. A little later, I watched him refill his cup without the coffee.

"Well, what do you think, Ivar?"

"I like it. Branded merchandise. A new revenue source, and maybe people will stop stealing from me."

"I meant about starring in our commercials."

"Oh that, of course. I've always loved a good promotion. Care to join me in a victory drink?"

The campaign was a success, and Ivar became a good friend.

• • • •

The other memory that came to mind was also with the bank, but with a different ad manager who was a great guy and very smart. He was an ex-agent for the Central Intelligence Agency and former marketing executive with Green Giant in Chicago. Very conscientious. Well, maybe a bit conscientious to the extreme.

We had a TV shoot scheduled in L.A. and his boss decided to come along. I didn't mind babysitting two clients, especially since they were polar opposites. Oh, they were equally smart, experienced, and conscientious, but Dave, the big boss, was also really easygoing and loved to have a good time. On the last day of a very successful shoot, Dave insisted on the three of us going to a fancy outdoor restaurant for lunch. George, the ad manager, said it was his duty to stay at the shoot, to which Dave called bullshit and ordered him along. It was a beautiful day and the traffic on Sunset wasn't bad. Dave ordered a nice bottle of Chardonnay and George ordered ice tea. Along with our lunch order, Dave got us another bottle of wine. George was going out of his skull with anxiety. Finally, Dave said he was going to catch an early flight back to Seattle, and I accompanied George back to the studio.

The wrap took a bit longer than expected, but George insisted on staying to the end. We dropped off our rental car and hopped on the shuttle, which would drop us at United Airlines. If you remember the old LAX, the United Terminal was the last stop for the shuttle. Needless to say, we were cutting it short. The bus was crowded and stopped to load and unload at the first couple of stops. George was concerned that we were going to miss our flight, which was the last of the day.

"Don't worry; if we miss the flight I'll treat for dinner."

"No, I can't miss the flight! I told my wife I'd be home tonight."

"George, she will understand."

"No, no, I can't miss that flight!" With that, George grabbed his overstuffed hanging bag, slung it over his shoulder, and jumped off the bus. It must have been about 90°, but George took off running toward the United Terminal. A few minutes later, we passed the panting George. A few minutes after that, he passed us. Each time he looked worse—hotter, sweatier, and panting more.

The first few times we were side-by-side, I urged him to get back on the bus. He wouldn't even acknowledge me so I just sat back in wonder. Of course, I didn't want to miss the plane, but neither did I want to run a mile-and-a-half in a suit with a bag over my shoulder.

We were in the home stretch and I could see George about a block ahead of us, but he was no longer sprinting. In fact, it looked more like he was staggering. We passed him just before the terminal. As I stepped off the bus, I saw that he was indeed staggering. I grabbed the bag off his shoulder and helped guide him all the way to his seat on the plane where he promptly fell asleep.

16.

BACK TO THE BEGINNING

My career took me from the creative department to the account side while Syferd worked most areas of public relations during his. A discipline that was completely off both our radars was the planning and buying of media. I had a good friend who had left Cole & Weber shortly before me. Her name was Terry Kirkland, and she was generally acknowledged as the market's Media Queen. She was very smart, tough as nails, and a great person. She became the third partner.

The fourth person to join the band was Pete DeLaunay, a PR colleague of Dave's from the bank. He was eager to become what he coined as the company's first PRAD—PR/AD guy.

Each of us admitted we had no clue how we needed to set up, let alone run an office, so we hired a wonderful lady named Robin as our office manager/administrative assistant/receptionist/mom. The importance of a skilled person in this position cannot be discounted. That is especially true in a startup.

The next thing on our list was to find office space. Although we had our hearts set on being in downtown Seattle, we quickly learned that we couldn't afford space in even the crummiest of buildings. We found that the further away from the city's central core, the cheaper the rent. We briefly considered Yakima, Dave's hometown, but we figured gas for the 300-mile round trip would kill us, so we settled for space in a building several miles beyond walking distance from the city in the lower Queen Anne neighborhood. The view from my office was a drive-in Kentucky Fried Chicken joint.

Without a single client, it was foolish to consider leasing much space. A saner group would have opted for a single room with one desk and four chairs. But with optimistic confidence fueling us, we took a one year lease on a space with twenty offices plus a small conference room and a large open production area. I convinced my partners that if we thought and acted small at the beginning, chances are we would end up that way. I was banking on the opposite also to be true.

Two weeks before we moved into our new space, I got a call at home from a friend who was the marketing director for the Seattle Mariners, wanting to know whether I was interested in pitching its account. I told him I was no longer at Cole & Weber. He said he knew that and had heard that I had already assembled quite an impressive team. If we were interested in pitching the account, he would make room for us. The pitch was to be in one week in their offices at the Kingdome. I was so excited I almost forgot to thank him. I called my partners with the good news that we'd have an account before we even had an office!

We showed up at the Kingdome on May 29 with everything each of us had ever done for every client during our careers. Actually, like all agencies, we only brought the good shit. Funny how a few great communications examples impress a potential client so much he hires you because of it and then makes you do work so terrible you would never use it in a new business pitch.

We also developed some pretty cool ideas on how to increase attendance for the perpetually last place Mariners. One of the better ideas was to suggest they "spend money on the field rather than on promoting their lame, half-assed team." After a few chuckles and high fives, the idea was shelved. We needed money more than the baseball players did.

The presentation was held not in the Mariners' office but in a huge room inside the stadium. Behind a dais on a slightly raised stage sat fourteen guys ranging from the community relations guy to the bench coach. The owner sat in the middle. Their introductions took three times longer than ours.

After introducing our team, I presented what we thought was the most relevant case study in our bag of tricks. It had nothing to do with sports and was only somewhat related to selling tickets, but I made a pretty good case for relevance. Dave, Terry, and Pete made a good case for our other examples. The presentation was going pretty well and we were getting a lot of head-nodding and smiles at all the right times. I was about halfway into my closing when a guy sneaked up to the stage and passed a note down the line to George Argyros, the owner, who shouted, "Goddamnit, the fucking union just called a strike!" With that, they all jumped up and stormed out without even saying goodbye. We had just learned the true significance of when they say the game is all about balls and strikes.

Two weeks later, we moved into our new office. Actually, it would be more accurate to say we occupied our new office. After paying the first and last month's rent, we had no money to purchase furniture. Little by little, we brought items from home, yard sales, and discount places.

Our newly installed phone rang. I picked it up and proudly answered, "Elgin Kirkland Syferd." My eyebrows went up as I listened. My partners could tell by my expression that it was a business call. Our first.

After a couple of more minutes, I said, "Thank you very much for your interest in us, but as much as we'd like an account of your size, we're not the right agency for you."

All three started shouting at once. "Who was that? What do you mean we're not the right agency for them? Was the budget too small?"

"He said it was a million bucks."

"Are you fucking crazy?"

"It was a discount waterbed chain with a sleazy name. I know we need money, but if we start down that road, we'll never win the kind of business we want."

Accepting the waterbed business may have made us instantly profitable, but it probably would have forever branded us as a bottom-end retail agency. Starting with a reputable brand, on the other hand, can establish an agency's position in the minds of potential clients, employees, and the community. When you're starving and wondering where you're going to find the next meal, please remember that you are what you eat.

17.

OUR FIRST PRESS INTERVIEW

We had our first media interview after being in business for a couple of months. Because of our combined reputations and Dave's contacts, we were asked to meet with one of the business writers from *The Seattle Times*. She asked some smart questions about our previous careers, our idea of presenting communications solutions that were discipline agnostic, and so on. The interesting part came when she commented that several agencies had been started within the past five years and the largest of them seemed to peak at about $5 million in annual billings. "How large do you think you can be?" At that time, Cole & Weber was the largest with about $60 million, so without hesitation, I declared "$100 million." Dave immediately kicked me under the table and asked that I join him outside for a moment.

"Why the hell did you kick me?" I asked.

"I kicked you because you said $100 million. You can't say $100 million. You sound like an arrogant jerk. She'll roast us in the article! Get back in there and apologize for saying something so stupid."

Dave is the best PR guy I know, so I swallowed my pride and made up some shit about not understanding her last question. She repeated the question, and this time my answer was that we hoped that if we worked really hard, that someday we could also be in that elite $5 million group. I'm sure Dave was right because the article turned out to be really good, but I was still pissed for not being true to myself.

Later in the book, I'll tell you about our follow-up interview.

18.

FINALLY, A REAL CLIENT

Our dialing for dollars had been relatively successful. Although we hadn't yet landed an account of significance, we had picked up enough revenue from some reputable PR accounts and consulting gigs to have the confidence to hire an art director, copywriter, and a couple of account executives. We even had enough to lease desks and chairs for the new employees.

When I left Cole & Weber, one of my favorite clients, Princess Tours (a division of Princess Cruises) volunteered that its account was staying behind because it neither knew me without Cole & Weber nor Cole & Weber without me. That was okay with me because I was told by a Cole & Weber lawyer that if I tried to take any of its clients, the company would sue my ass.

A couple of months later, Judy Palmer, the CMO from Princess, called and told me they now knew Cole & Weber without me and they wanted to talk. She made it clear that it was just a talk. The company wanted to learn about our capabilities, take a tour of our facilities, and meet our people before deciding whether our talk would go any further.

The meeting with Bob Brennan, President of Princess Tours, and Judy, went very well. Everyone got along and they were impressed with the portfolios from our creative team. Although they didn't commit on the spot, we felt good about the prospect of winning our first major account. They promised to get back to us within a day or so.

"Ron, can you come over to our office this afternoon? We've told Cole & Weber a couple of times that we're not very happy, but we haven't let them go and won't unless we can work out something with you. We'd like to discuss fees. By the way, until this is settled, please continue to be discreet."

"Of course," I replied. I hung up the phone and yelled, "Tom, help me put together a rate card for Princess Tours and grab a couple of pair of those funny nose glasses! We're going to convince them to hire us today!"

We arrived at Princess Tours' office that afternoon as requested.

"Mr. Brennan," said the receptionist into her headphone, "there are a couple of, ah, gentlemen, here to see you. They won't give their names, but they said you wanted to see them."

Bob walked into the lobby and immediately cracked up at the two guys dressed in conservative suits wearing funny nose glasses. "Why are you laughing, Bob? You told me to be discreet?"

After parading us through his office, explaining to everyone that this was our attempt at discretion, we sat down and discussed a mutually acceptable financial agreement. "Okay, you goofballs are hired! Hang on while I call the agency and fire their asses."

I declined his offer, saying we wanted to get back to the shop and share the great news. The real reason, though, was that my love for winning is matched equally by my hatred for losing. And not just for myself. Throughout my career, I could never get over a sense of sadness for the people at the losing agency. I've been on that side and know all too well the consequences.

Our initial assignment for Princess was to help it fill its company-owned and leased land assets such as hotels, motor coaches, trains, and escorted tours as well as berths to and from Alaska on Princess Cruise Lines.

Since I had worked the business for several years, I knew the details cold. I had been relying, however, on a creative team that knew the business as well as I did. Now I had a team that didn't know squat about Alaska or the tour business. I tried to be a good delegator and give careful direction and then step away. As I've said many times, if you knowingly delegate to someone not capable of the work, it's not delegation, it's the connotation of abrogation. I came to the conclusion that I had made a bad hire. Out of desperation (and a shortage of money), I hired a portfolio instead of a person. My immediate solution was to put on my rusty creative hat and let the writer finesse the copy. The art director half of the team was doing decent work and was fine with me stepping in. Together, we developed some acceptable work.

I told Dave and Terry that we needed a new partner for the art director. The writer simply wasn't what I was hoping for, and I wasn't good enough to make our work great. I started the process by approaching a person at Cole & Weber whose work I had always admired. I knew I risked my old company's wrath and possible legal action, but sometimes, you just have to roll the dice in order to win. Terri Small was not just a brilliant art director, but also a great writer. I also had a strong feeling she had the potential to become a wonderful creative director.

It took a lot of persuasion and quite a bit of money, but she agreed to become part of the family.

Then I had to have another hard conversation.

"Jeff, I'm sorry. I'm letting you go."

"What? You're kidding. I can't believe this. I could tell you weren't happy with my work a few weeks ago, so I prostituted myself and did everything exactly the way you told me. I gave up my identity for you!"

I realized that not only had I just taken away his livelihood, but I had emasculated and stripped him of his dignity as well. I may be insensitive in many ways, but I have always believed that a person's dignity means everything to him, and nothing to you, so leave him with it.

"Jeff, listen to what you're saying. You are better than that. I may not have liked your ideas or style, but I'm just one person with an opinion. Come on, man; you have to be true to yourself. Every time you don't do what you believe is right, you're living for others instead of for yourself. When you doubt yourself and don't do what your heart desperately urges you to do, you become increasingly numb. Desensitized. Robotic. That magical twinkle in your eye dims. Your mistakes make you who you are. Take chances, learn, and grow with each choice you make. Remember, it doesn't matter what any other person thinks. Say how you feel—always."

"Gee, Ron, do you really mean that?"

"Yes, Jeff, I really do."

"Okay, you're a fucking asshole. I hate you and I quit."

19.

PLEASANT SACRIFICE

Not too long after we started producing great work for Princess Tours, the company got news that it was being granted some of the very first American tourist visas for mainland China. This was a huge deal for the company and a great opportunity for the agency. Everything would be from scratch.

Bob called to tell me that officials from the Chinese government invited him and Judy to come to Beijing to discuss details, and they thought it would be helpful if I came as well. He cinched the deal by telling me that his wife Reba was coming, and he suggested I bring Bonnie. I told Dave the trip was a sacrifice I was making for the sake of our client relationship.

While the five of us were seasoned travelers, none of us had been to China. Truth be known, virtually NO American tourists had been to modern day China! We were given specific instructions as to visas, shots, recommended clothing (very casual), and so on. Bonnie suggested that perhaps the native food wasn't going to be the same as we got at our local Chinese restaurant, so perhaps she should pack some fruit leather, dried foods, and candy bars. She wasn't concerned about her husband, however, whom she referred to as the human garbage can.

A couple of weeks later, we were winging our way to Japan in luxurious first class seats on a Northwest 747. The itinerary had us changing to China Airlines at Tokyo's Narita Airport where our accommodations were about to change rather dramatically. At the end of the Jetway, we encountered a very old Boeing 707. These venerable planes entered service in 1958 and basically phased out of all known commercial carriers twenty years later. Our plane looked as though it had been reincarnated from an airplane graveyard. And then it got worse.

We had first class seat assignments in Rows 1 and 2, but where the first class section was normally found, there were two benches along the sides on which sat four nasty-looking Chinese soldiers in full combat gear, each with an automatic rifle! The only other thing in the compartment was a very large container that looked like a huge coffee urn. On the back side of that compartment behind a heavy black curtain, we found our first class seats. Actually, our first class seats were identical to all the other twenty double rows of 3 x 3 seating. We weren't about to complain to the guys with the guns.

The flight was actually uneventful. The flight attendants were polite. The food was bland, whatever the hell it was. As we started our evening descent into Beijing, I looked out the window, but all I could see was total darkness. I knew Beijing had to be at least a hundred miles inland, but it appeared as though we were landing in the middle of the Pacific Ocean. It got even scarier when we felt the landing gear lock into place. Then, all of a sudden like magic, the runway and terminal light burst into bloom. After a minimum number of bounces, we taxied to the terminal.

We deplaned past the guys with the guns, down the moveable stairway, into a rickety bus that ferried us to the main terminal. It's not that we stood out or anything, but as soon as we entered the mostly deserted terminal, we were descended upon by a cadre of military officials. As scary as it sounds, they were very pleasant and escorted us through customs, helped us with our luggage, and led us to a waiting bus. As we drove away, I looked back and witnessed all the lights of the entire terminal and runways go black once again. I decided then and there that our marketing materials would not feature the getting-into-China part of the tour package.

We were unbelievably tired and miserably jet-lagged when we checked in to the iconic Beijing Hotel with its white marble, dark mahogany, and richly colored fabrics. The front desk person found a staff member fluent in English who helped us register and escorted us to our rooms about midnight. The room Bonnie and I had was actually a suite, and it was magnificent with twenty-foot ceilings, overstuffed furniture, a huge bed, and heavy velvet everywhere. We called down for a seven o'clock wake-up call.

The phone chimed softly a few hours later. When I put the receiver to my ear, a voice shouted, "WAKE UP! WAKE UP!" We bolted out of bed, thinking fire or war. It was neither—

just the front desk's very literal response to our request; it was our WAKE UP call.

After calming our nerves and a good laugh, we heard the faint sound of birds chirping. I went to the window, drew the immense velvet drapes, opened the balcony doors, and was awed by the sound of 2 million bells on a million bicycles twenty stories beneath us. No shit, we were on an intersection of two eight-lane roads with no cars, but thousands and thousands of bicycles. They were very orderly, with no passing, shouting, or crowding—simply moving along as a single unit with everyone ringing their little bells. Oh, and every bicyclist was wearing either a gray or blue Mao suit.

While Bob and Judy went off to meet with some government officials and Reba opted to shed more jet lag, Bonnie and I were introduced to Li, our male English-speaking guide/keeper. To my pleasant surprise, rather than finding three bikes with little bells, we were led to a shiny new van and headed out to explore this fascinating historic city—all in the spirit of research for our ads and brochures, of course.

On our way to the Forbidden City, we passed Tiananmen Square, where we saw a crowd that looked like a Super Bowl mob, times a hundred. "Stop," said Bonnie to our English-speaking driver/guide/keeper. "We want to go in there!"

"Are you nuts, Bonnie?" I asked. "There has to be a million people over there!"

"Ron," she replied, "it's May Day."

I had no fucking idea what the hell May Day had to do with anything. But I also know when not to argue with my wife. So I sat back, shut my mouth, and listened while Bonnie convinced our driver/translator/guide/keeper to park the van, find a phone, and get permission to alter our itinerary so the crazy American lady and her husband could join the million Chinese in Tiananmen Square.

I found that I had slightly overstated the number of people because after securing permission to escort us in, our driver/translator/guide/keeper and soon-to-be protector explained the seemingly orderly crowd was estimated at only between 600 and 800 THOUSAND.

"Why are they all here?" I inquired.

"Because it's May Day," they both replied in unison.

I still had no idea what that meant, but I concealed my ignorance with a simple, knowing nod.

We had been told by a government official before leaving the States that we should not overdress but dress casually. He may not have been thinking bright blue Adidas sweats for me and even brighter red for Bonnie, but in the U.S. back in 1981, Adidas sweats were considered casual. Anyway, to say we stood out was an understatement. Especially since our driver/translator/guide/keeper/protector had us following him though the lines of the drab, blue and gray uniformed throng toward the square's center.

I thought any minute one of these mild-appearing comrades might freak-out and scream, "Wait a minute, you fucking round-eye; I've been in this line for two days; no fucking way are you crowding in front of me." That's for sure what would have happened if this were the Super Bowl. I feared that even the slightest push by one fed-up comrade might lead to a million people stomping the shit out of us. I don't know what our driver/translator/guide/keeper/protector said as we made our way through the masses, but everyone was exceedingly polite and courteous in clearing a path for us.

We eventually arrived at a very large pillared building. Just inside the entrance, we came face-to-face with a huge white marble statue of a seated Mao Tse-Tung. The memorial was remarkably similar to a famous monument in Washington, D.C. I guessed imitation was the most sincere form of flattery the world over.

Then it hit me. "Oh, I get it," I said. "Today is MAY DAY! This is the national holiday that marks the importance of working people! They're all here to honor Mao."

Bonnie rolled her eyes. She always acknowledges my brilliant insights that way.

We shuffled along in a single, slow-moving line around the statue toward what I assumed was the exit. Although I was happy we had made this half-hour detour, I couldn't help but be impressed that nearly a million Chinese citizens would stand in line for days to see a carved hunk of stone.

As we turned the corner, I looked down to my left. "Holy shit, Bonnie! That's him! That's fucking Mao in that fucking glass coffin! He's right there in front of me; I can see the fucking hair growing out of his fucking ear!"

"Ron, please, you're embarrassing me again." She says that a lot. "Did you think all these people come from miles around to stand in line for days just to see a carved hunk of stone?" She's so damn smart.

After Bob and Judy completed the official paperwork part of our trip, we were taken on escorted tours to the Forbidden City, the Temple of Heaven, and the Great Wall. After a few fascinating days in Beijing, we left for Shanghai.

Shanghai was equally fascinating but more progressive. We had not seen a single modern structure in Beijing. Although our hotel near the Bund was as old as the one in Beijing, there were new buildings sprouting up everywhere. And while we had not seen anyone without a Mao suit for the past week, about half the population of Shanghai was in what would be considered Western-wear.

I have three quick stories about Shanghai. The first took place in our beautiful Art Deco hotel. As I said, Shanghai was in many ways more progressive than Beijing. On our first night on the way to dinner, we heard some old Jimmy Dorsey music. Intrigued since we hadn't heard anything but traditional Chinese music on the trip, we followed the sounds into a cocktail lounge. On the stage were eight very old Chinese guys in tuxedos from the 1920s. You could smell the mothballs. We concluded the clothes and instruments were put away during the Cultural Revolution and just recently put back to use. We loved it. This was an ad in the making!

I forgot to mention the food. The food was terrible. For example, they served us what appeared to be stale birthday cake and orange Fanta for breakfast. When asked for eggs, they obliged by serving a plate of cold, hard boiled ones. Cracked open, the eggs revealed a black interior. They were called thousand-year-old eggs, and I believed it because they tasted like a pencil eraser gone bad. Of course, I was the only one eating them. Everyone else had been subsisting on Bonnie's stash of fruit leather, dried fruit, and candy bars.

Our first dinner in Shanghai was hosted by some local government officials. It was in a very fancy restaurant at a nearby hotel. After several toasts to each of our governments with glasses of baijiu, which we learned was the Chinese version of white lightning, the main course was brought into the room. Everyone in our group was starving, and each had lost several pounds except me, of course. A huge platter, on which sat an enormous fish, was placed on the center of the table. Our group was salivating. Salivating until the chef sliced open the belly and pulled out the innards. I was the only one who ate that night, too.

The next day, we visited a commune. I've never met nicer people or been exposed to more abject poverty. We walked by a group of huts that were constructed of some sort of stucco, and then we were taken to the community hospital. The staff proudly guided us through the small entry to the operating room. I silently prayed to myself to remain healthy. In the room was a stone table, a shelf with acupuncture needles, and an open window. Outside the window was a pig sty.

We adjourned to the communal dining hut. The food consisted entirely of overcooked vegetables and rice. It wasn't too bad so we all cleaned our plates. Each time we did, our hosts smiled and refilled them. Finally, after the umpteenth refilling and our bellies bulging, our guide whispered that as long as we cleaned the plates, the assumption was we were still hungry and they were obligated to continue feeding us. With the next course, we each took a couple of bites and thanked the host for his hospitality. The guide told us later that our hosts were amazed at how hungry we'd been. We didn't have to eat again until we got to Hong Kong where we gorged ourselves at the airport McDonald's. Burgers, fries, and milkshakes!

A few months ago, a friend told me he was really unhappy with the work from his new agency. I saw him again the other day and he reported his agency had turned it around and was doing some great work. I asked him whether he'd been assigned a new team. He said it was the same team but their work improved greatly after they had taken a familiarization trip on the product.

The work we did to promote the Princess Tours product to China was extremely effective. In our case, the cost of the immersion was only my time, but the result was such that *I vowed never to allow our agency to do work for a client without the team first experiencing the product—irrespective of who paid*

20.

OUR FIRST BIG WIN

Apparently, someone at the Western Washington McDonald's organization had heard about our fledgling agency because out of the blue we were invited to pitch its business. We were two months old, had grown to six people, and had boosted our annual billings to about $1.5 million. The McDonald's account we would be pitching was $3.5 million.

For the next month we lived, breathed, and of course, ate breakfast, lunch, and dinner at McDonald's restaurants all over the city and quite a bit of Western Washington. Once again, we were up against Cole & Weber, plus two big name agencies from out-of-state. We found out the latter two had been included by the McDonald's Corporation because each had McDonald's business in other parts of the country. Besides consuming tens of thousands of calories, we researched the category and the market from the Canadian border to Oregon and from the Pacific Coast to the Cascades. We knew we were big underdogs, but we were big believers that the harder you work, the luckier you get.

The McDonald's Regional Marketing Manager asked to schedule a tour of our offices with the Co-op Executive Committee to be followed by a brief meet and greet. Ouch. We had our twenty offices, conference room, and production area, but we didn't have a whole hell of a lot in any of it. Fortunately, we had some friends in the film business. Within two days, our mostly empty offices had been propped with desks, chairs, plants, and even fictitious family photos. We looked to be at least three times our actual size. During the office tour, we hinted that many of our employees were at client meetings. Fortunately, no one ever asked for a head count and our brief meeting went well.

The following day, we heard from a media source that most of the McDonald's owners really liked us, although some thought I was a bit formal and perhaps too upscale to be able to relate to its customer base. I immediately dismissed the concern. The rest of the team, however, didn't.

The concern led to some serious discussions. Agency people have a tendency to over-think and second-guess practically everything. I even got caught up in it. Should I not attend the presentation? But if the CEO didn't attend the presentation, what would his absence say about the importance of McDonald's business to the agency? Should we ignore the tip? Should I pretend to be something or someone I wasn't?

I decided I am who I am. Dave agreed and said you couldn't put lipstick on a pig. I told Dave I appreciated his support but resented the analogy.

McDonald's has three levels of advertising support: national, regional, and local. The $3.5 million we were seeking was a combination of the last two. The Western Washington Owner/Operator Association (WWOA) Co-op is made up of individual franchise owners and the McDonald's Corporation. Irrespective of the number of stores owned, each franchisee and the corporation has a single vote. WWOA had eleven owners plus the company, for a total of twelve votes.

The presentation was held at McDonald's regional office, and we were ready for it! That is until we walked into the room. There were at least twenty people from McDonald's in the room. Nearly twice as many as at the Mariners pitch. And not a suit or tie in the group.

My partners were dressed as casually as the owners. I, however, was in a black Zegna suit, white shirt, and an Armani tie. I absolutely typified the stereotype about which we had heard they had expressed concern.

Our pitch was going well despite my appearance. Terry was wowing them with her media prowess and the savings she could generate for them. Pete rattled off so many terrific promotional ideas that the group was having a tough time not buying them all on the spot. Dave was as articulate about the big picture as he was comfortably casual. I formally presented several case studies that I related to their business. They threw us some good questions that we fielded pretty well.

I pressured myself to believe the close would win or lose the business for us. I believe in situations like these, the more pressure the better. After warming up with all the logical reasons why they should hire this local, scrappy, smart group of people, I moved closer to the audience, dropped to my knees, pulled off my tie, thrust my hands skyward, and yelled, "PLEASE HIRE US! PLEEEEAASE! WE NEED THE FUCKING MONEY! WE HAVE SMALL CHILDREN AT HOME!" Here's this guy whom some thought might be a bit too stiff groveling around on the floor begging for the business. The McDonald's guys cracked up. Our team had mixed reactions to my surprise finish.

Funny thing about an important pitch—you're supremely confident that you nailed it, but at the same time, you're absolutely positive you blew it. We made ourselves crazy over the next two days waiting for the verdict. The rumor around the agency was that everyone knew whom to blame if we didn't win.

Fifty-two hours and twenty-seven minutes later, we got the call from the corporation informing us that we had won the business. The place went gunny bags. Everyone was running around, claiming he or she knew it all along. We had hugging, cheering, and people singing McDonald's jingles at the top of their voices. In the midst of all the madness, we got a call from the president of the co-op, asking whether the whole group could come over so it could congratulate us. Rather than have to explain again the empty offices, we met them at a local watering hole. All eleven owners showed up; the executives from the corporation didn't. Several of the more well-heeled owners insisted on ordering and paying for the most expensive drinks in the place. By the time we closed the bar, we had even more reasons to love these guys.

We found out a week later from an insider that all eleven owners voted for us, but the corporation cast its one vote against. We figured the key to our victory was that the owners saw us as small business owners like themselves. To be fair to the folks from the corporation, there was a concern about our viability. Truth be told, I was a bit concerned about the same thing. I'd read about the pitfalls of growing too fast.

The next week, everyone in the agency hit the road to get to know the owners while not under the influence of either the win or booze. My first visit was with one of the greatest McDonald's characters of all time: Pat Newbury. Pat was an ex-military guy who got his start with the company before becoming a multiple store owner; he had experienced both sides of the coin.

These were the first two of many sage bits of advice he gave me:

"Ron, your company will never be successful with McDonald's until both the Corporation and the owners hate you equally."

What an incredibly astute and memorable way to warn me that favoring one side over the other would bite us in the ass. In other words, speak up for what we believe and to hell with the consequences. That piece of advice worked well for the next thirty years.

"Ron, always remember that any dummy can lead a horse to water, but if you can find some way to make that sucker float on its back, you've got a winner."

I didn't say I understood all of his advice.

It took a while for us to comprehend McDonald's way of thinking and conducting business, but once we did, we discovered that working on the McDonald's business was nearly the equivalent of earning a Ph.D. in marketing.

McDonald's considers its agencies as the third leg of its marketing stool along with the owner/operators and itself. Most owners take great pride in being independent business people while at the same time realizing the Corporation largely controls their fortunes and future. The Corporation makes its money off topline sales. The owners make it from the bottom. This disparity is often the cause of at least a certain amount of distrust. Both the owner/operators and the Corporation constantly attempt to manipulate the agency to their own point of view. Hence, Newbury's famous advice. Over our thirty-year history, we suffered through a few really nice but not terribly marketing savvy co-op presidents as well as quite a few regional people who really, truly didn't give a shit about the welfare of the individual owners. At the end of my agency career, we had the unique opportunity to work with a co-op president who was both stupid and an asshole. Fortunately, most of his fellow operators knew it and together we were able to work around him. All in all, though, it's a great system.

• • • •

McDonald's was my first exposure to a client that used its agencies as true marketing partners rather than vendors. Together, several times each year, the three-legged stool came together to determine the most appropriate product and pricing for their individual markets. Time and again, this inspired innovation. For example, the Big Mac and the Egg McMuffin were not conceived at Oakbrook headquarters; they were the ideas of a franchise owner in the Pittsburgh area.

We had an idea for a new food product that we thought was an absolute killer. We even had visions of a tie-in promotion that would rock the world. The account team members had a connection in the meat-processing business. The idea was to offer a hand-held sandwich with a patty made of duck meat and served with barbeque sauce. And the name, of course, would be the McDonald Duck Burger. The obvious tie-in would be, of course, Disney.

When the team lead enthusiastically presented this killer idea, we were sure we had the next Big Mac. The co-op members were laughing and having a good old time. That is until they realized we were serious. Then all shit broke loose.

"Are you fucking assholes crazy?" screamed one of the owners. "You're suggesting our moms and their kids are going to be lining up to eat a McDonald Duck? You're crazy! They'll tear down are stores and set fire to the remains. Let's take a vote to fire these stupid assholes right now!"

It took quite a while to get the guys settled down, but we somehow averted the vote and kept the account. We subsequently found out that if we had convinced McDonald's to go ahead with our craziness, Disney would have sued and owned our children for generations to come.

Most of the co-op owners were enigmas. In any given meeting, a simple mistake could cause one of them to rip off the head of an agency person and shit down his neck. As soon as the meeting was over, the same owner would be back to being our best friend. I had a particularly good relationship with most of the owners. Probably because my people did the majority of the work so they were the ones who caught most of the shit.

Our co-op meetings usually began with a short operators only session where people from both the agency and corporation would mill around outside waiting to be called into the room. On this particular day, the operator's session dragged on and on. Being naturally paranoid, I asked our team whether we should be worried. One of the junior members fessed up and said, "The co-op treasurer thinks there's a problem with the budget."

What I learned in short order was alarming. The owners elect one of their own as co-op treasurer, but the agency is charged with maintaining the guts of the budget. Their budgets, by the way, are very, very complicated. I was told that, in this case, the problem was not in the agency's accuracy but in the treasurer's lack of understanding the process and procedure. He was a nice guy, but not the best when it came to our complicated spreadsheets.

After a very long hour, one of the owners popped his head out and asked me to come in. Alone.

I walked into the room and saw the grim faces. "Ron," said the co-op president, "we have some serious concerns about the budget."

"What's the concern?"

"There's a serious gap in what should be in the bank and what is in the bank. Some of our members couldn't help but notice that you just bought a new Mercedes 600, so they want you to tell us where our money went."

I couldn't fucking believe what I had just heard. Without directly accusing me of embezzlement, they were at least questioning my honesty and integrity. I was pissed. Seriously pissed. With fight-or-flight adrenaline flowing, I was shaking like a leaf in a storm.

As I stood there, I realized that I probably looked guilty as hell. Silent and shaking. The adrenaline flowing. I grabbed a side chair, threw it to the center of the circle, jumped over a table, righted the chair, stood behind it, and glared at my accusers.

The burst of activity had calmed me and allowed me to speak normally. "This accusation is absolute bullshit, but let your inquisition begin. Tell me exactly what you have found and believe."

I could tell they were pissed too, and not the least intimidated by my brashness. The treasurer took over and explained the money gap in what the agency had reported and what he had in the bank. Without boring you with the details, the "problem" was simply a matter of timing. It took no more than two minutes for me to explain away the discrepancy. After only about a minute into my explanation, I could tell by some of the sharper members' expressions that they got it. By the time I'd finished, everyone understood. Except the treasurer.

The president said, "Thank you, Ron. We'll work this out internally. Now get your team in here and let's get this show on the road."

I was no longer pissed. If I had thought someone was stealing from me, I'd have been upset too. *But I vowed never to besmirch a person or his reputation unless I had unequivocal evidence. And then I'd still never do it in public.*

• • • •

I'll share a few quick stories to give you a sense of these work hard/play hard guys. One year, the group voted to have its annual two-day planning session at the Alderbrook Lodge on Hood Canal. The rationale being that it was such a remote location, there would be little to no distraction during the meetings and a chance in the evenings for brotherhood bonding. The bonding sessions always included alcohol. The amount the group consumed on the first night was ridiculous. The next night was even worse. No one was well for the late morning checkout. All the expenses were handled by the agency. Everyone was free to pack up and leave at his leisure. Walking through the lobby to my car, I saw one of my favorite operators standing at the reception desk.

"Jesse," I said, "you don't have to check out; everything has been taken care of."

"I'm not checking out; I'm checking in. I'm so fucking hung over there's no way I can drive home. I'll go back to Seattle in a couple of days. If I live that long."

Another time, we held the planning session at a hotel in Olympia, the state capital, during the legislative session. The idea was for everyone to conduct a bit of lobbying on the side. We decided to save the co-op some money by renting a hospitality suite for pre- and post-drinking. In order to save even more money, the senior guy from the agency chose to use the bedroom of the suite for himself. About 2:05 a.m., shortly after the bars had closed, a couple of the guys decided to have a nightcap in the hospitality suite. Scott, the agency guy, had already turned in, and since the bedroom was at the far end of the suite, he didn't hear them knocking on the door. Not to be denied that final drink (or two), they actually broke down the door. Scott, roused in his p.j.'s, poured them a drink. After a few more, the two owners went to bed without ever mentioning the shattered door. The replacement cost for the door did appear on their final bill, however.

For the first ten or fifteen years of our relationship, the co-op hosted an annual Christmas party, and the agency was always included. This was the one event when the operators dressed up; it was always a classy affair. One particular year, several of the die-hards were stumbling out of the bar at closing time. I looked around for a couple of my favorite guys to say goodnight, but I couldn't find them. Someone said they had just stepped out the hotel's side door, so I went out to see for myself and found them sitting on the curb.

"What the hell are you guys doing?" I asked.

"There's no more booze in there, so we paid a cabbie to go get us some," was the reply.

"All the liquor stores are closed. So are all the bars. He can't buy you any booze at this time of night. He's gone and so is your money."

With that, one of them held up the torn half of a hundred dollar bill. "We'll see."

Moments later, a taxi pulled up and the driver said, "I hope peach brandy is okay; it's all I could find."

"That'll do," was the reply as he was handed the other half of the hundred.

I don't mean to imply that the owners drank a lot. They didn't. But most of them played almost as hard as they worked. And their wallets were almost as big as their hearts.

During a September co-op meeting, the president acknowledged our fifteenth anniversary working together. Ed, another of my favorites, stood and addressed me.

"Ron, fifteen years ago, you promised that you would attend each and every co-op and executive meeting. You gave your word."

Oh, oh. This could be bad.

"Yes, I did."

"Well, goddamnit, you kept your word. Thank you."

Either we missed the same meetings or Ed was being generous, but the group gave me a standing ovation anyway. It's those moments that build legends and loyalty.

21.

OUR OTHER FIRST BIG WIN

Just before the McDonald's win, on August 31 to be exact, we got a call from the Seattle Mariners telling us we had won its business! Two months earlier, and sixteen days before we were even a company, the selection committee had voted to hire us. Why they never bothered to tell us until the strike was over is one of those weird "only clients know" things.

We did some pretty good work and learned a few damn interesting lessons. Probably the most significant lesson was: *If your product sucks, it's pretty damn hard to sell it.* We tried humor, guilt, even begging. Nothing worked. The die-hard 5,000 faithful fans were there for every home game irrespective of what we did or didn't do. The only time our advertising positively affected the numbers was when we announced the Yankees were coming to town.

Several months into the relationship, we had a critical strategy meeting for the following season with the Mariners' top executives, including the owner, George Argyros. The primary issue was the need to increase attendance dramatically for the coming season. The client suggested that we needed a new, catchier tag line. Maybe even put it with some music this time. We had a feeling that would be their non-solution. Everyone knew the real answer was to increase the payroll and use it to get some superstars. But everyone also knew that wasn't about to happen. We were ready with our big idea. We told them that we were already working on some lines, but we were hoping that it could be based on a big idea that we absolutely loved. Our recommendation was they price a large section of the perennially empty outfield seats for a buck a person. Although the team had never been a winner on the field, we rationalized that if the experience were cheap enough, families could start building tradition without busting their wallets. Until they visited the concession stand, that is. The owner said it was a stupid idea and he wouldn't even consider it. I said they were stupid not to consider it. George reiterated his position and we ended up having to create a catchy tag line put to music with really no substance to support it.

Up to this point, the client had been paying promptly. If you don't already know, cash flow is critical for a start-up agency. After hearing "The invoice is hung-up in accounting," or "Could you resend the invoice?" or "Are you sure you sent that to us?" we started to panic. On paper, we were out several hundred thousands of dollars. Our cash reserves were about down to zero. I requested an immediate meeting with their VP of Marketing who was a great guy, but the one who had been giving us the runaround.

"George is mad at you." I looked at Billy like he was from fucking outer space. "Let me get this straight, Billy. You guys have us on the hook for nearly a million bucks, and George is pissed at *me*! Is this some kind of stupid fucking joke?"

"Remember the meeting a couple of months ago when you called him 'stupid'?"

"I never called George 'stupid.' I would have never said that. First of all, I know he's not stupid; people don't become as incredibly successful as he is by being stupid. I remember disagreeing with all of you at the meeting. I may have even said the reason for rejecting our idea was baseless and stupid, but I never said **he** was stupid."

"Well, he thinks you did and he's punishing you for embarrassing him in front of us."

I was flabbergasted. But even more than that, we couldn't work with a client who didn't want our opinions. I'm fine with a client who pushes his ideas or even disagrees with ours, but to disallow us from even expressing our opinions could not be tolerated. Since George also happened to own Air Cal, I demanded that Billy get me a comp ticket on the first available flight and arrange a meeting at his office in Orange County. Thinking I wanted to apologize for my egregious behavior, Billy made the call and booked my flight. I was to be George's first appointment the following morning. However, I was not going there to grovel.

"George, I understand your position. I don't agree with it, but I understand it. If I can't stand toe to toe with you in an honest discussion of what we believe is best for your business, we're of no real value to your organization. I'm sorry if I offended you in any way but I doubt you're going to change your position on this matter, and neither am I, so if you will cut the check right now for what is owed to us, we can shake hands and I'll see you at the ballpark." He smiled, shook hands, and wrote the check.

The resignation of the Mariners' business was not a testament to our philosophy of not working for assholes. They were good people in a tough business. If you take away anything from this episode, it should be: *Be true to yourself; know what you stand for and stand up for it.*

Let me say this last thing about George. Although an incredibly tough and shrewd businessperson, he's a really nice guy. Thirty-five years later, I still see him every year at Grandparents' Day at the school in Newport Beach where we each have grandkids in the same class. In fact, we were recently at a Halloween party hosted by his wonderful daughter, Stephanie.

22.

AND THEN WE WERE TWO

Early in our second year, Dave walked past Terry Kirkland's office on the way to his own. He could hear her on the phone yelling at someone and using extremely profane, foul language. He poked his head into my office and asked whether I knew whom Terry was screaming at. I told him I thought she was just having one of her normal screaming matches with one of our people. If it were someone on the outside, perhaps we should know about it. He said he'd find out and let me know.

A little later, he came into my office, pale and angry. He said he found out that she was yelling at the president of the McDonald's Co-op. We looked at each other and both said, "Oh, shit."

The next morning, I got a call from one of, if not *the* most powerful owner in the co-op. He was gracious but very firmly said, "Ron, we can call each other those names, but you can't. You need to talk to Terry. End of discussion."

We knew that, because of Terry's volatility, we'd have to have our conversation with her when no one else was around.

We asked whether she could meet after hours the following day to go over some work stuff. She agreed.

At the meeting, I told Terry about Mike's call and admonishment. She was very contrite and apologetic. We all hugged and sang "Kumbaya."

Later that evening on his way home, Dave saw Terry parked alongside the road with a flat tire. She didn't have a spare, so he removed her flat, drove her to a service station, had it repaired, and returned to put it back on. During the process, they had plenty of time to talk about the earlier conversation. He told me the next day that she was very apologetic, and apparently, we'd dodged the bullet.

One week later was Halloween and we had scheduled a happy hour with the staff in the conference room. Terry had been unusually quiet and reserved all week. Shortly after the party started, she left without a word to anyone. A few minutes later, a delivery person, who had asked for me, was shown into the conference room and had me sign for a registered letter. It was from Terry's lawyer. She was seeking to dissolve the partnership due to "irreconcilable differences."

The Articles of Incorporation set forth by our good friend and attorney, Bob Diercks of Foster Pepper, clearly established the procedure for such an incident.

The day for the drawing was set, and unfortunately—fortunately, depending on who's looking at it—I was on a previously scheduled Princess Cruise with our client. The first thing that happened was that Terry asked Dave whether he would side with her against me. I'll never know for certain whether he just considered me the lesser of the two evils, but he told her he was casting his lot with me. When it came time for the drawing, Dave and I were hoping to lose, requiring Terry to set the price. We did lose and Terry set a fair price to which we agreed, so we bought her out.

The lesson I learned was that a business partnership, especially an equal one, can be even more challenging than a marriage. *If you don't totally love and respect the person before entering an* ***equal*** *partnership, don't do it.* It's fine to go into business with people whom you only kind of love and respect, but for heaven's sake, don't give up control unless the person truly deserves it. If you're convinced that the future success will primarily or mostly be driven by your contribution, make sure you have the controlling vote. Time and again, I've seen situations where people's egos convince them they have the smarts, balls, or whatever always to be driving the bus. Bullshit. There's something about not legally owning the deciding vote that can ultimately rise up and bite you in the ass. Unless, however, you're comfortable being a passenger on the bus.

The other lesson is that a buy/sell agreement is like a prenup—the time to create and agree on one is ***before*** *the marriage, not during the breakup.*

The whole experience was very unsettling and painful at the time, but in the long run, it was one of the more positive milestones in the company's development. We're forever grateful to Terry for her enormous contribution to the organization and to Bob for our great buy/sell agreement!

23.

EXPANDING THE CONCEPT

During my last three years at Cole & Weber, I was given responsibility for all the below-the-line companies: public relations, graphic design, direct, and sales promotion. That sounds way more important than it was when given the assignment. My main job initially was to coordinate the approved advertising messages with the various departments to make sure their disciplines didn't hurt the integrity of the advertising work. Basically, I instructed the direct mail experts to take one of our ads, add a call to action, shrink it down to a number 10 envelope, and mail it to someone. Or I told the graphic design people to turn the ad into a brochure. And, of course, the PR folks needed to write a press release regarding the subject matter and a story about the brilliant ad and its creators. After all, these were "below-the-line" people who didn't have the right to an opinion. At least not in an advertising agency, they didn't.

A few months into the job, I began to see the flaw in this thinking. The more I worked with these department heads, the less inclined I was simply to direct them to modify the advertising messages to suit their disciplines. Eventually, I started to ignore completely the dictates from the ad side. Instead, I worked with the leaders of the "below-the-line companies to focus on the core idea and interpret it in light of the specific discipline. True, the core idea was usually defined by the ad people, but we tried to go upstream before it was articulated in "ad-speak."

I remember being nervous the first time I showed the agency's executive creative director work from the direct mail group that had "interpreted" his direction.

"That's not what I asked for," he said. After I explained once again how the work was still true to the core idea, he said, "Tell the shithead who did this that I hated it, but you begged me into approving it. But tell him to stop thinking for himself. I may not be as benevolent next time."

It was the thinking and comments from people like him that helped me become a firm believer that: *Each "below the line" discipline must be considered a separate but equal tool in helping with clients' communications problems or opportunities. The best programs should call upon as many of these disciplines as possible, and working with a central idea, each discipline should rely on its own best thinking, practices, and executions.*

24.

DON'T STEP OVER THE GARBAGE

During the third year of Elgin Syferd, my friend John Hornall, who ran the Graphic Arts Department at Cole & Weber, came to see me.

"I don't like working there since you left," he said. "They've gone back to their old ways of telling us how to do our jobs. I'd love to come here and work for you. A couple of my key people feel the same. What do you think?"

I had loved my time working with John and his staff, and I appreciated the work his group was capable of doing, so my initial thought was to jump at the opportunity. Instead, I told him I'd have to think about it.

My ego said a bigger agency is a better agency. John's design team was as good as or better than any in the market, and he had decided to leave the largest agency to join one of the smallest. My ego liked that, too.

Decisions based solely on ego usually end up sucking the big one. So I put ego on hold and tried impartially to analyze the opportunity. I thought back to our founding philosophy of honestly believing in the equality of the disciplines. If we hired this team, how long would we play nice with them? How many times would I allow them to argue their position against mine before I ordered them to do it my way? Or, looking at it from their point of view, how long would they fight for their belief before job insecurity took over? Dave and I had created the perfect equal partnership. Why not try to replicate it in a slightly different model?

"John, we've decided not to hire you," I said in a meeting a week later. "But we have a proposal that has the potential to work out even better for all of us. We want to help you create your own company. Elgin Syferd will provide office space and your salaries for three months or until cash flow covers costs, act as your initial new business team, and provide management support. For that, we want 50 percent of your company. Note, I said 50 percent. Not 80 percent, not 51 percent, but definitely not less than 50 percent. We're the ones taking the risk, and I strongly believe you should have equal voice in everything you do. The concept has been working pretty well here. I'm always trying to bully Dave into my way of doing things, but it hasn't worked once. I'll add the kicker that if our two companies are still in business in ten years, we'll sell our shares to you at a fair market price. What do you think?"

John consulted with his employees and Hornall Design Works was born. A year later, one of John's recruits left for health reasons and the other, Jack Anderson, was made partner and we added his name to the letterhead. The only thing

I ever regretted in our deal was my promise to sell back their shares. At any price.

When I was reminiscing with Jack recently, he said "Ron, I've known you for thirty-two years, more than half my life. You've been a boss, an investor, a partner, a mentor, and a friend. What I'm the most proud of, and what means the most to me, is our friendship. Through all of our highs and lows, ups and downs, and wins and losses, we've always been friends, and to this day, we continue to be the best of friends. So, knowing I'm probably going to end up in your book, I thought we should have a conversation to refresh your memory about what a great guy I have always been. Also, if you insist, we can also bullshit about our time together where I stood back and learned, marveled, participated, laughed."

"Go ahead and talk, Jack, but remember I'm the one who decides what my millions of readers will hear."

"It was through you, Ron, that I learned the difference between interdisciplinary and multidisciplinary. The model you guys initiated at Elgin Syferd was to bring together the best of class of different disciplines and get the parties to work in an integrated fashion. Sometimes that worked, and sometimes, it didn't, but it actually became a model for how we built Hornall Anderson."

Then he asked, "Do you remember the day we were standing at the urinals in the men's room?"

"You're not going to get all weird on me, are you, Jack?"

"No. You looked at me and said, 'Do you want to spend the rest of your life being a big fish in a little pond, or a relatively significant fish in a big pond?' You said the only way that could happen was for me to stop being such a control freak. I needed to start hiring people smarter and better than me and learn to mentor and partner instead of always just doing. I took that advice to heart."

Hornall's first account was working in conjunction with Elgin Syferd on Princess Tours. We helped them win a few other accounts, but their work was so spectacular from the outset that they grew independently, as well. Before long, my role as Chairman of HADW was largely that of financial overseer and business sage.

Most of our agency clients back then were either commission-based or on an annual fee. We had several PR-only clients that were project-based, but they didn't represent a big part of our revenue. This allowed us to be pretty accurate with our financial forecasting.

Although Hornall Anderson started making decent money, I was critical of its lack of forecasting and concerned about the pretty dramatic ebb and flow of its revenue.

"I know we're not very good at either forecasting or maintaining a steady flow of work, but that's because the two are tied so closely together," John reported.

"Explain."

"Well, all of us are heads-down and ass-deep in projects right up until the job's done. It's only at that time that we can get freed up to go out and scrounge up more work. Sometimes, we're able to find new work quickly, and sometimes, not so quickly."

"You need a salesperson," I advised.

"We're all salespeople. That's how design firms keep their overhead down."

"I don't care about how other design firms work. Hornall Anderson is already different, and I think we need to be different when it comes to the sales process, too. Let's hire a full-time salesperson. I'm not talking about just any salesman. Let's find a designer who is really good at sales and have him work at it full-time."

"I don't want a designer who's better with his mouth than his design sense representing us," replied John.

"Point well taken, John. So maybe it's not a designer. Maybe it's a great salesperson with good business sense and a gift of gab *and* a person who has a deep knowledge of and appreciation for good design." I knew the perfect person.

The decision to hire Jeff Baker as something between a chief marketing officer and director of global sales was everything we hoped for and more. He was a huge advocate for the work, a terrific business/salesperson and a great guy. Revenue continued to grow, but at an even faster clip, by having jobs in the pipeline waiting for designers rather than the other way around. Profits increased dramatically in spite of Jeff's additional cost.

One day, the Elgin Syferd creative director came to me with a complaint about Hornall Anderson. He said that although we were partnering with it for all our collateral needs, it was not reciprocating in directing its clients' ad jobs to us. He cited a couple of examples with which I was only vaguely familiar. I promised to look into it.

At the next HADW board meeting, I broached the subject. There was some nervous chatter that amounted to double talk so I let it pass. After the meeting, I pulled Jack aside and asked him what the fuck was really going on.

"We're doing some really, really good work for both those new clients," he said.

"And your point is?"

"Don't get pissed, but we've set the bar really high, and I don't think your creatives are capable of producing work at that level."

I didn't get pissed. I got embarrassed.

After reviewing their new work, I was forced to admit that he was right. We had a saying at the office, "Don't step over the garbage." I didn't. I marched directly to our creative director's office and told him exactly what Jack had said and what I had seen. No embellishments, but nothing held back, either. His first, second, and third comments had to do with Jack's character, heritage, and sexuality. I let him rail a bit longer, and then I told him I knew we were doing some really good work, but Hornall Anderson had really stepped up its game. You can imagine his first, second, and third comments to me.

"Look at it this way," I said. "It's like your younger brother was promoted from the JV squad and is now going to compete for your varsity position. Would you rant to the coach? Complain that it wasn't fair? Or would you up your game? I should think that if a person is at all competitive, he would up his game. I would think if he chose not to become better, the only option for the coach would be to put the guy on the bench."

Thanks to his competitive spirit, the creative director upped his game and Elgin Syferd became an even better company. *I suppose there are times when confronting a problem quickly and directly may not be the best approach, but I'm positive the opposite far outnumbers them. Never, ever step over the garbage.*

Ten years after starting Hornall Anderson, we were faced with living up to our handshake deal to sell our shares back to Jack and John. Dave sold his shares immediately and, quite frankly, did so without fully realizing the true worth of Hornall Anderson. Several months later, at Jack and John's insistence, we negotiated my shares.

"I definitely remember that negotiation," said Jack. I think it was one of the most defining, funniest, heartwarming, and most frightening moments I've had with you. When it came time to buy your share of our company, you didn't want to sell."

"I'm still pissed that you wouldn't let me keep at least one share," I said. "With even a single share, I could have continued to brag about being a part of what has become one of the most respected design firms on the planet."

"Ron, you know we didn't want to buy you out because you weren't a contributor or highly valued; we just wanted to transition ownership to our valued employees. I can still see you kicking and screaming while agreeing to begin the negotiations.

However, there was an incredibly huge difference in the share price of what we wanted to pay and what you were demanding. Remember that signature meeting in a hotel with our financial advisor whom you had agreed to and our shared attorney?"

"Of course I remember," I said. "I agreed to let your financial guy be the arbiter because I knew he was smart and would agree with me!"

"Whatever, asshole. I remember you and I sitting across from one another screaming and disagreeing and calling bullshit on each other and virtually spitting across the table. It was an extremely emotional, highly charged meeting. At one point, I even threatened to close down the company before paying your price. Your retort was that you'd rather see all of us get nothing than accept our offer. My partner John just sat over by the side, watching the war wage on."

"I was serious, Jack. It was a matter of principle."

"Well, to our attorney's credit, over the next few days, he was able to orchestrate a financial arrangement with you, John, and me that we thought was a very high price and you thought was a very low price. More importantly, it was a compromise that we could all live with and the deal got done. I know I can speak for you, Ron, when I say that it's hard to overstate the emotional toll this took on both of us because this was more than just a financial transaction—it was symbolic of a severing of our business relationship and maybe even our friendship.

"Ron," Jack continued, "I remember getting the call from our attorney saying that everyone had signed the papers and the deal was done. No sooner did I hang up with him than I got a call from you asking whether I had a moment to talk. I replied with a hesitant 'Sure' and walked across the building to your office. As you came at me from behind your big, fancy desk, I noticed a little tear in the corner of your eye."

"You were imagining things, butt-wipe."

"I don't think so, ass-wipe. And then, rather gruffly, you said, 'Get over here.' I rather timidly approached and you barked, 'Come here!' as you gave me a huge bear hug and said, 'Jack, it just doesn't get any better than this! I fucked you and you fucked me! We lived through it and are still friends. Don't ever forget this day. It doesn't get any better than this.'

"I don't think I ever shared this with you, Ron, but I also remember the many times in your office looking at the wonderful collections of photographs of Bonnie and Alison. I was always touched that at the center of this very busy guy's universe was his wife and daughter. That became somewhat of an aspirational model for the relationship I have with my own wife and daughter. As a side bar to that, I remember a time many years after we were no longer in business together that you invited Jeff Baker and me and our wives and daughters to your beautiful home and hosted a lavish dinner in celebration of families. I think that was just one more quintessential class act by a very classy guy. Thanks, Ron, for being such a great partner and friend."

To this day I consider Jack to be not just a great friend but a true brother. But I still wish I had that one share.

25.

FINANCIAL SHIT

From the beginning, Elgin Syferd encouraged competition between disciplines. We opined that competition for the best ideas to solve client problems would be a good thing. Instead, we found that competition for the budget and, therefore, the "most important" discipline, proved to be dangerously combative and came close to tearing us apart.

When we had zero revenue, the company was split evenly between advertising and PR. As income started to flow, it came in heavier on the advertising side, which resulted in more ad than PR people being hired. Understandably, the more disproportionate the ratio became, the more the PR folks felt like the hind teat. And, of course, the normal reaction to winning is gloating. This is especially true in the ultra-competitive agency business. Needless to say, the ad people started taking on an unwarranted air of superiority, which was not received well by any of the rest of us—especially the PR folks.

Our solution was simple: We eliminated the separate P&L statements. At least, we thought it was a simple solution.

Dave and I refused to share the details of our financials. We operated under the formula that 50 percent of revenue went for salary and related, 30 percent for rent and expenses, and we got to keep 20 percent for expansion, security, bonuses and the like. Our people were told only how we measured up to the last metric like "Sorry, folks; we missed our profit target" or "Great news kids: BONUS TIME!"

While the single P&L may have been good in theory to stop the "We're better than you" attitude in the agency, it sucked as a management tool. With a single P&L, we weren't able to determine in which departments we could afford to hire or how much we could pay. That meant Dave and I had to dissect the P&L. In other words, we had to look at the company as two separate entities and hire people where needed and subtract them when and where necessary. It didn't take our people long to understand that we had a single P&L in name only and the bickering returned.

Our next solution was to look beyond revenue into profit. Much to the chagrin of the ad side, our initial analysis showed that although its revenues were significantly larger than those from PR, the ad people were getting their asses kicked when it came to profit percentage. When I explained that raises, bonuses, and other perks came from profits and not revenues, we witnessed employees who had been financially naïve become profit whores. Then we began to see an even different dark side to the competition.

"The HealthPlus team is in the conference room screaming at each other," Dave told me one day.

"So what?" I replied. "As long as the screaming is productive and not demeaning to one another, it's a good thing."

Dave said that from what he could hear just walking down the hallway, it was not a productive meeting, and they were yelling things about each other's mothers.

I went to investigate.

"What the hell is going on in here?" I demanded.

Everyone answered at once. As the volume increased, so did the finger-pointing.

"We presented an idea that could generate more profit on this account," said the PR guy, "and all it would take is for them to reduce the media buy. We could take that money and bill the whole amount at our hourly rate instead of just earning the commission."

The ad guy countered, "If we reduce media spending, it will hurt both the reach and frequency of the buy."

"Bullshit," the PR guy replied. "What you're really worried about is that your margins already suck and you don't want to give up revenue because then your margins will suck even more and you'll probably have to cut staff!"

I ended the fight by telling them to forget the money for the time being and jointly decide which course of action would generate the best business result for the client.

"Dave, we've created a monster."

The money monster never really died. Conceptually, everyone agreed that solutions to client opportunities should be discipline agnostic. On the other hand, people can't help being territorial, especially if giving up revenue to another department meant losing one of your own staff.

And, of course, you can't ignore the personal pride factor. "I'm doing a 28 percent profit; what's yours?" "Fuck you, asshole!" The competition inevitably led to each division trying to outdo the other. As we added more disciplines and created more P&L's, we exacerbated the problem.

The good and bad sides really came to play at year-end when all the numbers were rolled up to a single P&L. To demonstrate, let's say that three of the five profit centers turned profits ranging from okay to great. However, the remaining two lost money ranging from bad to terrible. The end result was that the company made money but not enough to issue bonuses.

"What do you mean there will be no bonuses this year?" shouted the ad guy. "We turned in a 28 percent profit and our goal was only 20 percent. You said the bonus pool would be based on the profits earned above base. How can I explain to my people that they get nothing for busting their asses and exceeding their goal by 8 percent?"

"We're one company here," I replied, "and this one company did not make the company goal of 20 percent. Because of the loss of a couple of clients and cutbacks with a few others, two of our divisions lost money this year. The result is that the company made a profit but not large enough to support a bonus pool—for anyone."

"That's not fucking fair! Why don't you just penalize those assholes who didn't make their goals?"

"We are. They're not getting bonuses either. Remember how happy you were with last year's bonus? Let me remind you that your division only broke even and the four others had stellar years—especially the two that didn't perform well this year."

One of my full-time jobs for the next twenty-plus years was to navigate the treacherous waters between encouraging each division to exceed its profit goals and to be willing to give up revenue and corresponding profits to another division for the good of the client.

Later in this book, I'll tell you about another attempt to eliminate divisional P&L's. It's too painful a memory to write about it right now. In fact, I'm going to brighten my own day right now by sharing a little story that one of our former art directors and now an agency owner, reminded me about recently.

The local ad community had a softball league that played a dozen games or so each summer. It was appropriately named the RAT (Radio, Advertising, Television) League. We ad-types are oh, so clever. Anyway, I happened to wander into the production area one night after work and found a bunch of employees having beers and talking about the upcoming season. Either in spite of being new or because of it, Kevin had been elected as team manager. After talking about the schedule, who were the teams to beat, and having a few more beers, Kevin and I were the last ones standing.

"Hey, Ron, my goal for this season is to have the most fun possible!"

"Listen carefully, my new friend. I have two bits of advice for you. Having fun is very important around here. In fact, it's core to our culture. But I believe very strongly that it's impossible to have actual fun and be a fucking loser at the same time. The only way to have real fun is to win. Got it? The other bit of advice is that I don't want to tell you how to manage your team, but my partner, Syferd, thinks he's Ozzie Smith. He's not. He's old. He's slow and can't hit for shit. Put Phillips at shortstop and Syferd in left field. But that's only a suggestion, of course."

I think scaring the shit out of the new guy may have helped because our previously mediocre team went 10-2 that year and lost the championship game by one run.

"You were right back then, Ron," Kevin later told me. "It's a lot easier to have fun when you're winning. It was great to kick major league ass on all the other agencies. And you know what else? Over beers after our wins, we talked about bringing that same competitiveness and desire to win on the baseball field right here to work. In fact, we decided to have more fun here at work by beating the shit out of the other agencies both in new business and at the award shows. We're going to have major fun kicking their asses on and off the field!"

A guy once called me an asshole for being too competitive. *I believe it's impossible to be too competitive as long as it doesn't force you to ignore the rules.* Of course, that was the same guy who called me an asshole for being able to manipulate people.

26.

THE WORST DAY OF OUR LIVES—WELL, ONE OF THEM

Through our good friend and client Bob Brennan, we were introduced to a value-added reseller of IBM computers. The company, CDI, was started by a guy named Denny who had been a very successful salesman for IBM. His business model was to purchase mainline computers from IBM, load them with the appropriate software, and resell them to businesses. He was kind of a weird guy, but Bob vouched for him.

Since he was a startup, Denny's marketing budget was small. That was fine with us because we were a little leery of the guy's financial capabilities. We explained that our policy for startups was for them to pay for all media up-front on closing and within ten days of invoice date for all inside and production costs. He agreed.

Denny and his hot wife/CMO were really pleased with the direction we were taking them, and in fact, they kept pushing us even further into four-color, full-page ads in their trade journals. For the next month or so, the cost for creating and producing the ads far exceeded the cost to run them.

Importantly for us, our out-of-pocket costs were relatively small and their payments continued to be prompt.

They told us their sales were going great, so we were directed to expand the media coverage to include consumer publications such as the regional edition of *U.S. News and World Report*. They were definitely stepping up their monthly spend, and since we were on a media commission basis earning 15 percent of the cost of each ad, we were happy campers.

When the first really big invoice hit Denny's desk, he called and said that cash flow was a bit slow, and he asked whether he could send us the money ten days after the media closing date. This violated one of our hard and fast rules: *Never act as a bank for any client.* However, after considering the dollars involved, the greed in our heads and hearts made the decision for us. Fortunately, we received the check exactly ten days after closing. All was good.

Denny told us that orders were rolling in and they were making a ton of money. He and his wife had us produce a couple of more really expensive ads. Over the next couple of months, they had us expand the media buy to include the regional editions of *Time*, *Newsweek*, and *Sports Illustrated*. Each month, Denny asked for a bit more time to pay his bill and we relented since he had always delivered by the date promised. The obvious problem was that we were indeed acting as his bank and now paying the publications not just after closing but after the ads had already appeared. *Greed can make you do some really stupid things.*

The inevitable occurred. I got my usual monthly call from Denny, but instead of telling me when we'd receive our check, he casually announced that his company had just been forced into Chapter 7, an involuntary bankruptcy. I knew the definition of bankruptcy but definitely not what a bankruptcy would mean to us.

"Okay, Denny," I said. "I hear you, but you owe us nearly a million bucks. What about the million bucks? When do we get our money?"

"That's the point of bankruptcy, Ron. Our liabilities exceed our assets. We have no money to pay our bills. We're completely busted. In fact, all the money we've paid out in the past ninety days has to be returned to the court."

"Now just wait a fucking second, you mother fucker!" I screamed. "We're on the line for almost a million bucks. A lot of that has already been paid—by us! Are you telling me that not only are you not going to pay us what you owe us, but we have to pay even more for the privilege of being fucked by you?"

"Now you're starting to understand, Ron," he said in an all-too-calm voice.

"I'm going to fucking kill you, Denny!"

The agency immediately went into panic mode. We set up a crisis center in a spare office where we assembled all the CDI invoices as well as every media invoice. As close as we could figure, we were in deep shit. About $600,000 had already been paid by us to various media and production vendors, and we were on the hook for another $200,000 to $400,000.

We consulted with our attorney. He confirmed it. We were in deep shit.

Several of us immediately began calling the reps from the publications to which we had committed but not yet paid to share with them the bad news. Needless to say, they all promised to do what they could, but they said they had to take it up the ladder. We reiterated that CDI had no money and that neither did we.

A few days later, we got some good news in a very strange way. Our bank called to tell us we had bounced about $200,000 worth of checks "For Insufficient Funds." We were overdrawn because of the money we hadn't received from Denny. Much to our delight, those checks were to publications for CDI insertions. We immediately called those pubs and gave them the bad news, too.

Bottom line, after some serious begging and tough negotiating with the court and all the publications, we ended up with a $620,000 obligation. Although we had been doing okay financially, we were far from being able to pay a debt like that. We explained to our "creditors" that if they forced us into bankruptcy, they'd get nothing but the write-offs. Their option was to work with us. They all agreed not to force us into bankruptcy and to set up payment schedules. It took some very austere measures, but we paid off "our" debt over the following year and a half.

Some of our friends and associates asked why we didn't just close the agency and start over. The answer to us was simple; our names were on the door.

I have to share two additional anecdotes about the "bankruptcy" episode. First, the not-so-funny one.

About a month after Denny's bankruptcy announcement, we had our annual Christmas party for clients at my house. I had never even considered telling Denny that he had been uninvited. If I had thought about it at all, I would have thought he'd be too embarrassed to show up. Not so. Not only did he and his wife show up, but she made a grand entrance with a full-length white mink coat that Denny had just given her for Christmas. It took Bonnie, Dave, and me to hold back Dave's wife from killing her on the spot.

A few years later when we hired our first big-time accounting firm, the accountants talked about the period when we were technically bankrupt. Indignantly, we told them we had never been bankrupt—neither technically nor otherwise. "*Au contraire*," they replied. "You are technically bankrupt when your liabilities exceed your assets and you have no reasonable way out of the situation."

That response only confirmed for us that we weren't bankrupt: *When you have confidence in yourself and your partners, you can always find a reasonable way out of any situation.*

27.

SPEAKING OF STRANGE CLIENT EXPERIENCES

Back in my Cole & Weber days, Jacobi instructed me to get involved with the Seattle/King County Convention & Visitors Bureau. Actually, it went a bit further than just involvement. He not only wanted me to join the board; he told me personally to lead the business on a pro bono basis. He said the bureau's budget was too small for it to be a real client, but our involvement could pay dividends through the connections I would make.

The executive director was a guy named Hartley. At that time, I stood about 5'10" (I've been steadily shrinking back to my birth length) and Hartley was damn near a foot taller. As a superstar basketball player for the Idaho Vandals, he was an early pick by the Minneapolis Lakers. However, after discovering he'd make less as a pro basketball player than a beginning government employee, he turned down the contract. I'm sure that with each passing year watching the b'ball salaries soar, he must get more pissed about being born too early.

Anyway, over the years, Hartley became a good friend. Even though as a startup agency we couldn't afford him as a pro bono client, I acted as his personal marketing consultant. It didn't take much effort, and as I said, he was a good friend.

In fact, we were such good friends that we even bought a plane together as an investment. It was a Cessna 182 on floats. Neither of us was a pilot, but the idea was to lease it to our mutual friend's air service. We could make some decent money while realizing some excellent depreciation tax breaks.

It was a common courtesy of a few fishing camps in Northern Canada and Southeastern Alaska to host the owners of the leased planes the week after the last paying customers left. The custom was for those of us flying north to gather in the waiting room of the air service while the planes were being loaded. On this particular trip, I was the last to arrive and barely had time for a cup of coffee before it was announced that the six planes were ready to be boarded.

To my amazement, everyone jumped up and ran for the door, including Steve, one of my best friends. The only two left were Hartley and me. Strange behavior, I thought. There's room for everyone on the planes. What's the rush?

As Hartley and I ambled down the dock, I asked which of the company pilots was going to fly our plane.

"Surprise," said Hartley with a big shit-eating grin on his face. "I am!"

"What are you talking about? You're not a pilot."

"I am now," he said. "I've been taking lessons and I got my license yesterday. Isn't that great?"

Now I understood the rush for the planes as I ran for the other planes. I ran past our empty plane and tried to open the door of the next one in line.

"We're full; get in your own plane!"

By the time I tried to board the last plane on the dock, all five had fired their engines and I had received my final rejection. That final rejection, by the way, was delivered with a grin from my dear friend, Steve. He waved bye-bye as I dejectedly headed back to our plane.

Hartley was so busy with his pre-flight checks that if he noticed my late arrival or the panicked look on my face, he gave no indication.

"Are you sure you know how to do this, Hartley?" I asked.

"Absolutely! I did my first solo yesterday."

Shit. Do I bale like a coward or man up? Bale!

"Here we go!" shouted Hartley. Too late. Time to man up.

In case you've never flown in a float plane, the process is quite simple. After the warm up, the plane begins to taxi while the floats are still partially submerged. The idea is to build enough speed that the floats raise up to the point where they're literally skimming the water. This allows the plane enough speed for take-off. This process is called getting up on the step. Of course, the heavier the load, the longer it takes to get up on the step. And without being on the step, the plane can't take off.

In less time than it took for me to explain that, all the planes in front of us were airborne and heading north in the direction of Gas Works Park at the end of Lake Union. At that point, they would take a left turn and fly over the Aurora Bridge.

"Hartley, aren't you supposed to get the plane up on the step?" I nervously asked.

"I'M TRYING, GODDAMMIT!"

Shit. Why didn't I bale? I shifted my fixed focus from dead ahead to Hartley's face and nearly cried. He was beyond intense, which should have given me some sort of confidence except that he was ghostly pale and sweating profusely.

All of a sudden, we were on the step and the plane was accelerating. But we had been trying for so long that we were rapidly running out of lake. Finally, the plane broke free from the water and we started our ascent.

"WE DID IT! WE DID IT! WE'RE UP!" screamed Hartley. Not a huge confidence building announcement, I decided.

The next problem was that we had used up so much of the lake that we didn't have the altitude to go over the bridge. Not really a problem because before I could question our next move, we had flown *under* the bridge. Of course that's not only risky but illegal. But we were safely in the air and on our way.

We cleared both the Queen Anne and Magnolia hills and were flying north over Puget Sound at about 6,000 feet when we both began to relax a bit.

"Great job, Hart," I said.

"Thanks, Ron," he replied. "I don't know if you noticed, but I was a little nervous back there. This is only the second time I've flown without the instructor, and the first time I did a take off with a fully loaded plane."

"No, I didn't notice," I lied.

Things calmed down considerably as we headed north. In fact, we were able to relax to the point where we didn't have to keep our eyes glued to the "road" ahead and the instruments. Not exactly autopilot, but far from the sheer terror of a half hour earlier.

When six planes are all flying in the same direction, at the same speed, and at the same altitude, they're in somewhat of a cluster.

"HARTLEY, LOOK OUT!" I shouted as I looked past him to the terrified face of a friend in the plane next to us as the cluster had just become more intimate.

Hartley reacted immediately by turning sharply to the right and screaming like a girl. We didn't exactly do a barrel roll, but we weren't exactly in control either. Hartley pulled back on the yoke, and as we started to level out, I realized it was me screaming like a girl.

"Wow, that was close," said Hartley. "Why the hell didn't you tell me sooner?"

Because I'm an idiot, I thought. I'm an idiot for getting in the fucking plane in the first place.

The rest of the flight and landing were without incident. Thank God. My buddy Steve was waiting for us at the dock as we taxied in and tied up. Steve was the husband of our initial partner, Terry Kirkland. He was a Seattle Police homicide detective and a great guy. We grabbed our bags and headed to the cabin that the three of us were sharing. It was pretty late so we grabbed a little food and a lot of drinks and turned in. Hartley had volunteered for morning kitchen duty so we told him not to wake us until the food was on the table.

Clump, clump, thump, clump! What the hell is that, I thought? The whole cabin was shaking as the door burst open and Hartley shouted, "Someone stole our plane! It's gone. Someone stole it!"

"What the hell are you talking about?" Steve and I asked in unison.

"The plane, it's gone. I went down to get my recipe book and the plane is gone! Someone must have stolen it during the night."

"Come on, Hartley," I said. "We would have heard it take off. All we heard were crickets."

Steve, the cop, said in his official voice, "Let's go investigate" while giving me a wink. So we jumped into our clothes and headed to the plane.

It was gone. Seriously, the plane was gone. A couple of pilots were standing on the dock with shit-eating grins on their faces when we arrived. As we reached where they were standing, they pointed into the water and burst into laughter. We looked over the edge and there was our plane, still tethered to the tie-down rope, but completely submerged.

"What the hell happened?" asked Hartley.

One of the pilots cleared up the matter by explaining that the pilot had obviously parked the plane with the wind instead of against it. In that position, the wind can lap the waves over the pontoons, filling them, and when heavy enough, sink the plane.

"Ron, I'm so sorry," sobbed Hartley. "It's my fault.

"It's okay, Hart. We have insurance."

I didn't have the heart to tell him I would have scuttled the plane myself if I had known how. That was the start of one of the happiest days of my life. And I never again flew with my good buddy, Hartley. From then on, all my consulting for him was on terra firma.

28.

ANOTHER REALLY BIG WIN— I MEAN REALLY BIG!

In 1994, Bob Brennan, the guy who hired us at Princess, moved to Holland America Line as EVP of Marketing and Sales. I was sad because he was a great client and a close friend. But another dear friend, Judy Palmer, was still there, and we were doing some pretty good work together.

Six months into his new job, Bob called and invited us to pitch the Holland America Line business. "Chiat/Day is our agency, but they're in San Francisco. I want a local agency. Besides, I don't think they really understand our business. Are you up for it?"

"Tell me about the pitch," I said. "What's the timing and who else is going to be invited?"

"Just five or six of the usual local suspects. With your category knowledge, I think it will be a piece of cake."

"Let me talk with Dave and get right back to you."

The budget for Holland America Line was significantly larger than that of Princess, so it was tempting, but our decision came down to the proverbial bird in the hand. In order to pitch the business, we'd first have to give up Princess. If we didn't win, we'd have to lay off some really good people. We couldn't do that to them.

"Sorry, Bob; we're going to have to decline," I said the next day and gave him my reasons.

"You'd be a shoe-in," he pleaded.

"Sorry; we simply can't gamble with the livelihood of our employees."

A couple of weeks later, Bob called and said he had visited with the usual local suspects and was even more convinced that we were the right agency for them. Then he blew me away.

"I've talked with Kirk, our CEO, and Nico, our owner. They'd like to meet with you individually. By yourself. In secret. If you can convince them to hire you, you're hired. If you can't, no one will be the wiser and we'll proceed with the review."

It didn't take me long to say yes.

My first meeting was with Mr. A. Kirk Lanterman, who is one of the two smartest people I've ever known. He is also known for his dark humor. The combination makes him one of the scariest people on the planet.

The meeting consisted primarily of me bragging about our category experience, telling Kirk how smart we were, and explaining how we could have a strong impact on his sales. He cut me off mid-pitch.

"You sound like you're full of shit," snarled Kirk. "I think that's a good trait for an advertising guy. We'll see what Nico has to say about you. And, I guess, what you'll say about him. I'm the fifth president he's had in the last nine years. I'm the one he moved his whole fucking company from New York to Seattle for. He relies on me, but I'm going to push this decision off on him. I don't want a black mark on my perfect record."

Not exactly the response I expected from the CEO, but at least I was going to the next step. It was time to meet the company owner, Nico van der Vorm. The meeting was set for lunch the following day in the private dining room of Rosellini's.

Decked out in my nicest conservative dark suit, white shirt, and solid tie, I arrived early. Nico was already there. Shit. We were seated in a room set for thirty, but reserved for the two of us.

He stood as I extended my hand and said, "Nice to meet you, sir."

Nico said something. Actually, he said several things. None of which I could understand. I thought at first he was speaking Dutch. The closer I listened (while, of course, smiling politely and nodding enthusiastically), the more I realized he was speaking English but with a very heavy accent. Actually, it may have been a mild accent, but I am uniquely challenged to comprehend people from Texas or even Boston, let alone from a real foreign place.

As the meal progressed and my nervousness began to ebb, I realized a couple of things. First, Nico was a truly nice, cultured gentleman. Second, I was starting to understand him. He asked about me, my family, and my company. I pulled in my reins and answered as humbly as my ego allowed. As this very low-key meeting drew to a close, Nico looked me in the eye and said, "I see a cabin. A cabin deep in a snowy forest. From the stone chimney of this cabin, I see smoke. Smoke curling from the chimney into the sky blending with the falling snow." And then, nothing. He just sat there looking at me. What the fuck? After a couple of minutes of me staring back at him, waiting for the proverbial next shoe to drop, I broke the silence with "Interesting, Nico. Very interesting." He smiled and extended his hand. We shook and went our separate ways with mutual expressions of "lovely lunch," "enjoyed our conversation," and "must do it again sometime."

When I got back to the agency, everyone was lined up to hear how it went. "He's a really nice man. An authentic gentleman. I was even able to understand nearly half of what he was saying, but I'm afraid I blew the interview."

I went on to say that since Nico hadn't really seemed to want to hear about the agency's capabilities, our last exchange must have been his pass/fail test for us. When I described for them about the cabin in the snow and my response of "interesting," everyone started yelling about how stupid I was for not realizing it was allegorical, or mythical, or whatever, and I should have said this or that. My lame response was, "I guess it was a good thing that we didn't resign Princess."

The next day, Brennan called. "You're hired! You blew him away. He loves you. He said you understand him and his brand like no one he's ever met. I don't know what you said, but it had to have been perfect."

Sometimes more is said with less.

We celebrated for days. For the second time in three years, we doubled the size of our agency virtually overnight.

29.

AND THEN GOD SAID...

"Hey, you, agency guy at the end of the table," snarled Kirk Lanterman, "what the hell are you doing?"

"Taking very careful notes, Kirk," I answered.

The scene was the boardroom at the headquarters building of Holland America. The occasion was the weekly inventory meeting. Ever since winning the business, we were invited to sit in on this meeting as well as the monthly revenue meeting. The primary responsibility fell to me, but I was spelled once in a while by Dave, Jan Edmondson, and Tim Pavish. There were usually fourteen to twenty senior executives at each meeting which lasted four to six hours. The representative from the agency was the only "outsider" invited to attend.

The purpose of the inventory meeting was to analyze every departure of every ship in the fleet to determine what actions needed to be taken to ensure maximum capacity and revenue. That's a hell of a lot of ships, departures, and actions. The monthly revenue meeting was equally tedious.

Terror occurred when Kirk singled you out for a question or, more likely, a criticism. The key to living through these meetings was to stay awake and pay attention to everything Kirk said. The problem was those long periods of excruciating boredom when every number in a three-hundred-page document was carefully scrutinized. Out of self-preservation, I looked for ways to stay awake and not get fired. The first was to drink lots and lots of coffee. But Kirk charged a dollar a cup. Not just for me, but for his people too. When I asked why everyone had to pay, Kirk told me to shut up. That strategy was getting too costly, so my next was to commandeer the chair at the far end of the table on the same side as Kirk. That gave me some protection, but Kirk had an uncanny awareness about everything. As soon as my eyes reached half-mast, he'd bellow, "Hey, you, agency guy at the end of the table, what the hell are you doing?" So I started taking notes. Not just notes of which sailings needed support, but notes of Kirk's comments.

"Don't try to replicate my brilliant oratory," Kirk replied. "Just try to capture the essence of my direction with your limited knowledge of our written language. Best you stick with short, single syllable words. I don't want you interrupting every couple of minutes with spelling questions."

He can be so damn funny that I not only stayed awake to make sure I never missed a comment, but I actually looked forward to his meetings. I collected these comments for years, and for his seventieth birthday, I compiled them into a leather-bound book titled *And Then God Said...* Here is that book in part:

Foreword

A. "Kirk" Lanterman is the smartest person I know. He also has the most incredibly quick, dark, and acerbic wit. His beautiful wife, Janet, once said to me "Can you believe that some people are intimidated by Kirk?" Yes, Janet, most of us can believe that because he is also the most intense, best businessperson I've ever known.

Someone once said that sitting in one of Kirk's meetings was like playing goalie in a soccer game: When the ball is away, there can be long periods of boredom, but beware, inevitably they will be punctuated by moments of sheer terror. It's true. I've experienced them. And I've seen the panic on the faces of those employees who managed to live through his words. But I've also been amazed at his insight, wisdom, and most of all, humor.

Every comment, every exchange that you are about to read actually happened. Knowing Kirk, I'm certain that some of these comments were made with a twinkle in his eye. But the scary and, therefore, funny thing is that no one ever knows for sure.

Ron Elgin

AND THEN GOD SAID...

Kirk: We don't allow payroll deductions here. That concept is based on the assumption that employees will stay employed. I refuse to give false encouragement.

...

Kirk: Let's go ahead with your idea. Be sure, however, to leave us a forwarding address so we can let you know how badly it failed.

...

Employee: Can I go first?
Kirk: Believe me, you will be the first to go.

...

Kirk: I used to eat fish because it's brain food, but I got so far ahead of everyone else I had to stop.

...

Kirk: I've started eating fish again.
Employee: Are we catching up?
Kirk: No fucking way. I just wanted to extend my lead.

...

Employee: The travel agents will get very excited about this.
Kirk: Travel agents get excited if you put them in a pen and throw them shrimp.

...

Kirk: Where's Paul?
Employee: At home, resting up after his heart attack.

Kirk: I have forty-three field salespeople resting at home every day; I don't need my fucking inventory control guy doing it, too.

...

Kirk: Democracy is an interesting concept, but in practice, it just takes too fucking long. Dictatorships are much more efficient. Especially mine.

...

Kirk: Personally, I'm really quite wealthy; I don't have to worry about much. Unless you have a lot more money than it looks like, I'd put some serious time into worrying.

...

Kirk: I get the feeling from watching most of you that working here is like semi-retirement. Except that asshole sitting on the end who appears to be already fully retired.

...

Kirk: What are you doing?
Employee: I was going to sit with you because there are eight people sitting on the other side of the table.
Kirk: Get over there with the rest of them. I want this to be a fair fight.

...

Kirk: Your idea is ill-conceived and not well thought-out. You must be familiar with those words; you see them often enough on your employee evaluations.

...

Kirk: He eats people alive, but compared to me, people say he's a vegetarian.

. . .

Kirk: When I fire you, I'm going to replace you with a jar of flies. With you gone, I'll still be able to pluck the wings off defenseless weaklings.

. . .

Kirk: HAL's marketing department sells $700 million of beds with thirty-two people. Windstar's marketing department sells $30 million with ten people. My calculation is that Windstar should only have 1½ people. Since you are clearly the ½, which one of your people are you going to keep?

. . .

Kirk: The best way to train people is to punish them for their mistakes.

. . .

Kirk: After that comment, I'm not sure I'm going to miss you when you're unexpectedly gone.
Kirk: (said to a currently employed staffer) Since I'm nearing retirement, I'm curious: What's it like?

. . .

Kirk: (said to the head of the ad agency in front of the staffer) Ron, here's a chance for you to pay me back for all the nice things I've done for you: Hire this son-of-a-bitch and write off his salary as a charitable expense.

. . .

Kirk: Please, don't ever tell people where you work.

...

Kirk: Why don't you do something really positive to help increase sales...like locking yourself in your office and never talking with anyone ever again.

...

Employee: Would you like me to restrict capacity on that sailing?
Kirk: I have a marketing department and advertising agency that help me do that. I don't need an inventory control guy doing it, too.

...

Kirk: Does it ever bother you that you're the last one to know what's going on in the department I pay you to run?

...

Kirk: No one has effectively run your department since I fired your predecessor.

...

Kirk: Maybe I'm not as smart as I think I am. Perhaps I shouldn't have fired your predecessor.

...

Employee: Who was that poking his head in the door?
Kirk: Probably your replacement checking to see whether I'd fired you yet.

...

Kirk: I made a mistake thinking you knew what was going on in your department. Next time I'll just ask one of your employees.

. . .

Kirk: Have you heard about the Japs in World War II who hid in caves for decades without ever seeing the light? Makes me think about the people in our marketing department.

. . .

Employee: The pattern seems to be that a large number of our former employees return to us after six to nine months elsewhere.

Kirk: We simply can't allow that disruption to continue. I want a formal policy created that details the severe punishment imposed for all those who return. That will keep anyone from leaving.

. . .

Kirk: (said to the head of the ad agency) Ron, I'm looking to buy a business with high margins but that requires no talent, intelligence, or capital outlay. Is your agency for sale?

. . .

Kirk: Is the confidence in your proposal based on fact or stupidity?

. . .

Kirk: People have corrected me in the past. Of course, none of them are still with us.

. . .

Employee: We can't discuss that now because he isn't here.

Kirk: Why should that make a difference? He's never here mentally, anyway.

. . .

Kirk: I want to run a contest for our salespeople. All those who book one group get their names thrown in the hat fifty times; two groups, forty times; three groups, thirty times, and so on up to six groups where they get no chances. Then we draw and fire the fucking winner.

...

Kirk: How are you feeling since your last heart attack?
Employee: Better.

...

Kirk: Good. Maybe now you can stop dogging it by working only 6 ½ days a week.

...

Kirk: You have no balls.
Employee: I know. You took them when I first arrived.
Kirk: That's right. And anytime you start thinking otherwise, come into my office. I have them in a jar on my desk.

...

Kirk: You get only two weeks of vacation after ten years, not four like everyone else because you're only half as productive as the others.

...

Kirk: We should start a pool for Paul's next heart attack; both for when it happens and for how long he's in the hospital. Don't forget, though, I can control both.

...

Kirk: I want you to fire somebody today.
HR person: Anyone in particular?

Kirk: No. Anyone will do.

. . .

Kirk: This *is* a democracy. It's just that there is only one vote in my kingdom.

. . .

Kirk: Where is that stupid son of a bitch?
Employee: He has the flu.
Kirk: You didn't answer my question. Where is he?
Employee: He's home with diarrhea, vomiting, and a high fever.
Kirk: So, why is he home?

. . .

Kirk: The guy next to you says he's too sick to eat. With the numbers you're reporting, why are you eating?
Employee: I haven't eaten or slept in days.
Kirk: Okay. That will do as a start.

. . .

Kirk: I think Canadians take their long vacations only in the winter. I've not seen research to back this up, but now that I have issued the statement, it has become an irrevocable scientific fact.

. . .

Kirk: I want you to fire some of our accounting people now that we have less sales and, therefore, less money to count.

. . .

Kirk: Where is that asshole?
Employee: You gave him the day off.

Kirk: Don't you ever say anything again in front of people that implies that I have a human side!

...

Kirk: In an attempt to increase productivity, I've decided to replace each of you with an Energizer Bunny. There will be no difference in intelligence, and they'll last a hell of a lot longer.

...

Kirk: This Friday, we're going to fire all directors, VPs, and above. Next Friday, if I feel that I miss any of you, I will let you come back. At a lower wage, of course. Come to think of it, this is a great opportunity for us to promote a whole bunch of fuckers right now so they can qualify to get fired, too.

...

Kirk: You are quickly becoming one of those whom I won't miss.

...

Kirk: This is not a forum for good news. This is a management meeting.

...

Kirk: What the fuck are you doing?
Employee: Just doodling.
Kirk: Here's a thumbtack. Hang those doodles on your forehead as a warning to others who may unwisely choose not to pay complete attention to me.

...

Kirk: With you, bad news is a trend. Good news is a fluke.

...

Kirk: Your problem around here is that you've not learned to be subservient enough. Watch your coworkers and learn from them.

. . .

Kirk: I used to think you had a promising career. Every time you open your mouth, the chances of that happening are being dramatically reduced.

. . .

Kirk: That same shit was said by the last five guys who held your position. Now, would you like to reconsider those comments?

. . .

Kirk: James, if you ever make another mistake, I'll turn all your duties over to our ad agency guy. At least then I will be expecting things to be wrong.

. . .

Employee: We went forward with the plan because it had your initials on it.
Kirk: If something fails and my initials are on it, it means only that I saw it. When plans are successful, it means I approved them.

. . .

Kirk: This is very simple: We have an income problem; we don't have enough. The solution is that we need more. I order you to get more. End of discussion.

. . .

Kirk: Wake up down there. You look like you work for the fucking advertising agency.

• • •

Employee: This packet is being sent to our low and non-producers.
Kirk: Is our advertising agency getting one?

• • •

Kirk: James, take down everything he said word for word and then add, "I guarantee this and you should fire me if it fails" to all his fucking wishy-washy recommendations.

• • •

Kirk: Well, it's only my opinion. Is anyone here stupid enough to have a different one?

• • •

Kirk: You can save a lot of time by not attempting to teach the absolutely hopeless—like the dumb shits from our advertising agency.

• • •

Kirk: Well, it's time for our quarterly reduction in workforce. Do we have any volunteers? No? Then how about all of you worthless assholes drawing straws?
Kirk: Never attach your name to a success. I claim all of them. I want you to focus only on your failures.

• • •

Kirk: The reason I'm not in marketing is because I'm intelligent and not willing to have a lobotomy.

• • •

Kirk: It's difficult for me to relate to you employees because I'm rich and intelligent.

. . .

Kirk: I want all of you to stop talking so much about next year because so few of you will be here then.

. . .

Employee: Since we all agreed to it, we share equally in the failure.

Kirk: You're right. And I should fire the lot of you right now. But I won't. It's much more fun to fire you assholes one at a time.

. . .

Kirk: (said in a keynote speech at an American Bankers Association dinner) Frankly, I'd rather do business with pimps in purple hats than bankers.

. . .

Kirk: If you are going to continue letting your people take vacation, I want you at least to call the worthless fuckers every day while they're gone and tell them something to ruin their day.

Employee: Our bookings benefited this week from the latest snowstorm.

Kirk: If it will help, I'll make it snow more often.

. . .

Kirk: Where's Bill?

Employee: Vacation.

Kirk: Why did you let him do that? He's been here only six months.

Employee: It was one of his conditions to come work here.

Kirk: Bullshit. Just because you promise something, that doesn't mean you have to live up to it.

...

Employee: I was thinking about taking off next week.
Kirk: If your performance continues at this rate, you can take off a hell of a lot more than that.

...

Kirk: Amazing. You're only forty-six years old, been here eight years, and already you're winding down your career.

...

Kirk: I'm undefeated in debate. Of course, I've always been the scorekeeper.

...

Kirk: I see you, at best, as a human sacrifice in the overall effort to make me look good.

...

Employee: You weren't in this morning.
Kirk: I was at the zoo looking for new employees.
Employee: Did you find any?
Kirk: No. All I could find was a new advertising agency.

...

Kirk: Read it to our ad agency guy. He represents the lowest common denominator. If he understands it, anyone can.

...

Kirk: Are you naturally stupid or just too goddamned lazy to think?

...

Kirk: I want to change our marketing efforts from attracting old people to going after dead ones. We will save a fortune in food costs and they won't complain about the price of shore excursions.

...

Employee: I've talked to a ton of people about it.
Kirk: How many is a ton?
Employee: About three.
Kirk: Asshole.

...

Employee: I think the long-term effect—
Kirk: Why the fuck should you be concerned about a long-term effect?

...

Kirk: Is that shirt a gift from your wife or from someone else who hates you?

...

Kirk: Congratulations on your four-week anniversary. The best part of your career here is now over.

...

Kirk: Have you ever considered that perhaps your main function in life is simply to serve as a warning of what can happen when everything goes wrong?

...

Kirk: I hope you understand that I'm not being rude: I just consider you insignificant.

...

Kirk: Do you see these meetings as an opportunity to humiliate yourself in public?

...

Kirk: How about this, asshole? I'll try to be nicer if you try to be smarter.

...

Kirk: I don't think you should get married.
Employee: Why not?
Kirk: You might accidentally breed.

...

Kirk: Because I'm so intelligent, I can see the point you are feebly attempting to make.

...

Kirk: Thank you. We were all refreshed and challenged by your unique point of view. Now quit wasting my time and do what you're told.

...

Kirk: Good teamwork is a lot of people doing exactly what I say.

...

Kirk: You don't understand. If I wanted it tomorrow, I would have waited until tomorrow to ask for it.

...

Kirk: You'll get a lot further in this company once you learn to grovel.

...

Kirk: Just tell me what it is that you need so I can tell you how to get along without it.

. . .

Kirk: You're having delusions of adequacy again.

. . .

Kirk: It's our patriotic duty to help get our economy back on track. Therefore, our new marketing strategy is to order consumers to buy our cruises at more than retail. Your job is to sell my brilliant strategy.

Truly an amazing, amazing man that Kirk Lanterman.

30.

THE DIVERSIFICATION CONTINUES

A few years after we created Hornall Anderson Design Works, two guys showed up at our door with a proposal. Bill Fritsch and Ron Christiansen had heard about our arrangement with the design group and wanted to know whether we would be interested in adding a direct marketing company. After talking with the pair for about an hour, we were hooked. These guys were not only smart, energetic, and mucho savvy, but they seemed a perfect fit with our culture.

Bill has a monthly column in *Marketing NW Magazine* where he imparts wisdom. At the end of 2011, he shared his version of how he and his partner became a part of the Elgin Syferd family:

> In its heyday, just a few years ago, Elgin Syferd employed more than 200 people. And over the years they had the best account retention record in Seattle. McDonald's and Holland America were with the agency the last 30 years. This is an amazing accomplishment in the age of procurement mentality.

I had the honor a long time ago to work directly with Ron Elgin and Dave Syferd. In 1988, Ron and Dave both personally guaranteed a $150,000 line of credit that became the financial foundation that allowed Ron Christiansen and me to found Christiansen and Fritsch. For this act of faith, we gave them a fifty percent stake in our enterprise, and when we sold the company to FCB, they both made a great return.

There were two "ideas" that seemed to guide Elgin Syferd that I believe are the reason the shop had such a long and productive life.

Trust in the right people.

Our deal with Ron and Dave was essentially a handshake deal. We didn't have big contracts or detailed term sheets. They made the investment in two young people who had built good reputations and trusted that we would honor our word by building a profitable business.

They knew that no contract on earth could ensure integrity. They were guided by good instincts in people and we knew they trusted us to do a good job. This trust became a very big responsibility for my partner and me. We did a great job in keeping our "partners" up to date. Our financial records were impeccable and open at all times. And when we had problems we sought their counsel. But I don't recall a single time that Ron or Dave intervened.

Over the years, DDB did one of the better jobs of keeping its key people. I attribute this to Ron Elgin's

> inherent trust in the right people and in allowing them to do their jobs.
>
> Keep your word. Period.
>
> Over the years, we've all worked with people who are quick to make promises but not so good at following through. This lack of personal integrity is very destructive to long-term relationships.
>
> The opposite was true in all our dealings with Elgin and Syferd. If we shook hands, things happened exactly as intended. We never had to ask for something twice. This created a bond of trust that meant we never had to watch our backs or document every last detail of a business deal. We considered their word golden. And we were never disappointed. As we built our company, we tried to emulate what we had experienced. We were rabid about keeping our promises. And I'm convinced that this was the primary reason for our success and the ultimate sale of our company. And we owe this to our association with Ron Elgin and Dave Syferd. I believe that organizations reflect the behavior of the leadership, and when promises are not rigorously kept at the top, organizations cannot excel. Nor will they retain their best people.

Well, Bill's version is essentially accurate, but he should have emphasized the fact that we were smart enough to *hire and partner with really good people and stay the fuck out of their way.*

31.

MORE ABOUT PITCHES

Because of the work we had done for Princess Tours and Holland America Line/Westours and the connections made through those clients, we won the Anchorage Convention and Visitors Bureau (ACVB) account.

Like most association-type accounts, there were several clients within the ACVB client. Primary funding for marketing activities came from the downtown hotels, hotels on the outskirts of Anchorage, and the resorts miles from the city. So everyone had a say. Even with that cross to bear, we created a pretty good campaign based on the theme "In town, around town, and just out of town." Our main client and the primary funders liked it. But with a big association like the ACVB, even the local gas station guy has a say, so we were asked to develop a presentation to sell the campaign to all 250 "clients."

Back in those days, real audio/video innovation was to have more than one slide projector and a tape recorder operating at the same time. A friend of ours was a cutting edge kind of guy and had created a system that operated *four* slide projectors *and* a coordinated audio as well! Hot damn. We created a killer presentation complete with great photos, a dynamite script, terrific voice talent, and even nice music. Of course, being an agency, we were still putting the finishing touches on the show the night before our crack of dawn flight to Anchorage. But being a good agency, we completed our portion in time for our friend to program the components. Since my job was to be on stage while Dave ran the equipment, I took off for home about 10 p.m. Dave was to load the gear into his car and meet me at the airport at 6 a.m. for our 7 a.m. flight.

The next morning, 6 a.m. came and no Dave. 6:05 a.m. and no Dave. 6:10 a.m. and no Dave. I started to panic, found a payphone, and called his home. After several rings, his wife answered and told me they had overslept. She said that when Dave heard the phone and saw the time, he ran from the house while putting on his pants. Mind you, in rush hour traffic, he was an hour away.

Since this was well before cell phones, I couldn't call the asshole. So I paced and cursed. At 6:30, I asked the woman at the counter whether the plane was on-time. She said it would be boarding in ten minutes. Shit. Since I had previously worked on the Alaska Airlines account, I knew many of the senior executives. "My partner is arriving any moment with some audio/video gear for Jim Johnson's meeting in Anchorage this morning," I lied. I used Jim's name because he was not only a senior vice president at Alaska Airlines, but he was also known as Mr. Alaska and everyone loved him. "Your friend had better be here quick," she replied.

Just then, I saw Dave's BMW sliding sideways to a screeching halt. As my half-dressed, frantic partner leaped to action, I grabbed a porter and the three of us rushed to the counter with the equipment. Dave said, "I have to go park the car."

"Fuck the car; let's get to the plane!" We left the car, engine running, and ran through the concourse. When we got to the gate, the door had already been closed. We told the agent a similar bullshit tale about having to hand-carry Mr. Alaska's presentation to Anchorage. She immediately opened the door and rushed us down the Jetway and had the plane's door opened for us. You would not have believed the look on the other first-class passengers' faces when presented with these two sweating, disheveled guys, one of whom was unshaven, hair askew, and smelled bad. Just as we buckled up, the flight attendant made an announcement that the flight would be delayed a few minutes so they could load some important Alaska Airlines gear.

I'd love to say that was the fairy tale ending, but it wasn't.

We got to the hotel in plenty of time, and I began setting up the equipment in the ballroom while Dave went to the restroom to try to look a bit less like a homeless person. We ran through the presentation a couple of times with the client, and finally, we began to lower our blood pressure.

Curtain time. You can see this coming, can't you? After introductions and some pre-mumble about the campaign, Dave hit the button and…nothing. Then, after rewinding and hitting the button a few more times, the presentation started, but the four projectors were now completely out of sync. After making the standard apology about technology, the client and I left the stage to help Dave. Our quick fix was to unplug the coordinating cables, allowing the audio to run independently while the three of us operated the four slide projectors. The audience had no idea of the problem and loved the show. Finally, we had our fairy tale ending.

32.

A FEW MORE NEW BUSINESS STORIES

I'm sure most people in the agency business could write volumes chronicling their new business adventures and misadventures. I know we had plenty of good ones, bad ones, and we also had a few just plain weird ones.

Although I had been involved with new business throughout my time at Cole & Weber, a win is never more crucial than when it is for your own company. The new revenue is the main thing, of course. On the other hand, it's really shitty to see your name in the press in the "losers" column.

We pitched a relatively interesting, decent size account during our first year, whose owner told us we'd hear from him in a week. Waiting for the good news or the dreaded "Sorry, but you came in second" is one of the worst parts of our business.

Agencies live and die by new business. In our business, you must win just to stay even, and you must win big and often in order to grow. *The day you win a piece of business is one day closer to when you lose it.* Seriously, new business is that important.

By the seventh day after that particular pitch, I was experiencing the normal paranoia. By the eighth day, I couldn't stand it anymore, so I placed a call to the marketing director.

"Hi. This is Ron Elgin from Elgin Syferd just checking to see whether you have made a decision yet."

"About what?"

"About which advertising agency you are going to hire."

"Oh shit," the guy said. "I forgot all about that. We were supposed to get together to talk. I'll check to see whether anyone has time soon."

A few weeks later, they did get together. We didn't win. With the importance those assholes placed on the decision to hire an agency, I was happy we didn't. But it did make me realize an agency's relative importance in the lives of some clients. *Not everyone thinks as highly of us as we do.*

When thinking back to the following story, I find it hard to believe it really happened, but it did. This bright sounding guy convinced me over the phone that he had a new product that was a hundred times better than sliced bread. He told me it was such a big idea that he couldn't even give me a hint about it without us first signing a non-disclosure agreement. He'd bring the form to our meeting, and after signing, we'd be privileged to witness his world-changing invention.

Since he wouldn't divulge a thing about the product over the phone, I asked three account types representing a variety of product categories to join the meeting. After everyone signed the NDA, he started his presentation with a single, bold statement.

"As you know, the use of cell phones causes brain cancer—"

"Ah, excuse me, I'm not sure that's exactly been proven...."

"Oh, but it has. Definitely. There are tons of documents that conclusively prove that sustained use of cell phones definitely causes brain cancer!"

The four of us looked with concern at one another. The cell phone industry was still relatively new, but it had advanced well beyond the "big bricks," and all of us were using the newer models as much or more than conventional landline phones. The concern about cancer currently growing in my brain was somewhat offset by the thought of representing the company that would prohibit future users suffering from the same fate. And, of course, the millions we could make alerting the masses.

"Can you share some of the research that proves the direct link between cell phone use and brain cancer? We'd also like to see your patent info, please."

"As to the first part, here are just some of the most recent newspaper articles and a few of the scholarly papers on the subject. Take a look."

He divided the pile among us and we started going through them, looking for anything that substantiated his claims. Anything other than the *National Enquirer*, *Star Magazine*, *The New York Post*, *The Sun*, and *The Mirror* that is. We searched for a single positive story that wasn't next to a tale of alien abductions or men giving birth. Failing in that, we started scanning the "scholarly articles," hoping they could be our saving grace, but instead, they looked as goofy as the tabloids.

"As to the patents, I haven't filed for them yet. But here, let me show you my invention—one that will save millions and millions of lives for generations to come!" With that, he whipped out a strange-looking phone. "This started as a regular, cancer causing Motorola cell phone. My brilliant invention, the secret sauce if you will, is the lead shielding! I've completely encased the phone with industrial strength lead. Not a single cancer-causing ray can be emitted from the phone!"

He handed the phone to me.

"Wow, it's pretty heavy," I said.

"A small price one must pay for prevention."

I turned the phone on and put it to my ear. "Is the battery dead? I don't hear a dial tone."

"No, it's not dead. You can't hear the dial tone because the lead is shielding it. That's the protection against cancer."

"Is this a joke? Are we on *Candid Camera* or something?"

"I don't know what you mean."

"If you can't hear the dial tone, you won't be able to hear voices either."

"Well, I haven't solved that part yet."

33.

A LITTLE HELP FROM YOUR FRIENDS

About 10,000 words into writing this book, I was driving to Ballard to meet a good friend and former employee. On the way, I had an inspiration. One of the biggest reasons for my success was because of my and Dave's ability to hire people much better than us. This guy was definitely in that category.

After a few beers, I said, "Vandy, I'm writing a story about our company. Could you send me a few words about one of the most memorable things that happened while you were copywriting for us? Maybe something funny, weird, or even something that turned out to be a good learning experience for you. It doesn't really matter what you send; my real reason is to get some professional writing into my book."

"I'd be honored, Boss." I love it that he still calls me boss. "I had some of the best experiences of my life there. I'll send something in the morning."

Here's Vandy's new business story. He wrote it as the dialogue actually happened.

"Ron, remember when we were invited to pitch the Northwest Ford Dealers?"

"How could I forget that one, Vandy? The meeting was to be down in Portland. This was a very visible piece of business, so basically every agency of consequence was there trying to win it."

"That's right, Ron. Typically, pitches of this magnitude often relied on stunts or 'attention-getting devices' to augment (and more often than not, to supplant) the actual work being presented. So there was no shortage of marching bands, monkeys driving Fords in parades, balloons shaped like cars, personal pizza deliveries, elephants on unicycles, and other crazy, attention-getting stunts. But we had decided to let our work speak for itself, so instead of spending time in Presentation Dreamland, we concentrated on showing them a full-blown campaign that would actually get potential buyers into dealerships.

"Now since Northwest Ford was a broadcast-driven account, we put the majority of our spec creative work on videotape. And understanding that we did all the right things leading up to the presentation…arranged to have a ¾ inch videotape machine ready and waiting at the Portland Marriott, made a backup ½ inch Video Home System (VHS) tape just in case, tested the rental ¾ machine the day of, cued up the tape, retested, recued, re-retested, and re-recued one last time. We were up most of the night rehearsing.

"So you probably remember where this is going?"

"I was there, Vandy."

"You're getting in the way of my story, Ron. Anyway, the time for the presentation finally arrives, we go through introductions, do a couple of ice breakers, explain how we're all about doing good work with no distractions to get in its way, direct everyone's attention to the monitor, press the play button and...

"Nothing happens.

"Okay, this brings out the prerequisite half-hearted joke about technology, a few nervous chuckles, and a very emphatic touch of the play button.

"Still nothing.

"It was at this point that I started to push all the buttons on the machine. Some of these buttons had exclamation points on them; some of them didn't. I didn't care. I pressed all of them; I pressed all of them very hard. Meanwhile, Dick Hadley did the greatest tap dance in the history of advertising and marketing. He talked about the auto industry, trends, research, how everything related to baseball, while we called in the AV company, and watched as the AV company guy pressed all the buttons on the ¾ inch, did some interesting things behind the ¾ inch, unplugged that ¾ inch, brought in another ¾ inch, watched interestingly as that one didn't work either, panicked, panicked some more, and walked over to me and whispered, 'We don't know what else to do.'

"By this time, Dick was talking about his childhood in Seattle and a friend's first sexual experience with somebody named Doris and then something equally idiotic about a nun.

"I looked over and saw your head buried so deep in your hands that your fingers were molded to your skull."

"I was in a lot of pain, Vandy."

"Okay, there was actually one last final resort. For one reason or another, I had made the VHS copy of the entire presentation. Why, I don't know. The ¾ inch was so much better in quality than VHS, but I did it as an afterthought. So I told the hotel rep, who told the maintenance crew, who went and raided one of the hotel rooms for a VHS tape player. They brought it down, hooked it up, and just as Dick was finishing his story about a prostitute, a camel, and a Turkish prison, up came the video.

"And of course, the way this story should end is the Ford people were so impressed with the work and how we handled a five-alarm emergency that they awarded us the account on the spot. But of course, they didn't. They gave it to their incumbent agency, JWT. Said it was because they had the best work out of any of the four agencies that presented. Yeah, sure, whatever; we all knew the real reason. Well, at least a friend of someone's neighbor said he saw all the Ford dealers emerge from the last meeting with a set of new golf clubs in bags with JWT logos. Free golf clubs beat a binder with your presentation in it every time.

"What I learned from this incident is to be prepared for everything; have a backup plan to your backup plan to your backup plan. And more importantly, don't beat people up when they're beating themselves up enough as it is. See, when you cornered me after the presentation, you said not to worry;

shit happens. You brought me a beer, and it was never mentioned again."

"Vandy, it was six beers."

Laughing at Vandy's story, I knew I was right in wanting help in writing the book. I was tempted to ask him to send me about 90,000 more words. I decided instead to ask other former employees for their stories. Their recollections give a balanced reflection of not just my memories, but the crazy agency world in general. You'll be able to pick out their contributions; they're the well-written ones.

34.

PITCH, PITCH, PITCH

Elgin Syferd had some successful pitches, some miserable losses, and some maddening experiences. We also had a few that were downright bizarre.

One in the latter category started with an invitation to pitch a hotel/casino in Las Vegas. We had zero category experience, but the prospective client said it wanted to talk because of our strength in media strategy, planning, and buying, as well as creative. I asked Sydney Hunsdale, one of our managing partners, to head up the effort. She assembled a team, and within days, it was on its way to Las Vegas to see the properties, meet the marketing team, and understand its goals, challenges, and competition. At that time, we presented our answers to their Request for Proposal and gave a short dog and pony show about the agency.

Everything was pretty standard up to this point.

A few days later back in Seattle, we got the word that we had made it to the finals and set a date for the team to return to Las Vegas. We were told that at this meeting, we'd be presenting to the owner and his key managers, who together would make the final decision. They asked us to keep the meeting and materials informal so we scrapped the idea of multimedia and put everything on handouts.

On the day of the presentation, Sydney's team was told to meet the marketing team for lunch and be briefed for the big meeting. The first surprise happened at the end of the lunch when the team learned that the presentation would not be at the hotel/casino as before but at the owner's home. The second surprise was that the meeting would be in the owner's bedroom because he was a bedridden paraplegic. The third was a complete bombshell. The marketing team explained that the owner would be mostly naked because his skin was so super-sensitive!

Sydney didn't know whether to laugh, cry, or bolt! After her initial shock, she realized none of those were options. The team was in place and she wanted to win the business. But wait—everything was on handouts. Sydney asked, "How in bloody hell" (she's Irish) "does a paraplegic hold a handout?"

The owner's home was a beautiful two-story villa on a lush golf course. The marketing team introduced our people to the senior managers while in the living room area. After a few minutes of introductions, the entire group was led to the second floor bedroom. There he was, just as described.

Well, not exactly. Our team had not been told that the owner also had a tracheostomy tube for breathing and speaking, which meant he had to speak in small bursts. Think Christopher Reeve after his accident. He was also hooked up to a number of machines.

Needless to say, our team members were stressed to the max, but they gamely began struggling through the presentation, carefully showing the owner pages from the handout, one at a time. It didn't help their flow when one or more of the machines signaled the man's vitals were registering stress. Nurses kept interrupting to fix this or recalibrate that.

Our team was a fucking mess. It couldn't have been worse; presenting ads and commercials, media charts and graphs and budgets to a naked man who could die at any moment while machines were ringing and chiming. It helped that the owner was very smart and asked incredibly good questions. It helped but not enough.

One of the cardinal rules of pitching is to know your audience. Another is to know the physical layout of the room where you're going to pitch. In our haste, we followed neither rule and suffered the consequences. We vowed never again to allow a client's schedule to get in the way of doing a thorough, professional job. We kept our word—well, most of the time.

I told this story to my good friend Mike Doherty who runs Cole & Weber United. "Whoa, we were in that pitch and made the same mistakes."

• • • •

Then there was the time when a friend offered us the opportunity to pitch a start-up being created by a mutual acquaintance. The company, a white labeler of chocolate products for a number of local companies, had been offered the opportunity to partner with Jim Beam to produce a whiskey-filled product. The marketing folks at Jim Beam had given her the authority to help select the participants for an agency competition. We loved the idea of having this famous brand on our roster.

Although a lot of us at the agency had a great deal of experience eating chocolate and swilling whiskey, we had zero case studies that even came close to the category. We ended up having to build our presentation around the strengths of our departments, divisions, and people. In other words, the usual bullshit.

When the day came, we decorated the main conference room with dozens of our most visibly appealing ads. I was chatting with our pitch team, which included a couple of account people, an art director and copywriter, a planner and a media person when our receptionist informed me that our guest had arrived.

I greeted the prospective client at the reception area and was more than a little surprised to find that she had brought her newborn to the meeting. She explained this was her first child and she was so totally enraptured that she couldn't bear to be separated for more than a few minutes at a time. I figured that might be doublespeak for the sitter didn't show.

I have to say, the baby was cute, and the mom was even cuter. Of course, I didn't notice the latter. I was, however, a little put-off when she handed me the diaper bag, some sort of sleeping contraption, and something like a playpen. She marched ahead to the conference, with me trudging behind with my arms full.

After brief introductions and several of our all-male team "coo-cooing" the baby and ogling the mom, I offered refreshments, presented the agenda, and explained that the Ladies Room was right outside this room to the right. Then I asked to hear more about her company and the joint venture with Jim Beam. It's common knowledge that clients are more interested in themselves than in what agencies are pitching, so it's always best to let them go first. I've been in meetings where the client talked for an hour without hearing a word from us and walked away thinking we were brilliant. With the foreplay over and the fact that her baby was asleep, she spent the next half-hour telling us the history of her company and the Jim Beam opportunity.

When it came time for us to present, the baby woke up and immediately began screaming. Not crying—screaming. The mom tried to pacify the child to no avail. Finally after several excruciating minutes, the mom said, "He must be hungry." With that, she opened her blouse, pulled out a teat, and plugged in the kid. I have absolutely no problem with a woman discreetly breast-feeding a baby in public. But there was nothing discreet about the way she pulled out her teat and plugged in the kid.

After a couple of minutes of adjustments, which didn't include the mom doing anything to shield us from her activities, she asked us to proceed with our presentation. Immediately after her request, she started singing to the baby. Not humming, singing. What with the double distraction of breast-feeding and singing, the team was understandably underperforming.

The louder we presented, the louder she sang. I was thinking this presentation had to be not just the worst one ever, but also the most bizarre. That thought was etched in my mind until she switched breasts without bothering to cover up the first. Everyone was trying to maintain strict eye contact, but it became impossible when presented with an unobstructed view of a naked breast. No one seemed to have the slightest idea of where we were in the presentation when she began trying to burp the baby without bothering to button her blouse. At this point, we were seven speechless, gawking guys as she alternated between singing and talking baby-talk to the kid.

Finally, the baby let out a man-sized belch, was silent for a moment, then started screaming again. "Does Mommy need to change her little snookums' diapers? Goo goo gaw gaw?" she asked, or something like that.

When she asked me to hand her the diaper bag, I asked whether I could carry it to the Ladies Room for her. She said not to bother; I should just spread the changing mat onto the conference table. She continued to jabber nonsense to snookums while changing a foul-smelling dirty diaper in front of a group of gagging ad guys. No longer was either the baby or the mom thought of as cute. We couldn't get them out of there fast enough.

I'm sure if I had insisted on pursuing the business, I would have been handed at least six resignations posthaste.

Fortunately, Jim Beam pulled the plug on the project so I never got tested.

• • • •

Obviously, not all pitches go the way we'd like. In fact, relatively few do. That's one of the reasons why agency people need to be out there every day seeding opportunities. Someone once told me that .200 was a winning percentage for new business. That may be optimistic.

One of our first pitches was when flip charts were on their way out and slide projector presentations were the new hot thing. We had been on a roll with our flip chart presentations, but we decided to join the tech ranks for our next new business opportunity. The opportunity came with a cattle call for a regional bank's business.

It was decided to go high tech all the way. We weren't just going to load samples of our work onto slides, but give it the whole fucking she-bang, including script and black screens for when we wanted to engage the audience in conversation.

We rehearsed this new technology several times and were feeling pretty damn good. Unfortunately, the rehearsals took place at the production counter in full light. The morning before the prospective client was to arrive, we set up the projector in our small, interior conference room, clicked it on to make sure it worked, and congratulated ourselves on being so tech-savvy.

The prospective client showed up with five people plus our six, which made the cozy conference room even cozier.

With formal introductions over, we turned on the projector and turned off the overhead fluorescent lights.

Light from the projector made the room bright enough to see clearly the expressions on the guests' faces. Until the first black slide, that is. Remember, the black slides were inserted so there would be no distraction while we looked intently into the clients' eyes and espoused profundities. However, the room was now darker than a coal digger's ass. Someone stupidly started talking as though this were planned. After a very uncomfortable minute or so, I flicked on the overheads and the room went from pitch-black to eye-squinting bright. We flipped the projector to the next slide and turned off the overheads. It went along okay until we ran up against another fucking black slide. After two more episodes of this insanity, the client said, "Thank you. We've seen enough. I can confirm right now, you won't be advancing."

• • • •

Another of my least favorite pitches was also held in a too-small conference room. This time, however, the meeting was in Ketchum, Idaho where Dave and I were making a presentation to our existing client, the Sun Valley Chamber of Commerce Board of Directors. The meeting's purpose was to unveil our following year's campaign.

This was going to be a full-on presentation: slides, flip charts, foam core, and even a tape recorder for the radio spots. We had everything set up around the small room when the client crowded in. Dave was lead, so he started the meeting.

After a brief intro, he turned it over to me with a wave of his arm, which immediately knocked over the first easel, which fell into the next and on around the entire fucking room. The Three Stooges could not have choreographed it better. The slide projector not only went to the floor, but the top ring came loose and all sixty-four slides scattered. Even the tape in the recorder jammed. I'd never seen Dave do a better presentation using just foam core charts while using me as his easel.

• • • •

Perhaps my all-time least favorite horrible presentation took place in an equally exotic destination—Steamboat Springs, Colorado.

Dave got a call from a long-time PR colleague who invited the agency to participate in a review for its tourism business. He explained that as head of marketing, he had been empowered to select the agencies for the cattle call and assist the committee in narrowing to the finalists. When asked specifically who was going to make the final decision, he admitted it would be a committee vote, but he would be "extremely influential."

The more we talked with him, the more excited we became. For example, he told us not to worry about our initial submission because we were already in the final six. Even better, he said that he and his wife wanted us to stay with them at their condo in Steamboat when we came down for the pitch. I wanted to suggest they just skip the formalities and send us a contract, but Dave said it would be more fun to spend a couple of days after the pitch "learning to know the client" by skiing their slopes.

A couple of weeks later, we got our official notification that we had made the finals and we were given the date, time, and place for the final round. We assembled our presentation materials and arrived in Steamboat just in time for pre-dinner cocktails with our "new client/old friend" and his wife at their lovely condo. After about a bazillion cocktails and no business talk, we went to their favorite dinner place for more cocktails, a lot of wine, and a little food. One of the funny things about booze is the more you drink, the less you care.

Way after midnight, we stumbled back to their condo and kind of giggled about the fact that our presentation was at eight o'clock that morning. That, of course, called for a few rounds of after-dinner drinks and talks about how fun it was going to be to work together on such a cool piece of business. Everyone was hammered.

I staggered off to my room while Syferd was mumbling something about using his watch as an alarm to wake him at seven because the "client" was leaving even earlier to help set up the meeting room.

Seemingly minutes later, Syferd was violently shaking me. I screamed at him in a voice so strange to both of us that we each continued to scream. We were both fucking messes.

"We're late," apologized Dave. "I didn't believe my alarm the first few times it went off. We have to be there in a half-hour!"

"No, I can't do it," I moaned. "I'm sick. Really, really sick. I know I'll die if I even move."

"You have to," Dave begged. "The company is counting on us. Look, I'm up and I'm as sick as you."

"Fuck."

Somehow, I dragged my sorry ass out of bed into the bathroom where I splashed water on my face and discovered I looked worse than I felt. At least I was still fully dressed. We were out the door within ten minutes.

Apparently, Dave's adrenaline was fading faster than his color because by the time we got to the meeting hall, he told me that I was going to have to carry the burden because he knew if he opened his mouth, he would be projectile vomiting. Great, just what I needed.

The first thing I noticed upon entering the room was a dais with about a dozen guys staring intently at us while drinking coffee. The second, even more scary thing—no, correct that, the MOST scary thing was that not only was our "client" not one of the twelve, but he was sitting in the back of the room looking worse than the two of us.

Dave and I proceeded to the table in front of the committee. I introduced us while Dave opened the portfolio case and promptly fell over into a chair. I didn't need a mirror to know what the guys in front of us saw and probably smelled. As each person introduced himself, you could see disdain and revulsion on his face. Before starting my pitch, I noticed the chairman nodding to the guy on his right and pointing to where our "client" sat slumped over in his chair, snoring rather noisily.

I started off rather shaky and then proceeded to get worse. I honestly don't remember much after the first few minutes. I must have been kind of on autopilot or something. I do remember sitting down next to Dave while still talking, thinking that was preferable to falling on my face.

I was holding a foam core mounted ad with my head twisted in order to read the copy when all of a sudden I got a sharp rap on the side of my head. In a flash, I thought that either Dave had hit me or the chairman had thrown something at me. In the next instant, I realized that I had momentarily passed out and hit my head on the fucking table.

The good thing was that the jolt completely woke me and pumped enough adrenaline through my system that I could finish the pitch on my feet. I thanked the committee, gathered our materials, picked up Dave, and left. The "client" was still snoring as we walked past him.

We found the first open café and convinced the proprietor to serve us Bloody Marys. Dave asked how I thought we did. Rather than hit him, I ordered another round.

Several hours later, we were starting to feel almost human. We had some food, bought a couple of cowboy hats, and talked about how we hoped the high altitude had adversely affected the other five agencies as well. As if that had been the problem.

A short time later, we ran into the committee chair on the street. He looked as if he were trying to ignore us, but I stopped him anyway and asked whether they had made a decision.

He turned to me and said, "We haven't selected an agency yet, but it sure the hell isn't going to be you. Your presentation was pathetic. Let me put it this way; we haven't finished seeing all six of the agencies, but I can guarantee your finish will rank somewhere between eighth and tenth."

If I had been a judge, I would have given us the tenth place finish. *That was the last time I ever took for granted any aspect of a new business pitch. No matter what anyone said or even implied, we forever approached each step in the process as though it might be our last chance to win the business.*

35.

WE PROMISE TO BLEED FOR YOU

"Wow, look at this!" I yelled. "It's an RFP for the state lottery! This is huge. If we win this, it will be a complete game-changer for us."

"You say that about every account we go after," said someone from the peanut gallery.

I knew he was right, but the Washington State Lottery was a big and very visible account, so I really did want to win it. My enthusiasm became contagious. Everyone in the shop chipped in to help create our initial response. All eight copies were perfect bound and placed in a very cool, handmade box resembling a safe. We ad types are oh, so clever.

A few weeks later, we received notification that we and five other agencies had made the final cut and would be presenting in Olympia at one of the state capitol campus buildings.

The big question we faced was: Do we do spec creative or no creative? That's always the quandary in the agency business. Creating speculative (spec) ads can cost the agency tens if not hundreds of thousands of dollars in inside time and hard costs. Prospective clients hardly ever make the decision an easy one for an agency. One of the standard instructions is "Spec work is not required." However, they never say, "You will be disqualified if you even think about including spec creative," or even "Don't include spec creative or we'll fucking kill you." So, even though an agency can only guess at the prospective client's wants, desires, and taboos, most of us include spec creative because everyone else does.

We believed we had an edge because out of the six agencies, only two offered advertising and public relations under the same roof, and we were the only one truly integrating them. Our spec campaigns had multiple components from TV to point of purchase. Although the presentation team had grown to ten people, we figured that was okay because the client had at least that many, and a consultant had once told us that bureaucracies could relate to big numbers.

We carpooled three vehicles to Olympia and got there in plenty of time to sit in the lobby of the designated building, twiddling our thumbs for an hour while another agency finished its meeting. We were given a half-hour to set up while the client took a short break. The room was extremely large and had two tables to seat ten on each side with a head table of about the same size. We would present from the middle of the horseshoe.

The presentation got off to a great start. We were lively, energetic, and the State people were friendly and receptive. About halfway through the meeting, I looked to the table facing me and noticed a spot of blood on the shirt collar of one of my coworkers, Marc Delaunay. A few minutes later, the spot grew to cover most of his left collar. Then the blood began spreading from the collar to the front of his shirt. Marc was excitedly making his points, and with every jerky movement, the blood continued to spread. I kept trying to catch his attention, but he was really into his presentation. The more he gesticulated, the more the blood ran. Everyone in the room was staring at him and his formerly white shirt. Finally, I couldn't take it anymore, so I said, "Marc, you're bleeding all over yourself."

He looked down at the red mess, touched the neck wound, displayed his now red fingers, and said, "In conclusion, if you hire us, I promise to bleed for you with every promotion we undertake." With that, he got up and abruptly left the room.

A half-hour later, we closed with the promise that everyone on the team would be proud and honored to bleed for the Washington State Lottery account. We then rushed out to see whether Marc had either bled to death or fooled us all with a fake blood sack. We were relieved to find him alive and no longer bleeding from his shaving cut.

About a week later, the State narrowed the field to us and another agency. I got the call saying we had a slight lead on points, but it was very close, and the final decision would be determined by the best financial proposal. I expressed confusion because we had already told them our compensation would be based on the standard agency commission. (Back in those days, the "standard" was 15 percent commission from media and a 17.65 percent markup on production.) The guy told me our competitor had agreed to what amounted to a 12 percent commission, and if we would at least match it, we would be awarded the business.

When we had a team meeting, Terry Kirkland was adamant. This was a government account. All government business is public business, she said. If we cut our commission to the state, sooner or later we'd be forced to do the same for McDonald's and every account in the shop. Not only would we make less money, but all the reputable clients and agencies would consider us no better than scabs. She convinced us with her passion. I called the guy from the lottery and told him we weren't whores, and we were sticking to the standard agency commission pricing model. The State selected the scab agency.

A couple of months later, I bumped into the head of the winning agency. "Damn, I'm sure happy you stood by your principles," he smirked, "as fucked up as those principles may be. You lost because you refused to lower your commission. We didn't lower our commission. We shit-canned the entire commission concept and just proposed a monthly fee. All the big shops back East are doing it. We're already making a ton on the business. I'm buying a new Mercedes that's way bigger than yours."

He may have been an obnoxious asshole, but he now had a bigger Mercedes than me. I vowed never again to let a financial structure get in our way.

I have always been amazed at agencies that either resign or argue themselves into being fired by the client who has had to cut its budget from say $5 million to $1 million. I can assure you, the recipient of the new $1 million account is one happy agency. *The size of the client's budget doesn't dictate the percentage of profit that can be made. In most cases, an agency can make a decent return if it can get the client to agree to a prescribed scope of work and staff accordingly.*

36.

NOT SO FUN LOSING

Part 1
A Really, Really Dark Day

Holland America Line had been doing great financially ever since Kirk took control. He and his team dedicated themselves to filling every bed on every cruise at the highest possible rates. We helped by enhancing their image with beautifully effective brand ads in lifestyle magazines and hard-hitting retail newspaper ads strategically placed in key markets across the country.

"Ron, this is God," said Kirk. "Are you standing?"

"I am now," I replied.

"We're putting our account up for review."

I sat down. "Review?" I asked. "Are you kidding? How can this be? Bookings are strong, you're the most profitable cruise line in the industry, and your people are consistently telling us how much they like and appreciate our work. We're always on time and on budget. We have at least a dozen people in your offices every day, seven days a week."

"Yeah, yeah, yeah," replied Kirk. "I know all that, but you know that we hired the Boston Consulting Group to help us determine what type ships we should build in the future."

"Of course I know that. We've been working with them for weeks," I said. "What does that have to do with putting the account up for review?"

"Well, they have this checklist of things we have to do, and number 67 says, 'Review Agency,' so that's what we have to do," he said.

"Just tell them no," I pleaded. "Tell them you're happy with your current agency."

"Ron, we are happy, but we're paying them a million bucks for their advice, and number 67 says, 'Review Agency,' and that's what we're going to do. End of conversation. If you're as good as you're always telling me, the review shouldn't be a problem." That was his final comment before hanging up the phone.

The next day, we received the formal letter announcing the review. We were devastated but confident that we could retain the business. But not confident enough to sit back and rest on our laurels. We assembled the team and set about to analyze any and all possible weaknesses, especially in light of our insights into the recommendations that would be made by the Boston Consulting Group.

We were confident in the strength of our creative. We believed it would stand up to any shop's anywhere. It was a complicated account, but we knew we had every aspect covered in spades. Based on who Holland America Line was at that moment in time, we were golden. But where was the company heading in the future?

One of our team members made a casual comment that a junior person from the Boston Consulting Group said that one of its recommendations was going to be that Holland America advertise nationally on network television. Under different circumstances, we would have been elated because a national TV campaign would mean larger media and production budgets. But with the account in review, it exposed a huge weakness about which we'd never before had to worry.

Although we were a big fish in the Seattle pond, we'd be lucky if any of the major television networks would even allow us an audience. Our media department was good, but we had no clout at the national broadcast level. We now had a good idea where Holland America Line was heading, but if we didn't do something quickly, it would be going there without us. We needed to find that clout.

For years, we'd received overtures from several of the global agencies seeking a strong presence in the Northwest. We kept those channels open, knowing someday they could be our exit strategy. With our largest account in jeopardy, we knew it wasn't time to sell the agency, but we needed help, so I started a dialogue with four of the global agencies looking for a strategic alliance.

All four agencies were eager to help. Three of the four wanted to know how much of the budget they would get once we retained the business. Two of those also wanted to know how we would divide the costs for pitching the business. One of the four was simply eager to help. No strings attached. That agency was DDB Needham Worldwide.

My initial contact with DDB Needham was through Alan Pando, an icon in the advertising business and President of DDB Needham West. When I explained why I was interested in creating a strategic alliance, he said, "Let's do it." I asked him how much it would cost me for his company to partner with us for the pitch. He said, "You worry about how much you spend and I'll worry about how much we spend. There will be no cross-charging for anything from us." Ever fearful of being swallowed, I asked what it was going to cost me after we retained the business and sought a permanent working arrangement. He said, "Let's win the business first; then you can figure out how you can use us in the future and how much you want to pay for it." I fell in love with Alan and his agency.

After settling on the preliminaries, Alan put me in touch with Keith Reinhard, Chairman and CEO of DDB Needham Worldwide. Although I'd never met Keith, I'd been reading about this living legend for years. My nervousness about talking with *the* Keith Reinhard disappeared after about ten seconds into our phone conversation. He had this authentic way about himself. I was incredibly delighted to find out he was this real, genuine guy, eager to help us. Not just in making DDB Needham's vast media resources and clout available to us, but to offer his personal involvement.

"I began my career as a creative person and I'm still pretty good at it," Keith said to me. "I'd love to come to Seattle and work with your creative team if they wouldn't mind. I'll even be in the final pitch if you want me." I fell more deeply in love.

Once we advanced to the finals, our strategy was to stand on our record, but with a twist. We would also present a brand new TV campaign and an efficient and effective national media buy. We would also, of course, flesh out the campaign with ads, radio, outdoor, and even appropriate geegaws.

Keith showed up at our office three days before the pitch. He humbly asked for a desk and computer so he could help writing copy. He was so smart; within a day, our creative leaders were over their awe and intimidation and saw him as a working partner. Together, we created work that was beyond our hopes and expectations.

From one of our many friends at Holland America, we learned that the other finalist was the San Francisco office of Foote Cone Belding (FCB). It wasn't much of a surprise; FCB was one of the hottest shops in the West. It also handled the State of Alaska Tourism account. It was a formidable opponent.

I was surprised when we walked into the presentation room to find about twenty people seated at the head table. There were even a few people whom none of us recognized. I was also surprised to see a couple of executives from the Boston Consulting Group.

Our presentation was terrific. Keith was awesome. So were the rest of the team and the work. Dave and I were pretty good, too. The Q&A went smoothly. Holland America thanked us and promised a call with its decision by the next day.

The call came and it wasn't good. Despite all the nice words about how great we were, how close it was, and what a difficult decision it was for them, we came in second. You're always prepared for something like this, but you're never really prepared.

The account represented about a third of our agency's revenue and an even larger percentage of our profits. Contractually, all of it would be gone in ninety days. In reality, we knew the revenue would start diminishing immediately and work its way to zero in three months. We were suddenly facing the first layoffs in the company's history.

Everyone at the agency knew layoffs were inevitable; the big question was: Who would be leaving? The answer wasn't a simple one. Some of our very best people had been 100 percent Holland America. You can't afford to get rid of your best people just because of a cut in revenue. Even one as deep as this one would be. But if you don't cut the Holland America team, who do you cut? And if you make room for someone on another account, will that person be right for that account? These monumental decisions had to be made quickly and not just because of economics; *lack of action in the face of a crisis can be paralyzing and crippling.*

"Let's take a list of all our people and our problems over to the Mexican joint and figure it out over beers," Dave said to me.

"Best idea you've had all day," I replied.

About two beers into solving our seemingly unsolvable problem, I asked the waitress to bring us six tequila shots—each.

"What the hell are you doing?" asked Dave.

"We're not getting anywhere with beer," I replied, "and I think the tequila will help bring clarity. The other reason is that tomorrow morning we're going to tell twenty or more of our valued employees that we can no longer afford to help them support their families. I want us to be able to look them in the eye and tell them honestly that we feel worse than they do." He called me a sick fuck as he threw down his first shot.

The next day was terrible. Hung over and with incredible guilt for letting the agency down by losing the account, we prepared for the worse. It turned out to be even worse than we anticipated. But in an unexpected way. All but one of the people we had to let go was absolutely wonderful about it. They honestly appeared to feel even worse for us than they did for themselves. All but one of the people asked whether he or she could come back when we replaced the revenue. The exception was a media person who was a complete bitch about being laid-off. She screamed and ranted that she was better than anyone else in her department. She made us feel a little better that we had unwittingly discovered and eliminated an asshole from our ranks.

Even having to suffer through the worst experience of my agency career, I still loved the Holland America Line brand and its people. Of course, I was devastated, but I was also grateful for having had the opportunity to partner with such a remarkable company. A week after losing the business, we took out a full-page ad in the *Business Journal*, thanking Holland America Line for our four wonderful years together and wishing it continued success.

Part 2
The Sun Returns

The agency slowly began to recover both financially and emotionally when, nine months later, I got a call. "Ron, this is God; are you standing?"

"I am now," I replied.

"I need your help," Kirk said. "These new fuckers haven't a clue how to put butts in bunks. They don't even understand that our target audience is the parents of really, really old people. They're wasting my money. Can you do the butts in bunks part and let them do the pretty pictures shit?"

"Let me talk with the team and get back to you," I said.

I was surprised by the team's mixed reaction. Half were excited to begin working with Holland America again while the other half ranged from "To hell with them" to believing FCB was in trouble and claiming that if we held out, we'd end up with the whole account again. After considerable discussion and debate, I made the decision.

"Kirk," I said, "while we'd love to manage all aspects of your business, we'd be delighted to help in any way we can."

FCB was not happy. In fact, it threw such an absolute shit-fit about sharing the Agency of Record responsibilities that

Kirk asked us to agree that Elgin Syferd would be a contractor to FCB. I agreed, with the provision that all direction and approvals for the work would come directly from the client.

At that time, the media budget was about $10 million. FCB had allocated $9 million to TV and $1 million to retail newspaper. At my urging, Kirk ordered another million shifted from TV to newspaper. With the additional targeted exposure and dramatically different creative approach, bookings immediately began to increase.

Over the following months, the client shifted more and more of its budget from TV to newspaper, supplemented by our image ads placed in key lifestyle magazines. The last straw for FCB was when it was told to create a media plan for the following year with 90 percent of the budget devoted to retail and 10 percent to brand building. FCB told the client if it were forced to do that, it would resign the business. The client said, "Bye, Bye."

We happily welcomed the full Holland America Line account back to the family after nearly a year of separation. *Burning a bridge may create a good feeling at the time, but it can prove to be a huge detriment to reconciliation. Playing nice isn't just the right thing to do; sometimes, it even pays off.*

One of the first meetings after we took back control of the business turned out to be quite interesting and, in retrospect, pretty damn funny.

Jan Edmondson and Tim Pavish were responsible for the daily running of the business. Both were extremely bright guys who knew the business cold. In preparation for the following year's marketing plan, they conducted extensive interviews with HAL's top management—especially, Kirk—discussing their goals and objectives. Based on the information gathered, the team spent at least a month developing strategies, tactics, and a fair amount of spec creative and media recommendations. The agency team worked closely with its counterparts at the client to iron out the wrinkles and ensure that every aspect was on target.

On the day of the big presentation, Kirk and the top five officers of his marketing group showed up at the agency promptly at 9 a.m. Kirk was never big on chit-chat, so after a couple of minutes of pre-mumble by me, I turned the meeting over to Jan.

"Thanks, Ron. We're extremely excited about the work you're going to see over the next few hours. Our team, alongside yours, has been working tirelessly for the past month on strategies and tactics derived from your very specific goals and objectives to produce what I'm sure you'll agree is work that will set Holland America Line apart from that Sea of Sameness out there and fill your ships at the highest possible rates."

"Jan," Kirk said.

"Yes?" replied Jan.

"On the way over here this morning, I decided to change all of those goals. Now, go ahead and make your presentation."

Stunned, we looked to the marketing staff as it looked to us with similar expressions of bewilderment. All those many hours of crafting a program based on specific goals, gone.

"Kirk," I said, "would you care to share those new goals with us?"

"Of course," replied Kirk, "but not right now. Finish your presentation, Jan."

Without an option, we did finish the presentation, and it was applauded by Kirk. Well, not exactly applauded—that's not Kirk. Let's just say his lack of criticism was considered a win for us. By the way, his change of goals was to raise all the revenue goals to make them harder to achieve. I learned a lot about stretch goals from Kirk.

I should mention that all of Kirk's meetings ran longer than most human bodies could handle. He's a stickler for details and a voracious consumer of data. He could spot a number on page 312 of a deck that didn't foot with something on page 34 seen five hours earlier. Anyway, it made him crazy that people would leave his meetings for restroom breaks. He wouldn't prohibit the breaks, but he would ridicule the people who had to use them as pitiful weaklings who couldn't control their bodily functions.

About five hours into a different presentation, Kirk scowled at me and said, "This is bullshit, Ron. I want to see you privately outside. Now."

As soon as we stepped outside the conference room, he marched to the restroom with me in tow. "If you ever tell anyone I had to use this room before you, I'll disown you." Sorry, Kirk; that story is just too funny not to tell.

Another time, I got the following call from Kirk.

"Ron, this is God. We need more bookings. I think the problem is that your advertising isn't working hard enough. And now that I think it, I declare it to be fact. But I have also solved the problem. I want you to stop inviting people to take HAL cruises. Order those assholes to buy my cruises! And make the type larger. Make it really big. Yell louder to those dumb shits. Intimidate them. That should do it."

Telling Kirk, "No" is never a good idea. Working with his marketing team to target even better potential cruisers usually worked enough that Kirk would shift his focus to harass another group.

Terri Small, our creative director, was due to have her first child around the time of one year's annual creative presentation to top management. As luck would have it, Terri went into labor the morning of our scheduled meeting. The other suits and I gathered up the materials and headed over to Holland America. A few minutes after we had set up in the conference room, Kirk walked in, looked around, and gruffly growled, "Where's Terri?"

"She went into labor this morning and is now at the hospital."

"Why are we still meeting then?" he asked.

"We have some imminent deadlines looming," I replied.

"Who's going to show me the creative?" he asked.

"We are," I answered.

"Bullshit. I refuse to be subjected to your account-speak mumbo-jumbo. We'll have to wait until she's back."

Just when I was about to explain that because of the critical deadlines, we couldn't wait, Dee Keegan, Kirk's executive assistant, came into the room and announced that Terri was on the phone.

Dee set up the speaker phone and Kirk said, "Terri, these meatheads said you're having your baby; is that right?"

"Not until after I present our campaign, Kirk!" she replied. "OW, UHH, OHHH! I think we better get right into it." Never had one of our creative presentations gone as smoothly with Kirk smiling from beginning to end.

A couple of weeks after the creative presentation, we were back in the room with our media team headed by Sydney Hunsdale. At one point, Kirk questioned some of the numbers. "No, they're correct Kirk," Sydney said.

"How the hell would you know?" asked Kirk.

"Because I have an accounting degree and worked as an accountant before becoming media director."

"Holy Mother of God!" shouted Kirk. "Finally, someone at the agency I can relate to! Okay, now I have two rules: you know the first one; every piece of creative has to be blessed by Terri before showing it to me, and my new one is that Syd has to see and approve everything else before I see it. Got it?"

• • • •

I have to tell you about the time four of us went to one of HAL's sales meetings in San Francisco. After the meetings ended, we had a few cocktails at the hotel with the clients, which stretched into dinner with several bottles of wine. A bunch of nightcaps later, the clients retired because of early morning flights. The rest of the night was ours; we were lubed and ready.

I vaguely remembered from a previous trip visiting a strange bar in the basement of a hotel. From my muddled memory I described it as having a lake and a pirate ship and occasionally it rained inside the room.

"I think you've either had too much to drink tonight or during the night you're describing," opined Tim.

"No, really," I replied. "Let's ask at the front desk."

"Well, sir, it's not exactly a lake, but you're thinking of the Tonga Room in the basement of the Fairmont Hotel."

"See, I told you! Is it within walking distance?"

Gauging our condition, the desk clerk politely recommended a taxi. As we headed out, Jan suggested we save the fare and take our rental. Stupidly, we all thought that to be an excellent decision.

The Tonga Room wasn't quite as monstrous in size as I'd remembered, but the Polynesian décor was even more kitschy. The mini-tropical storm began as we were being seated. Really. The combination of the heavy night of drinking with our client followed by a sampling of just about every exotic drink on the menu pretty much resulted in four blind mice. Well, four blind mice without the combined intelligence of even one.

Somehow, we found the car and headed in search of more alcohol. Jan was behind the wheel. It would be giving too much credit to say he was driving. I was in the passenger seat with Tim and Jane in the back. The Fairmont hotel was at the top of a hill and the alcohol was at the bottom. If you've been to San Francisco, you know that some of the hills are very steep. I think we found the steepest. Jan was normally the safest driver I knew. In fact, we used to tease him about driving like a little old lady; that's why we let him get behind the wheel in the first place. Well, the little old lady came out of her shell that night. As the car began to pick up speed, a strange transformation came over Jan. Instead of just not using the brake, he started using the gas pedal. By the time we reached the bottom of the hill, we were really moving.

"Wasn't that great?" exclaimed Jan. "I felt like Steve McQueen in *Bullitt*! Let's do it again!" We, of course, were crazy enough to agree.

This time, Jan hit the gas right from the start. The intersections literally flew by with the only indication being our heads hitting the roof and our butts smashing the seats. We actually left the ground, and the last two intersections were marked by metal scraping concrete sounds and sparks flying behind us.

"One more time!" shouted Jan. I turned, looked at the pale faces in the backseat, and said, "Maybe not quite so fast this time."

By the time we got back to the top, three of us seemed sober enough to think perhaps this time wouldn't be the charm. Fortunately, Jan pulled over and said he had to take a leak. As he went in search of a clean wall to foul, I told Jane to get behind the wheel and get us the hell away from this Mario Andretti doppelganger. We were a block away when Tim asked whether we were just going to leave Jan there. After debating it for a few blocks, we agreed to go back and maybe put him in the trunk. When we returned to where he got out of the car, there was no sign of him. We assumed he had started walking, but just as we started moving, Tim spotted him lying on the sidewalk, partially covered with old newspapers.

I lowered the window and said loudly, "Jan must have hailed a taxi; let's go."

About a half block later, Tim said, "He's still chasing us but losing ground. We better stop and let him in or you may have to hire a new executive vice president."

37.

180° FROM ORDINARY

In 1988, Holland America Line purchased Windstar Cruises, which, at the time, was a fleet of three of the most beautiful sailing ships in the world. The *Wind Star*, *Wind Song*, and *Wind Spirit* were each 440 feet in length and accommodated 148 passengers. They had teak-lined decks, towering white sails, luxurious amenities, gourmet cuisine, exceptional service, and because of their shallow fourteen-foot draft, the ability to visit the world's most exotic and unique ports of call. With the purchase, HAL inherited Windstar Cruises' visionary founder and CEO, Jean Claude Potier.

Jean Claude was a character. The first time I met him was at Holland America Line's weekly inventory meeting. Kirk Lanterman was usually the last person to join the fifteen to twenty person meeting. We all had our regular seats.

Jean Claude entered the room with a flourish and announced, "I am Jean Claude Potier, visionary founder of Windstar. Where does Kirk Lanterman sit?"

Someone pointed to Kirk's regular chair. Jean Claude immediately walked over to the two empty chairs (no one had the balls to sit right next to Kirk) and sat in Kirk's chair. Someone pointed out he had chosen the wrong chair; he smiled and intentionally ignored the remark.

Moments later, Kirk entered the room, looked at Jean Claude sitting in his chair, and without a word, sat in the empty seat. Everyone was stunned at both Jean Claude's audacity and Kirk's passivity, but each privately predicted that Jean Claude was not long for this world.

Before Jean Claude's ultimate demise, however, Kirk told him to move his advertising account from his long-time agency in New York City to Elgin Syferd. He also told him that David Geirsdorf was going to be his CMO. Jean Claude's adamant objections held no weight with Kirk.

I had known and admired David's father when he was a major player at Alaska Airlines. I quickly learned to admire the son as well if not even more.

Both David and I realized that the Windstar product was actually superior to the manner in which it was being positioned and marketed. David got Kirk's approval to reposition the brand and have the agency create all new marketing materials. Jean Claude's argument against giving the agency the assignment once again held no weight with Kirk.

David and the agency team took a roadtrip to Florida for a visit aboard the *Wind Spirit* while she was in port. Several of the team members had become very familiar by this time with a variety of cruise ships from spending multiple years working on Holland America Line and sampling several of its competitors. None of us were prepared, however, for the majestic beauty and elegance of this gorgeous sailing ship. It was so different from every cruising experience previously encountered. It made us realize how important it was for us to see the ship before we tried to market it. *You can't effectively sell something you would not buy for yourself. Even if you can't afford the product or service, you must desire it above all its competitors. The most effective selling ideas must come from your heart as well as your head.*

Our heads told us Windstar represented a unique cruising experience; our hearts helped give us the words for the position. To this day, there are at least three of us at the agency who take credit for the now iconic tag line: "180° From Ordinary."

David loved the line and how it came to life in subsequent ads and brochures. He made some brilliant suggestions that made the materials even better, and with those changes made, we arranged a date for a presentation to Jean Claude.

We expected that since Jean Claude had had a heavy hand in the creation of the old materials and nothing to do with the new, it would be a hard sell. It was even more difficult than we imagined. Jean Claude hated everything. He took great delight in telling us that his disappointment did not surprise him since we were simply a "small Seattle agency, not a big, famous New York City agency like the one he had worked with to create the brilliant work we were trying to cast aside." He instructed us to scrap everything and go back to the original materials.

David was pissed and wanted to go directly to Kirk. Not knowing how long we were going to have to work with Jean

Claude, I convinced David to give me a couple of weeks first. I had a plan.

I called Keith Reinhard in New York and described the situation. He asked that I send the materials to him. I told him it would be more credible in Jean Claude's mind if I actually brought the old and new materials to New York City for an assessment by one of the largest and, arguably, the world's most creative agencies. Keith agreed and we set a date for the meeting. Unfortunately, neither David nor Jean Claude could make the trip, but Jean Claude was so certain of his position that he blessed the trip.

Keith *loved* the new line, made a few helpful suggestions about the ads, and sent me on my way. But not before skillfully crafting a letter for me to present to Jean Claude, congratulating him on his brilliant leadership in evolving the brand position from merely good to one of the best he'd ever seen. He went on to say how proud he was that his Seattle agency had developed "not just New York City, but global quality creative materials."

As soon as Jean Claude read the letter, he became the fourth person taking credit for "180° from Ordinary." That line, by the way, is still being used twenty-four years later.

38.

WALKING THE WALK

We had an early incident at the agency that tested our resolve for the "No Asshole Rule."

Tom, one of our senior account people and a really great guy, told me that a client had been verbally abusing one of the younger account people. The account was not huge, but it had a respectable budget, and even more importantly, the client was allowing us to do some really nice work. We had been hired by the company owners, and after we had worked directly with them developing the initial campaign, they hired a marketing director and turned the function over to him.

I counseled Tom to use the experience as a teaching tool for the junior account person. "Tell LeAnn not to take any shit from him," I said. "Tell her to argue her position passionately, but professionally. If he tries to take the conversation into areas she considers inappropriate, teach her how to get the conversation back on track."

A week later, Tom was back in my office. He told me that he had coached LeAnn and even taken her through a couple of rehearsals where he played the part of the asshole. The result of her subsequent meeting was even worse than before. She came back in tears.

"Call him and set up a meeting for yourself. Explain that we will not tolerate the abuse of our people. Try not to lose the business, but tell him he's acting unprofessionally and that's unproductive for both of us. Get him squared away, Tom."

A few days later, Tom showed up in my office. If I had to guess, Tom probably started shaving at age nine. He had played college football and could be one scary mother. But he actually had tears in *his* eyes. He didn't have to tell me how his meeting had gone. I picked up the phone.

"Harold, this is Ron Elgin at your former agency."

"Hi, Ron. What do you mean, 'former agency'?"

"Just that, Harold. You're fired. We don't work for assholes. And you're an asshole."

It was a proverbial shot heard round the agency. That may be a bit of an exaggeration, but it was a pretty big deal within the company. We didn't exactly have dancing in the aisles, but there was a huge sense of pride that reverberated throughout our halls. Not only had management demonstrated that we would back our employees to the extreme, but I had also proved that we lived our philosophy of not working with or for assholes.

• • • •

Tom Phillips is one of the greatest public relations guys ever. He's also a damn good manager. So good, in fact, that he managed a couple of bad clients right out the door.

Tom worked for us twice. The first time almost didn't happen.

He was new to Seattle and didn't know that our office was only a block away from his Queen Anne apartment. He left an hour early for his interview, and due to some faulty map reading, ended up fifteen miles away in Bellevue. Thanks to a savvy gas station attendant, he backtracked across the lake and ended up parking in the same spot he had vacated an hour earlier. I've often wondered whether, if he had told me this story at the time, I would have even considered hiring him.

Anyway, I remember him asking, "Why did you decide to start your own agency, Mr. Elgin?" I looked him straight in the eye and said, "Because I got tired of working for assholes; it's something we don't tolerate around here." Apparently, that was enough for him to want the job.

Tom grew from a snot-nosed kid to a polished professional who then shit on us by starting his own agency with another former employee. Several years later, I got revenge by luring him back to head up the entire PR group. The other day, we were reminiscing and he reminded me of some of his best highs and very funny lows. Sometimes, they were one-and-the-same.

Tom claims the agency's worst client ever was the CEO of a dating website. He believes the client's primary reason for hiring us was his infatuation with one of our female employees, whom he took to calling "Gaby Baby." To this day, Tom refers to him as the "Arrogant Fat Fuck."

"Ron, the guy was barely tolerable as a human being," said Tom, "but when he started his own smarmy site, he was over the top. After not seeing his company immediately profiled on *NBC Nightly News* and headlined in *The Wall Street Journal*, he took great delight in sending me late night emails that were sarcastic and vicious. It got so bad that I told the team we were going to fire him, and I did, with great pleasure. But wait; it didn't end there. He told me he wouldn't 'allow' the termination unless we abided by the ninety-day out clause. He insisted that we continue working for him for three fucking months!"

Tom knew that this clause was typically written to protect the agency by allowing it adequate time to make any necessary staffing changes. None of us had ever seen it used by a client to prolong an abusive relationship. Being a greedy bastard, I said, "Tom, just grin and bear it, and continue billing the $25,000 retainer for the next three months."

"No way," Tom argued. "We are so sick of this abusive cretin that he can keep his $75,000, and you can take it out of my salary!"

I pushed my greed aside and let Tom sever the relationship and didn't dock his pay. The guy threatened to sue, but nothing came of it, and Tom became legendary around the agency for walking the walk.

"I really hope the Arrogant Fat Fuck ends up totally broke and his next job is cleaning toilets in gas stations," a smiling Tom added.

Tom's second "worst client" story went like this.

"In this guy's case," Tom reported, "he was truly a horrible client, but I honestly think it had to do with a chemical imbalance in his brain. I remember one call in particular. Scott Janzen was running the business, but the buck stopped with me, and this asshole knew it. So the guy decides he needs to have a come-to-Jesus conference call with the entire account team at 4:00 p.m. on the Friday before Memorial Day weekend. We get on the call and he proceeds to shred us verbally non-stop for the next forty minutes, calling us amateurs and the biggest waste of money he'd ever seen. He screamed he could get more press by cold-calling reporters himself. That he could get better work by hiring monkeys from the zoo and giving them typewriters. The team members' faces had turned white by this time, and I was about to tell the guy to go fuck himself when he paused the tirade for about three seconds and then said, 'Okay team, keep up the good work and have a great weekend' … click, end of call. It was like something straight out of *Saturday Night Live*."

Tom fired the client soon after the long weekend and kept alive our tradition of walking the walk.

39.

A REMARKABLE NON-CLIENT FREE TRIP

Dave and I were having lunch and a bottle of Italian red wine with Bob Walsh, an old friend, on the terrace of Il Terrazzo Carmine. Bob is one of the most interesting people ever; his remarkable career included: on-air radio personality, General Manager of the Seattle Supersonic basketball team, best friends with Bill Russell the basketball legend, and promoter extraordinaire. Bob had just regaled us with the latest on his venture, which he co-founded with his friend Ted Turner. It was 1986 and the venture was called the Goodwill Games, which were to be held in Moscow from July 5th through the 20th. The Goodwill Games were a response to the Olympic boycotts of the period, which saw the U.S. refuse to attend the 1980 Olympic Games in Moscow and the Soviet Union refusing to attend the 1984 Summer Olympics in L.A. This was to be the first time in eleven years that elite athletes from the Soviet Union and the U.S. competed against each other in a major summer multi-sport event.

At the end of the meal, Bob said he had an opening for two people to join the Seattle contingent going to the games.

He first invited Dave and his wife Trudi to be his guests on the trip a couple of weeks hence. Dave thought about it for a minute and declined, saying he was too busy. Bob then asked me whether Bonnie and I would like to join him. I considered it for about a second and shouted, "YES!"

By the time Dave realized that if I could make time for the trip, he could as well, it was too late. We had our visas, shots, and plane tickets.

When I saw who made up the Seattle contingent, I was even more excited. It was like a giant buffet of new business opportunities. The names, positions, and even the companies on the list aren't important to this story except for one person who is key to the tale: Randy James, who was then Vice Chairman of Seattle First National Bank (Bank of America).

I arranged a lunch with Randy to talk about the trip. Although I didn't know him well at the time, I knew him to be a hell of a guy in many ways. First of all, he doesn't look like the stereotypical banker. One might guess from his build and the strength of his handshake that he could be a very terrifying nightclub bouncer. He doesn't have the stereotypical banker's personality, either. He's charming, funny, nice, and extremely decisive.

He told me during the lunch that he'd been approached by a local Jewish group with an unusual request. Apparently, the Soviet government had some very strict and hurtful rules, regulations, and laws against the majority of its Jewish citizens. A particularly onerous one was the restricted sale of baby formula. The Jewish group had told Randy that baby formula was desperately needed because the Jewish mothers were so severely malnourished it was nearly impossible for them to breast-feed. The group asked Randy to purchase as much baby formula as possible and deliver it to the country's most notorious dissident. Since it was impossible to carry that much formula in his suitcase, it meant buying it in Russia. I said, "You gotta be kidding." He showed me the guy's name and address. On the slip of paper, someone had written that if the window shade were half-drawn, it was safe to approach. I said, "You GOTTA be kidding." He assured me he wasn't.

The flight was long and uncomfortable. Since the tickets were gratis, we were in coach the whole way. By the time we finally reached Moscow, Bonnie informed me we were flying home First Class, and she didn't care how I arranged it, but it would be arranged. After flying for nearly two days sitting straight up in a hard chair, I saw her point.

At the last minute, Randy's wife was unable to join us, so Bonnie and I adopted him. On the way to the hotel, he explained to Bonnie his mission and promise to the Jewish group. She immediately bought in and said she knew great alternatives to the specified formula and started suggesting other things like bottles, nipples, and diapers. Finally, I exerted myself and proclaimed that we were not getting involved.

They both looked at me with curiosity and Bonnie said, "You may not be willing to help, but you're not speaking for me."

Taken aback, I said, "This is not America. Not even close. This is a police state. What you're threatening to do is probably against the law. When people break the law here, they are sent to a gulag in Siberia. They go there and never come back."

They said in unison, "Be a wimp if you must, but we're helping these poor women and their babies." I tried all that night to dissuade Bonnie, especially after Bob and other senior executives from the games gave us our list of must-do's and must-not-do's. A few that really hit home were that we were "relatively free" to visit the city with our guides from InTourist, a Russian travel agency, but we would be shadowed by KGB agents to insure good behavior; that our rooms would probably be bugged; and we should not fraternize with citizens of the USSR—the government officials would introduce us to the people they wanted us to meet.

After a sleepless night wondering what my life would be like without Bonnie, I sucked it up and decided I'd rather be in Siberia with her than anywhere without her. She took my heroically romantic decision in stride and said, "Hurry up; we're late."

We met Randy outside the hotel entrance. He said, "I've already spotted the KGB guys. We're obviously not high priority because they're just kids."

"Where are they?"

"My guy is over there behind the black truck. They all have on Hawaiian shirts, trying to look like Americans. The problem is, all the shirts are exactly the same, and they're so ugly I can't imagine them even being sold in America. I've been watching them following our other friends, and I think I know a way to ditch him."

I thought, "Shit. Siberia, here we come."

I have no idea where a banker, even one who looked like a linebacker, learned his tradecraft, but within minutes, we had lost the poor KGB kid. Randy then led us to a taxi stand. We couldn't find a driver who could even come close to understanding English. Randy then started showing the written address. That didn't seem to help either. In fact, the drivers appeared even more confused. Finally, one of the drivers took the address over to a guy who had been watching with a great deal of interest. To our dismay, the guy was a cop.

"Perhaps, I can help," suggested the cop in very broken English. "You want to go to this address, yes?"

"Yes, sir," answered Randy.

"Well, as you discovered, none of these drivers speak English. They also cannot read English. Our language is spoken and written in Cyrillic. I can translate it for you if you wish."

"That would be great, officer," said Randy, while I was thinking to myself, "Why the fuck doesn't he just ask him to have the cabbie drive us straight to Siberia?"

We arrived safely at the designated apartment complex about 8 a.m. Following the written directions obtained in Seattle, we counted windows, and to my dismay, the correct one was signaling that we could enter. The foyer to the building was dismal. Not dirty, just dark and gloomy. We walked up two flights lighted by a single bulb hung from a wire in the center of the stairwell. Randy rapped on the apartment door, which was immediately opened by a middle-aged guy in a bright blue Adidas sweatsuit and Nike sneakers. Oh, and a huge gold medallion around his neck. He looked like an out-of-touch hip-hop artist.

We introduced ourselves, but our host, Lev, already knew who Randy was, and that was all that mattered. After hugs and kisses all around, he invited us to sit while he plopped down a bottle of vodka and four glasses.

"We must drink to your courageous and selfless act to help our poor mothers and their babies," he proclaimed as he poured generous shots into our glasses. Bonnie and Randy declined while I was thinking a little liquid courage might be just the thing. Lev, almost to the point of anger, insisted we toast. So we toasted. Three vodkas and one water for Bonnie.

Over the next hour, we learned that Lev was the USSR's undisputed number one dissident. He proudly showed us his face on the cover of *TIME Magazine*. The headline and feature story verified his claim. Lev had been the highest ranking official in the USSR's meatpacking industry. When their son reached college age, Lev and his wife decided they wanted to migrate to Israel. Their request was declined. The government claimed it would be detrimental to the security of the USSR if his knowledge of putting meat in cans were ever to leave the country. After many failed attempts, Lev hit upon a unique solution. He divorced his wife, and as soon as it was final, she applied for exit visas for herself and their son. Since she didn't possess any State secrets, she and her son were able to jump on a flight to Tel Aviv. Needless to say, when the government figured out what had happened, it was pissed and immediately fired Lev and closed that particular loophole for all other Jews. Fearing for his life, Lev devised a novel strategy. He would become the outspoken voice of Jewish oppression in the USSR. He would be audacious in his efforts. His rationale was two-fold: He wanted to help better the lives of his fellow Jews, and he reasoned that with enough loud and obnoxious behavior, the world attention could discourage the government from making him disappear. The strategy appeared to be working. His end-game was the hope that international "fame" would someday translate to international pressure to allow him to join his family in Israel.

That part of his story took the three of us guys through about half the bottle of vodka. Apparently, women were exempt from the mandatory toasts. Either that or Lev was smart enough not to push his luck with Bonnie. In any event, he launched into our assignment. The government had recently banned the sale of baby formula such as Similac to Jews. No one explained why, but it was a law. Our job was to go to as many stores as possible and buy every can we could find in the next few hours. It had to be fast because as soon as the government figured out what was going on, shit was going to happen.

"Ah, excuse me, Lev, but to whom would this shit be happening?" I asked.

"Why you, of course. You need to strike fast, bring the formula here to me, and disappear back to your hotel."

"We're not doing this; we're fucking out of here, guys!" I said.

"No we're not," said Bonnie. "Give us the addresses of the stores and get us a dependable driver, Lev. We'll make it as fast as possible."

Our shopping spree went without incident—just a lot of anxiety on my part. We returned after a couple of hours with bags full of formula, bottles, nipples, and diapers. We politely but firmly refused to toast our success and instead bid a hasty farewell.

When we got back to the hotel, we were met by a massively pissed off Bob Walsh. "I commend your act of kindness, but are you guys crazy? You can't believe the shit Turner and I had to go through to keep you from going to jail! Please, please, I desperately want you to be able to go back to Seattle with me. Do not do anything more that's going to make the Soviets keep you here!"

If you think that would keep Bonnie from doing what she thinks is right, you haven't paid attention to my previous descriptions of her.

A couple of nights later, we were invited to a big deal dinner with Ted Turner, Bob, and the rest of the leadership group. About fifty people were supposed to be there, but because of late games, jet lag, and a variety of ailments, only about half that many showed up for transportation to the restaurant. When our vehicles arrived, we assumed it was a pretty popular place because a significant line was waiting outside, including a young lady in a wedding gown.

We were led to the front of the line and entered through the door to a completely empty restaurant. It was explained that the entire place had been reserved for us. That didn't seem to bother Ted, but it did Bonnie.

"Why can't you let those people in?" she asked the waiter. "There's plenty of room and it's starting to rain outside."

The broken-English answers we got back were variations of "Not permitted" and "They don't mind waiting." Anyway, the food was typically terrible, but there were multiple bottles of the ubiquitous vodka and even champagne, so I was having an okay time listening to Ted hold court. Bonnie, however, was not only bored but getting angrier by the minute watching the crowd outside. After Bonnie had a toe-to-toe with the manager, he sought permission from Ted to allow the wedding party to go into the banquet room, promising they would be ejected if they proved troublesome. Ted didn't give a shit, so the party was carefully escorted to the private room.

A few minutes later, Bonnie picked up a couple of bottles of unopened vodka and champagne, instructed me to do the same, and told me to follow her.

"What are you doing?" I asked, suspecting the answer.

"The manager told me that Ted had paid for the booze on all these tables and there's no way even he can drink all of it, so we're going to present it to the wedding party as an apology for making them stand out in the rain."

"Did the manager say that was okay?"

"I didn't ask, but if you stop talking and grab a bunch of bottles, we can get in there before anyone can stop us."

I remember wondering whether it was always cold in Siberia.

When we walked into the room occupied by the wedding party, the conversation went from hushed to silent. All eyes were on Bonnie and me and twelve bottles of booze. No one appeared hostile, but neither did they look hospitable. By that time, the broken-English manager caught up with us with a look of "What the hell are you doing?"

Bonnie said, "Please tell these people that these bottles are a wedding gift from the organizers of the Goodwill Games." While translating, he actually smiled at us for the first time. As we turned to leave, the manager said they would like to take a picture of us with the bride and groom. We agreed and a really old guy with what looked like an even older Brownie box camera stepped forward to take our picture. Then pandemonium broke out—everyone wanted in the picture. The now good-guy manager took photos until the film was gone, and then we once again made our way to the door. We had just about made it when the manager said they had one more request: Would we do the honor of having the first dance with the bride and groom? It made our day. I'm certain Bonnie's thoughtfulness stayed alive, not just in the photos, but in the hearts of everyone in the wedding party.

40.

THE PERILS OF FAULTY COMMUNICATIONS

One of our earliest accounts was an HMO by the name of HealthPlus. Dave won it as a PR-only account. Based on some really good work, we quickly were able to capture additional areas of their business. Multiple disciplines meant multiple touches by multiple people. Because the account wasn't very big, all that multiple stuff was making the account complicated. Although the work was pretty good and our people reported that the client was happy, my paranoia had me check for myself. I arranged for a lunch with HealthPlus' CEO, who was smart, personable, and friendly. We had a good chat over lunch about world affairs, the local arts scene, and the economy. After talking for a while about the state of her business, I asked whether she had heard how the agency was performing. She said everything was okay, but I could tell there was something troubling her. Sometimes you can learn more from nonverbal conversation than you can from what is verbally communicated. But I needed to be sure.

"Come on, Margaret," I urged. "There's something bothering you. We're partners in this relationship. Lay it out. Tell me what's wrong."

"It's really not that big of a thing," she said. "It's just that some of my people have expressed concern that they wished the agency's left hand knew what the right was doing. Apparently, they're getting mixed messages."

"Thanks for being honest with me, Margaret. Let me look into it," I promised.

It was pretty much what Dave and I had feared from the start about our concept. When the two of us tackled a problem, we did so with years of experience as well as knowing beforehand what to expect from one another. The agency had some relatively inexperienced people who were running while learning and not taking the time really to communicate with one another. The fix was just a matter of forcing regular face-to-face status meetings and making sure everyone was copied on all reports. It was a simple matter of making sure the left hand knew what the right was doing.

A couple of weeks later, I got a call from Margaret.

"Ron, I want you to know that our people are raving about the agency's recent performance," she said. "I don't know what you did, but our people are happy campers. Thank you so much."

Doing good work is not enough to keep good clients. Constant care, contact, cultivation, and asking the right questions are essential.

"Thanks for the feedback, Margaret," I said. "Our promise to all clients is that once we know a problem exists, big or small, we will address it. If at all possible, we will even fix it. It's those damn things we never hear about that always bite us in the ass."

• • • •

A friend of mine at a big-time New York agency told me a story about a client for whom the agency was doing stellar work. Sales were at record highs; the work was receiving accolades from the general public; they were winning big at creative and marketing award shows; all was seemingly good. My friend was invited to fly across country to have an audience with the client's CEO at year's end. With visions of bonuses dancing in his head, he headed to the meeting. After a short preliminary conversation, the CEO fired the agency. My bewildered friend went through the impressive list of accomplishments and basically demanded to know why they were being fired. The answer was simply that his people found it just too difficult to work with the agency.

Someone at the agency was either not reading the situation correctly, asking the right questions, or both.

41.

THE INTERVIEW REDUX

The reporter from *The Seattle Times* asked whether she could do a two-year follow-up to her interview with Dave and me. She suggested the day and even the location for a lunch. Her choice was an outdoor restaurant near Gas Works Park on Lake Union. It was a nice day and she had a table reserved right next to the boat dock.

"So, I hear that your new company is doing really well," the reporter said. "Word on the street is that you've been tagged as the hot shop in town. To what do you attribute all this early success?"

"It's actually a combination of a lot of things," I began. "As I told you before, our founding philosophy is to deliver communications solutions that are discipline agnostic. When we've been able to put this into practice, it has yielded good results for our clients. And their successes seem to have bred even more success for ourselves. Another thing we told you was we'd hire people better than ourselves and try to stay out of their way. We've been really good at the hiring part and we're getting better about staying out of their way."

"How long do you think you can stay on this roll?" she inquired. "I mean, you can't expect to continue at this pace."

I was starting to get bored with her and pissed at her nervy attitude. So I took Dave's earlier advice and just sat back, enjoyed my beer and the weather, and let the PR professional handle the rest of the interview.

Dave was gracious and humble in his answers, but I could tell he was starting to get bored as well. I started thinking that perhaps she wasn't the sharpest tool. I didn't care. I had made my initial points and was content to wait until the end of the interview to deliver my final point. I just smiled contentedly, drank my beer, and watched the boats cruising Lake Union.

She finally asked the question I'd been waiting two years to answer: "During our first interview, you said that your ultimate, long-term goal was someday to grow to be a mid-size agency. I think you said back then you'd like someday to have $5 to $10 million in billings. If I understand correctly, you've already surpassed that goal. What does that mean for your future? Have you reached your plateau? Can you realistically expect further growth?"

"Dave, please let me handle this," I said, "and please don't kick me this time. Ms., I wasn't really honest with you about how big I thought we could grow our agency. What I really should have said was that Cole & Weber is currently the largest in our market with $60 million in billings. If it intends to keep the top spot, it better start cranking because I fully expect us to be at least $100 million within ten years. And we're going to do that by being the best in the market. You can quote me on that."

The table went silent while she scribbled in her notepad. I took a sip of beer and looked at Dave. He was smiling because he now believed it, too. I turned back to watch the boats on the lake. One in particular was packed with very loud, obnoxious drunks heading for the restaurant's dock. It was probably the inevitable result of some stupid CEO's decision to allow his employees to go drinking on a boat during working hours. While pondering the stupidity, I saw one of our employees leaning over the boat's railing. A moment later, I spied a couple more. Was I that stupid CEO?

"Dave, some of our people are on that boat," I said. "Did you give them the day off or something?"

"Hell no," he answered. "Did you?"

Just then, the boat turned sideways into the dock. Draped along the entire side was a huge banner with the words, "Happy Anniversary, Ron and Dave!" Then we realized it wasn't just a few of our employees; it was all of them, and they were waving beers, yelling, and laughing over the loud music blaring from the ship's speakers.

The reporter smiled and said, "Well, they finally got here! I ran out of questions twenty minutes ago and felt idiotic going back over the same ones! Your people invited me on the cruise as payment for my part in the surprise. I told my boss the interview was going to be lengthy and might take all afternoon. After suffering through this interview, I think he would agree that I deserve the rest of the day off."

We were absolutely blown away and honored that our unbelievably terrific people had chartered the boat and stocked it with booze and food at their own expense to celebrate our anniversary. I was so touched that I barely gave thought to the day's lost revenue opportunities. Barely, that is.

Everyone had so much fun that day that we decided to allow our employees to pay every year—just kidding. But it did become a tradition and one of our best Kumbaya events for the next twenty years.

Over those many years, we had some notable experiences on the cruise. Most of which were the result of hiring wonderfully crazy people who were fueled by generous amounts of alcohol and love for one another.

One particular year on a lovely, warm afternoon, we were cruising on Lake Washington. An employee had alerted her parents that she would be coming by their waterfront home on the company cruise and to watch for her. About the time we were within sight of her parents' home, two of our people decided to jump off the top deck for a little swim. I shit you not. No thought whatsoever about how the hell they would get back on the boat. They were just so hammered they simply jumped.

"Man overboard!" shouted about a dozen laughing and screaming drunks. Several others started pitching beers to the frolicking swimmers.

The boat captain took immediate action by throwing the old diesel engines in reverse, which caused a shuddering halt to our forward progress. Seconds later, an immense black cloud belched from the boat's smokestack. Meanwhile, our crazed employees were have a rip-roaring good time: laughing, drinking, shouting, and jumping up and down with drunken glee.

From the shore, however, it looked to be a catastrophe in the happening. The parents of our employee, fearing the life of their beloved daughter, immediately called the police, the Coast Guard, the Shore Patrol, and probably the White House. "There's been a terrible explosion on a boat right in front of our house," they reported. "It's on fire and people are abandoning the ship. And our daughter is on it!"

By the time we were able to pull the two drunks back on board, we were surrounded by two police boats and a fire boat with some very pissed off public servants. Since no laws had been broken, no citations were issued, but we were promised by the police that there would be a welcoming committee when we docked. Fortunately for our many drunks, the cops must have had something better to do that night. That particular charter company refused our business the following year.

As the event evolved, each year we had a new theme with the requisite T-shirts, signature drinks, and food. We would gather the staff shortly after lunch for what evolved into a half-assed pep rally. I would explain the origin of the tradition and show slides and video of the highlights from previous cruises. One year, someone decided my boring little speech needed a punch line, so while I was talking, people handed out plastic cups of tequila. After knocking back a few shooters and an appropriate toast, we headed to the boat and more booze.

Attendance was strictly limited to current employees over twenty-one, plus the gorgeous Bonnie Elgin and Trudi Syferd. Bonnie was wearing a navy top and jeans, and Trudi was in an immaculate white outfit. These are important points to note because of what was about to happen. Our intern that year may have been legal, but she turned out to be not much of a drinker. Or maybe she just wasn't used to tequila shooters in the early afternoon.

About midway through the cruise, the intern staggered over to our wives to meet them. While reaching for Trudi's hand, she upchucked about a gallon of red wine all over the previously pristine white outfit. I mean like all over. It was like a fire hose had been hooked to a wine barrel. By the end of the night, our drunks had elevated the incident to mythical and legendary proportions.

I'm sure that if Dave and I had been smart enough to think of having an annual party cruise, it would have been successful, but because it was employee-inspired, the employees owned the cherished tradition from womb to tomb.

42.

A COUPLE OF DREAM RETAIL CLIENTS

A media rep informed us that a regional chain of retail fashion stores was looking for a new agency. When we heard it was Jay Jacobs, I jumped all over it. The chain was based in downtown Seattle, founded in the year of my birth, 1941, by Jay Jacobs. It specialized in trendy clothing for teens, mainly targeting girls. Although the company's first twenty years saw slow growth, by the mid-1980s, it operated 288 stores in twenty-two Western states. One of the reasons for my excitement was that I knew Jay's daughter and son-in-law, Shelly and Doug, who were both key executives with the firm. With their help, Elgin Syferd was able to be included in the pitch process, and with the excitement of everyone in the agency, we ultimately won the business.

All the people we met at Jay Jacobs were wonderful: From the young "shoe dogs" all the way up to Jay himself. Since most of our people were barely over half the age of Dave and me, they all wanted to work on the business. We spread it out as best we could and learned a lot about fashion, fashion merchandising, and retailing.

Most of our contact was with the merchandising managers and the president, but on special occasions, we got to present to Mr. Jacobs. We began to understand and appreciate the world of fashion merchandising and began doing some best of category work together.

A few years and a lot of creative awards later, I got a call. "Ron, this is Linda Toschi at Nordstrom. I'm head of advertising. We'd like to come over to meet you and take a look at your agency."

I could hardly believe my ears. Nordstrom? The most iconic brand of all retailers? I could also hardly believe the words that fell out of my mouth, "I'd love to meet you, Linda, but I'm afraid we have a conflict. We handle Jay Jacobs."

"I know that, Ron. I'm not asking for you to do work for us," replied Linda. "We'd just like to meet."

We arranged for a meeting at our office. Although we knew it wasn't a pitch, we assumed Nordstrom wanted to get to know us through our work and our key people. Linda ("Call me, L.T.; everyone does!") and her people were every bit as wonderful as their company brand. They were friendly, inquisitive, and sensitive to the fact that we handled one of their competitors. We shook hands and vowed to stay in touch.

A few weeks later, I got another call. "Ron, this is L.T. We need to talk."

Over coffee, L.T. said, "Ron, we've talked to several agencies and have decided that we really want to hire you as our broadcast partner. I feel bad about the conflict, but not bad enough not to ask you to join with us."

"L.T., I'm flattered," I said, "but we didn't even pitch you. How do you know you want to hire us?"

"We like your work, but even more importantly, we think you guys are Nordstrom kind of people," she replied.

How could anyone say "No" to flattery like that?

I truly felt bad about having to resign Jay Jacobs, but we knew what the Nordstrom brand on our roster could do for our reputation and what the increased billings would do for our balance sheet. As tough as it was going to be, I chose personally to deliver the message to Mr. Jacobs.

Jay was a man of small stature but huge personality. I'd been in his office for presentations but never in a situation like this. Perhaps that's why I noticed things I'd never noticed before. Like the fact that his big desk was positioned in front of a very large window with the sun behind him. And that his desk wasn't just wide, it was tall. Or at least it looked that way from the small chair he had positioned in front of him. After a nervous hello, I told him how much we enjoyed working on his brand with his people.

"Get to the point, Ron," he urged. "You may not be busy, but I am."

Mr. Jacobs didn't get to where he was by being slow, slovenly, or stupid.

"We've been asked by Nordstrom to be its advertising agency, and with your permission, we'd—"

Before I could finish my sentence, he jumped up from his chair and ran around his desk, right for me. I thought, "Shit, this is all I need—a fight with someone as old as my dad!"

Just before he got to me, I realized he had a huge smile on his face and his hand was extended in friendship. As I stood and took his hand, he said, "Ron, this makes me so incredibly proud. When we started working together, you and your company didn't know shit about fashion or retailing. Just think, in just a few years working with us, you've become good enough to become Nordstrom's agency. I can't wait to tell everyone the great news!"

Jay Jacobs passed away recently at the too-young age of 101. Bonnie and I are still friends with Doug and Shelly and our kids are friends with theirs.

I loved Mr. Jacobs.

43.

FISCAL (IR)RESPONSIBILTY

Dave and I constantly preached that all disciplines are equal and everyone deserves to be treated with dignity. Because of this, we had pretty good partnerships between departments—even between account management and creative. But it's just natural that when strong-minded people passionately believe their way is best, polite debate can get out of hand. I know because it happened to us more than a few times.

If you've been in the business, you know about write-offs. Although there are no good write-offs, sometimes there are good reasons for them. Most times, not.

One day, our McDonald's account director came to me with a request for a write-off. I took one look at it and asked, "What the hell is this?"

"I know it's a lot of money, but it's all inside time," he stammered.

"I can see that, but it's for twenty-five-thousand fucking dollars!"

"Actually, it's only $24,546."

"You fucking asshole! What the hell is this?"

"It's for the creative time developing ideas for a tray liner."

"A tray liner? A fucking tray liner? You let the creatives rack up $25,000 of time on a fucking tray liner? What was the original budget?"

"Five hundred. For the whole job, including production."

"I'm going to fucking kill you."

"Hey, I had no idea they were spending that kind of time on it. They knew the budget. I've been more concerned about keeping the TV shoot on track; I had no idea anyone was even working on the tray liner until yesterday's internal creative review when all four teams presented their ideas."

"All four teams! Has this place gone completely nuts?"

With that, I stormed off to see the creative director.

"Laurie, did you know there's a $25,000 write-off on a tray liner job for McDonald's?"

"I didn't know the money part, but I guess it's understandable because I put four teams on it. What's the problem?"

"You authorized four teams to work on one lousy tray liner? What were you thinking?"

"Ron, just last month you told me that we had to up our game. Do better work. Win more awards."

"But this was just a $500 tray liner, for God's sake!"

"Whoa, I'm getting crossed signals, Ron. On the one hand, you tell me to take pride in every piece of creative that comes out of here, and now you're saying it's just a fucking tray liner?

"I didn't mean for us to invest $25,000 in a $500 job."

"Please explain," she asked.

"Of course I want you to do great work, but what you did was fiscally irresponsible," I said. "A good agency should strive to have at least 5 percent of its work be of the quality to win at Cannes. Because I want us to be recognized as a great agency rather than simply a good one, I'd like 10 percent of our work to be great. I fully expect the other 90 percent to be best of category."

I said that if her people couldn't create within a reasonable budget a tray liner that was better than anything done by the agencies for either Burger King or Wendy's, perhaps she should find better people. "That's what I mean about best of category work. We pay our bills with the money earned on the 90 percent. If we do that wisely and do NOT go over budget, we will have the ability to invest on projects for which we can win gold at Cannes. I didn't say it is impossible to win an award for a tray liner, but I am telling you to be more responsible in allocating our resources." Until the day Laurie left, years later, she guided some of the best work we ever produced. And most of it was done in a financially responsible manner.

• • • •

An acquaintance approached me at a cocktail party and asked whether our company had the capability to produce brochures. I told him that under most circumstances, we didn't accept clients with billings less than a million dollars, but for a friend, I might be able to find a way to help.

"Well, I need a brochure that tells a little about my company and presents a variety of our offerings. I want it to look nice, but I don't want to spend much on it. I'd like to get it as cheap as possible."

"Oh, I'm so sorry to hear about your troubles," I replied. "Are you just trying to stay afloat, or are you actually going out of business?"

"What the fuck are you talking about?" he practically shouted. "My company is doing great! We're not going out-of-business; we're making a lot of money!"

"Really? Then why would you want to give the opposite impression to your audiences?"

"I don't want to give that impression to anyone!"

"You are your communications, and your communications are you. Most people aren't stupid, especially your customers. If you create a piece of communications that's poorly designed and shoddily produced on cheap stock, your customers must assume the work is representative of the company and its products. The logical conclusion is that you can't afford to do it the right way. Do yourself a favor; if you're not willing to spend the money to produce something befitting the company you say you are, don't do anything at all. That way, at least you won't confuse your customers."

I'd love to say my conversation convinced him to produce a magnificent piece of work, but the truth is I was so turned off by his attitude that I never followed up. The whole conversation reminded me of the famous line I urged our people to use in situations such as the one I just mentioned. "There are a number of ways we can get this project done. We can do it fast. We can do it cheap. We can do it good. In fact, we can do any two of those, but only two. You get to pick." Invariably, clients say they want all three, to which we have to respond, "No, we can do it fast and good, but that means we'll have to put a lot of talented people on it, so it can't be cheap. Or, we can do it fast and cheap, but in the rush using less expensive talent, we can't promise it will be our best effort. We can even do it good and cheap, but we'll have to work it into our schedule so it won't be fast."

We didn't invent the saying but we sure used it.

It reminds me of another idiotic request from clients who ask for an original, completely out-of-the-box, revolutionary idea—and three examples of how it worked before.

44.

SOME GROWTH OPTIONS

Part 1
Reasons to Grow
by Ron Elgin

Along about our seventh year in business, we started losing some of our best and brightest employees. Although in total the loss represented a small percentage, to us it represented a significant crisis.

In most cases, departing employees graciously told us how much they loved our company, it was the toughest decision of their career, blah, blah, blah; and if it weren't for an even better career opportunity, they would be happy to stay forever, blah, blah, blah. Of course we enjoyed hearing that part, but it didn't change the fact that we were losing some of the primary reasons for our success. We decided to put aside HR rules and policies and conduct our exit interviews in bars after many drinks.

"Okay, Nancy, if you're not leaving for more money," I asked, "then why the hell are you leaving us?"

"Ron, you know I love this place and everyone here," she answered, "but the fact is our growth has slowed and you and Dave aren't leaving anytime soon."

"I'm sorry; what does our growth rate and us not leaving soon have to do with anything?"

"Simple, silly. Right now, I report directly to you. My only real growth opportunity is to take your job. Are you willing to give it up? And if not this minute, any time soon? You don't have to answer that; I know the answer. I'm not blaming you or Dave; you both love what you do and have many years ahead of you. I was serious when I said I wasn't leaving for a salary bump. At my new company, there are about twenty levels above mine. My incentive is to climb that ladder. Please don't be upset; be proud that you have helped me grow to this point, and be happy for me when I climb to the top of a company a hundred times the size of Elgin Syferd."

Once again, it became apparent that we had hired people smarter than ourselves. I hated hearing it, but I couldn't disagree with any part of her thinking. So how could Dave and I ramp up our growth curve to retain our superstars in light of our own realities?

One of the reasons our growth had slowed was because of this horrible little thing in the agency business called "conflict of interest." In professions such as accounting and legal, when a specific firm becomes an expert in a certain category, everyone else in that category wants to take advantage of that expertise. That rarely happens in the advertising agency business. It's kind of like people believe that accountants and lawyers are too ethical to share a client's specifics, but those slimy ad people aren't. I've debated my entire career with clients who believe that an agency's loyalty could only be to one master at a time. Not all clients are so narrow-minded, but most are.

I'm not necessarily talking about an agency handling direct competitors. I once attended a high level McDonald's meeting at its headquarters in Oakbrook, Illinois where the conflict of interest subject was brought up by a fellow agency owner. "I've been forced to accept McDonald's policy that restricts us from handling work for any other restaurant. Although including high-end white-tablecloths where the tab could be $100 or more per person seems to be a stretch, but what's with this new rule that we can no longer handle supermarket chains?"

"That should be obvious," replied one of McDonald's marketing officers. "As you know, our target market is anyone who eats. Supermarkets are now selling ready-to-eat meals. We're not saying that our agencies can't handle supermarkets; we're just saying that if you choose to do that, you won't be one of our agencies."

That bizarre, narrow-minded decision was eventually overturned by top management at McDonald's, but it gives you an idea of how tough it is for agencies to grow within a category. Our problem at Elgin Syferd was that we handled the biggest or one of the biggest clients in damn near every category in the Northwest. So the question became: How do we continue to fuel our growth in order to keep key employees?

Mulling this over, Dave and I were reminded of one of the strategies our favorite airline had once employed. Alaska

Airlines wanted to expand its route system, but it knew it had neither the financial wherewithal nor the customer base to compete with the bigger carriers on either the Seattle-San Francisco route or the Seattle-Los Angeles route. So what did it do? It started flying from Seattle into Oakland, Burbank, and Orange County. With this strategy, it attracted plenty of customers who settled for or desired these destinations over the bigger, more congested airports. Eventually, Alaska Airlines built up enough financial strength and a customer base to be competitive in San Francisco and Los Angeles. Perhaps, the seven-year-old Elgin Syferd could do something similar.

Because of Dave's love for skiing and his many contacts in Sun Valley, we had already handled some business in Idaho, so our first choice was to explore the possibility of starting an agency in Boise. Considering our extensive experience in the Great Land, our second option was to explore the possibility of starting an agency in Alaska.

Initial exploration indicated that Boise had the greatest potential because of the large number of significant businesses headquartered there such as Boise Cascade, the Idaho Potato Commission, Simplot, Albertsons, and so on. Although we felt Alaska had potential, we put Anchorage on a back burner and delved more deeply into the mindset of the Boise business community.

We learned that Boise businesses had always cast their eyes westward to the economically dominant cities of San Francisco, Portland, and Seattle for services that dwarfed the small business community in Boise. Similarly, its ad agencies looked to their larger, more successful brethren agencies in these cities with a sense of envy and awe. But mostly, with fear. Often as businesses grew in Idaho, they reached a point where they thought they were too big for the small agencies in Boise. Far too regularly, clients would leave for the big city and bright lights where the streets were lined with talented creatives and well-dressed account executives would impose their erudite and articulate jargon with impunity. Inside these coastal agencies, Idaho clients were certain they would find advertising campaigns worthy of national attention, which would improve sales for their cash registers back home. Elgin Syferd was determined to be one of those agencies.

After fiddle-farting around, we bought the largest agency in Idaho, WR Drake & Company. In Bill Drake's words, this is how it happened.

Part 2
Bigger Must Be Better
by Bill Drake

When I returned to Boise from a short career in public relations in Philadelphia, I worked on the Idaho Potato Commission at Cline Advertising, which had the account in a joint agreement with Botsford/Ketchum in San Francisco. Working closely with the people at Botsford, I saw a much higher level of professionalism than anything I had experienced in Boise. In 1982, I was invited to join AAAI network, and once again, I saw the rich resources and high level creative work coming out of my new West Coast "partner" agencies:

Borders Perrin; Kraft/Smith; and Ball & Company. I soon realized that all the awe, envy, and fear were well-earned and that the West Coast agencies did, in fact, have better talent and produced better campaigns founded on better strategies than anything I had seen in Boise. If I were ever going to expand my skills and abilities in this business, it became clear to me that somehow I needed to connect and tap into one of these West Coast agencies, while at the same time live my life in Boise. I had started my agency and was sorely in need of someone with whom to collaborate to get the best for my clients. I was alone at the top of the heap. But in Boise.

"You went with who?"

"Elgin Syferd…up in Seattle," came the reply from Jack, my now *former* client. Jack ran Chappelle USA, the marketing arm of a small winery in Idaho, and he had been my client for a couple of years. Chappelle USA was not a big client, but it represented a great and exciting category and had one of the few consumer products produced in our home state. Jack and I had gone to school together, and we were doing some pretty good work for him. He said he wanted to "expand" and conducted a competitive review "to see what's out there."

"They're getting me on television."

I said, "Did you increase the budget from the miniscule one you had with us?"

"No, it's about the same."

"Then, you won't get jack, Jack. There is no way they can get anything of any consequence in Seattle for your budget, Jack."

"Later, when I saw the work, I knew we had been beaten in strategy. Elgin Syferd planned to use a small TV schedule of ten-second commercials, placed carefully to conserve the budget. Then, at the retail level, merchandise "As Seen on Television" on each bottle, thereby giving some cache to an otherwise unknown and unheralded label. Instead of an Idaho wine, the focus was on *"Sunny Slope, the newest growing area to be added to the world's great wine growing regions."* Later, after our merger, we continued to show that brilliant work on our sample reel for years.

"My conversation with Jack wasn't the first time the caller at the other end mentioned Elgin Syferd. A year earlier, the Sun Valley Visitors Bureau had hired Elgin Syferd after a competitive review in which we participated. I told the review committee afterward, "There is no way Elgin Syferd can adequately service your account from Seattle…its travel costs you will pay for…one way or the other." What I didn't know at the time was the account was a red herring. Syferd was an avid skier and outdoorsman so trips to Sun Valley would include a combination of work and pleasure. Elgin Syferd didn't need to make any money on the Sun Valley account. It just needed an excuse to vacation in Sun Valley.

In the course of the agency's work on Sun Valley, I became acquainted with Dave Syferd. We had handled the Idaho Travel Council since 1981, and occasionally Dave would attend Council meetings. Our paths also crossed at McDonald's conventions since we each handled a McDonald's co-op. Dave's easygoing ways were easy to like. He was client-focused, smart, and a bit of a smart ass…all likable traits in this biz. He and I also shared a love of Idaho, skiing, wine, and trimmed mustaches.

While I liked Dave, I was worried about having a crafty fox in my Idaho hen house. Elgin Syferd had established a small beachhead on my little island where our firm was the dominant player. I needed to keep an eye on these guys. And it didn't take long to receive yet another call from a prospective client, the Southwest Idaho Travel Association.

"Naturally," they said, "you will be included in the coming review. After all, Bill, you are the expert in marketing travel in Idaho. Why wouldn't we hire your agency?"

"But," they went on, "we are seriously looking at this Seattle agency that has plans to set up an office here in Boise. Do you know them? Elgin Syferd?"

"Sure…I have heard a little about them…but promises are cheap and they've been talking about coming to Boise for over a year…."

The client delayed the agency selection process for five months while waiting for a decision to come from Seattle about opening an office in Boise. In the meantime, we also waited.

While we waited, we received an invitation to compete for the largest bank in Idaho, West One Bank. We had to assess this opportunity carefully because we handled two competitors of West One: Idaho Bank and Trust and Provident Federal. But, West One was big…over $3 million in budget…huge by Idaho standards. The client contact was an old friend of mine. We had lots of banking category experience. We had won a bunch of awards for our work. We knew West One's market area better than anybody around. But we had just finished an exhausting and unsuccessful campaign on behalf of our governor, trying to unseat a sitting U.S. Senator, so I was physically spent. But for $3 million, I could get it up.

We put all we could muster into the review…a PR plan, a solid creative approach, an efficient media plan, even some clever swag. A cover story in *Adweek* magazine revealed the competitors: WR Drake & Company from Boise, Davies & Rourke from Boise, McDonald/Babb from Portland, and Elgin Syferd from Seattle. Following the appearance of the article, Davies & Rourke withdrew. In the course of our preparation, we learned Dave Syferd was a close personal friend of the bank's president. Undaunted, we persevered.

"McDonald/Babb won."

"Why?" I said, in a download meeting with the client, my friend, Mike.

"They just seemed to have the right combination of good chemistry and capability we were looking for, and the knowledge of other northwest markets, which will be helpful as we expand."

Mike continued, "We like you and your media and creative…but Bill, you have a weak bench. If anything were to happen to you, our advertising program would be up shit's creek. It's a risk we can't take."

"Okay, Mike, you're telling me I'm too small for a $3 million account?"

"I'm telling you that you have no depth beyond you and a couple of top people and no backup!"

In the course of the review of West One, I made a classic mistake in not telling Provident Federal or Idaho Bank & Trust prior that we were in the finals for one of its toughest competitors. It didn't matter to Provident, but IB&T was really pissed off and immediately called for a competitive review of its account. After a few weeks, my client, Jack, confessed that he was unable to find any local agencies as good as us. I took a breath.

"But," he continued, "there is this Seattle agency that is going to be opening a Boise office soon. It is really good, and big enough for us. So we have asked it to compete against you for our account."

"Jack, don't tell me…it's Elgin Syferd, right?"

"Exactly! You know them?"

"Not exactly."

A week prior to the oral presentation for IB&T, Dave Syferd called me.

"Drake, we're tired of beating our heads against the wall every time we come to Boise; we need to talk," he said. "Every time we look at an account here, we encounter you dogs, and we're tired of getting bit. We all will be better if we can somehow work together. You open to talk?"

"Sure."

"Elgin and I will be back in Boise next week for the IB&T pitch. Let's meet then to move this ball down the field some more."

For my first meeting with Ron, I arranged a dinner at Boise's nicest restaurant in the historic Idahna Hotel. From the start, it felt like a scene from *The Odd Couple.* Ron: right out of the pages of *Gentleman's Quarterly,* impeccably dressed in the Armani suit, Zegna tie, gold cuff links, monogrammed shirt with an "E" on the cuff, and perfectly combed hair. Dave: right out of the pages of *Outdoor Backpacker,* in a wrinkled navy blazer and khakis, penny loafers, and no socks. Could these two guys actually be partners?

Our two agencies had a lot in common. They were just way bigger than us and operated in a market ten times our size. Ron, Dave, and I put a pencil to the basics of a plan and I made several negotiating trips to the Emerald City. I took an attorney, the only one I knew. Not a corporate attorney, but a close friend whose law practice consisted of chasing ambulances for personal injury cases. The meetings were held in the well-appointed thirty-fourth floor offices of Foster Pepper, a big time, downtown Seattle law firm. We were like rubes from Ideeho in the castle palace. Eventually, we worked out all the bugs and WR Drake & Company would become Elgin Syferd/Drake. Elgin Syferd would own 90 percent, and I would still have a 10 percent ownership of the new entity.

The new Boise office was to be the first expansion of Elgin Syferd into other northwestern markets. It was also talking to an agency in Anchorage, Alaska, had its eyes on agencies to acquire in Spokane and Honolulu, and eventually, planned to expand into Portland. It was going to be a powerhouse in the Pacific Northwest, and I was happy to be part of a growing empire—all I needed was a Versace tie.

Coincidently, the lease on our office space was soon to expire, so we needed to find brand new offices for our new venture that would reflect well on our mother ship in Seattle. One of the senior guys in Seattle, Tom O'Rourke, was to come to Boise to run the operation, where, he was told, "You can live like a king on your salary." I was to go to Seattle to fortify some unscripted senior position. Scott Manning was transferred to Boise to work on McDonald's. He only agreed to come to Boise with the help of a cattle prod and a quick snap of a rubber hose to the back of the head. We ramped up the staff even though we had lost a couple of clients in the merger. We made fancy tenant improvements to our new space. We added a couple of staffers so we would be on par with Seattle. It didn't take long to be rolling in red ink. But we were part of Elgin Syferd International, and we were on a roll.

O'Rourke coming to Boise fell through, so I would remain in Boise. The Seattle office sent some hand-me-down computers, some duplicate media resources and surveys, and helped out where and when it could. I made quarterly trips to Seattle to take part in "management meetings." With help from the Seattle creative team, we won the Idaho Lottery account. We secured another contract with the Idaho Travel Council and picked up a few smaller accounts. We just needed one more big client to make up the losses we were encountering. Maybe Ore Ida Foods?...or the Idaho Potato Commission?...or another co-op of McDonald's? *Just one* was all we needed.

"What the fuck are you doing, Drake? Are you out of your goddamned mind? Why didn't you tell us you were resigning McDonald's? Are you crazy? Do you realize how this makes us look to McDonald's Corporate?"

Syferd's acerbic tirade only lasted a couple of minutes and was the only time Ron or Dave raised their voices to me. In hindsight, it was a mistake not to advise Dave or Ron before about a move that made perfect sense to me. We had a great relationship with the McDonald's co-op, but it was requesting significantly more time from the agency without agreeing to any plan to compensate us for the extra time demands. To me, the decision was obvious. We had a lean, mean staff, and our precious time and talent were needed on accounts that would adequately pay us. Since Boise was now on its own financially and had only an arm's length relationship with DDB Seattle, it was not necessary to demonstrate a unified world to McDonald's. So, I cut the cord and re-deployed our staff on more profitable client work, and within months, we enjoyed an improved bottom line. And McDonald's Corporate may have yelled a bit, but it didn't fire DDB Seattle.

Our improved bottom line continued during the '90s. As the company settled down, Ron and Dave wanted to sell their stock in Elgin Syferd/Drake. While we had the ability to retire their interest, we couldn't seem to agree about how to value the company because we had a negative net worth from the shareholder loans that were in place. We each engaged our lawyers and accountants to help establish a fair value. Ron and I continued back and forth for several years, but we never quite found the right formula. In the meantime, Dave wanted his interest retired, and he and I were able to find a valuation, which had so eluded Ron and me.

With Dave out of the company, I had assumed a majority interest in the company, and that caused Ron's role to change. He took a vital interest in what we were doing and became a solid and trusted advisor to us. He offered advice and used the experience that he was gaining in the leadership of DDB to our advantage. He became a good partner and a good friend.

After almost a full decade had passed since Ron and I discussed his equity, the time finally came to get a deal done with him. We had a much larger enterprise and the wherewithal to commit to a fair deal. After a few months, we agreed to a long-term note.

My wife and I see Ron and Bonnie on their way to or from Sun Valley or when we have extra time when in Seattle. Now it's just a nice, pleasant friendship we share. We share family photos, an occasional dinner, and some great wine.

45.

MY COLOSSAL FAILURE

Still in search of new ways to grow revenue, I told Dave about an idea I had been contemplating for several years—a purely retail advertising agency.

Back in the 1960s, the days of the "Creative Revolution," advertising agencies were even more arrogant than were the high tech start-ups of the dot.com boom era. For those agencies that considered themselves "creative," it was heresy to use something as vulgar as a price point as the big idea. It was acceptable to mention price in the body copy of a print ad, but never as the main selling point.

During the Creative Revolution, Bill Bernbach encouraged people to forget words like "hard sell" and "soft sell," saying those terms would only confuse. He stressed that advertising should always say something of substance—something that will inform and serve the consumer—and to be sure it's being said like it's never been said before. But even with those words of guidance from the master, when clients had a price point advantage, most so-called "creative" agencies of the period were convinced that by featuring price, it cheapened the brand. Many of the rest of the agencies convinced their clients that the louder you yell, the more you sell.

Anyone turning on a TV during non-primetime was exposed to a massive amount of hard sell retail advertising from local companies. Much of it was price-driven, and most of it was bad. I wondered whether we could find a way to subscribe to Bernbach's intent by combining "hard and soft sell" in a way that might create an entrepreneurial opportunity for us.

While sniffing around the periphery of this opportunity, I went to my close friend, Glenn Wright, who was the number two executive at the local CBS affiliate. I figured if anyone knew about retail advertising, it was him. Perhaps not surprisingly, many of the affiliate's most prolific local advertisers were car dealers. Also not surprising was that a lot of that advertising was very much in-your-face, hard-core, price-driven, starburst, huge type, amateurish voice and on-air talent. I couldn't help wondering whether at least one or two wouldn't be interested in investing in a campaign that moved merchandise while creating a positive halo for their company. I asked Glenn whether he could help me get close to some of these guys.

One of the traditions started by Glenn's boss, Ken Hatch (whom I mentioned earlier as one of the first people I interviewed with for a job), was to offer to the station's biggest advertisers all-expense-paid trips to various exotic destinations around the world. Although Elgin Syferd had always qualified for this trip, it was because of the money we placed on behalf of our clients. Because of that, we felt morally obligated to pass on those trips to our clients.

"Ron, we have a station trip coming up soon and there will be a lot of retailers going; why don't you and Bonnie join us?"

"Thanks, Glenn, but we already passed that opportunity on to our McDonald's client. It sounds like it would have been the ideal opportunity."

"I know your agency's posture on the trips, Ron. Your McDonald's client Bob Roth and his wife Barbara have already confirmed. I'm asking on behalf of the station for you and Bonnie to come along as our personal guests. We just had a last minute cancellation and Sandy and I would love the company. Besides, there will be quite a few owners of retail agencies whom you should meet as well."

Bonnie was over-the-top excited because she loved Hong Kong from our Princess trip and this one included Bangkok and Singapore, which neither of us had visited. I agreed with her, but I also looked forward to being able to spend a week learning from the hard-core retailers and their agencies. In addition, the Roths were great people and dear friends. The four of us celebrated the upcoming trip over dinner as three of us talked excitedly about exploring new cultures.

"I want to spend a lot of time visiting as many McDonald's as possible," said Bob.

"That will be interesting," I replied as both Bonnie and Barbara rolled their eyes. I loved Bob, but I was starting to think this trip might not be a good idea.

"There's something else I want to do while we're there," added Bob. "I've been looking at a new limited edition Rolex that sells here for about $20 grand. One of my friends told me that prices for watches and jewelry are cheaper over there than here. He said there were thousands and thousands of jewelry stores that we can check out. What do you think I could get it for at one of them?"

"I have no idea, Bob," I said as I carefully contemplated the pointy end of my steak knife.

Hong Kong was our first stop. Bonnie and I had been there before, and we were eager to show Bob and Barbara the sights, eat some exotic dishes, and go shopping for handmade clothes and shoes. Jet lag be damned; we were in Hong Kong and ready to roll.

Bob hadn't been kidding that night over dinner. We hadn't been in this wonderfully exotic city an hour before he insisted that we search for and eat breakfast at a McDonald's restaurant. Don't get me wrong; I love McDonald's, but breakfast and then lunch on our first day? Bob suggested that before dinner at a different McDonald's, we shop around for his watch. The ladies declined the opportunity and said *sayonara*. I reluctantly set off with Bob.

Fortunately, the special "limited edition" watch wasn't quite as limited as Bob thought. At the first jewelry store we visited, Bob showed a picture of the watch, and within ten minutes, a runner came in with it. Bob asked the price, which started at $17,500 and ended at $15,000. However, rather than taking that deal at any of the stores we visited and ending my misery, Bob asked whether I thought the watches might be even cheaper in Bangkok.

I should have used the steak knife on one of us when I had the chance.

With the exception of having to visit a half-dozen more McDonald's stores, the rest of our Hong Kong stay was fabulous. By the way, in case you didn't know, I can confirm that an Egg McMuffin is an Egg McMuffin and a Big Mac is a Big Mac the world over. Most interesting to me was the fact that the in-store merchandising was pretty much the same as back home but with Asian subtitles.

Our first day in Bangkok was the same shit all over again. McDonald's for breakfast, then clothes shopping for the ladies, and watch shopping for Bob and me. It was agonizing but finally rewarding. We found the watch and Bob negotiated a price of $14,500. I spent forty-five minutes over three beers convincing him he'd never find a better price anywhere in the world. He finally bit the bullet and handed the guy his credit card.

Bob and I returned to the hotel where we met up with the ladies in the lobby bar. Bob couldn't stop talking about and looking at his new toy. After one drink, Barbara decided to do more shopping before dinner. Bonnie wanted to rest her feet, and Bob wanted to sit and admire his watch. I wanted to do anything other than eat at another McDonald's or watch Bob looking at his limited edition Rolex, so I told Barbara I'd join her.

About two blocks from the hotel, we walked by a street vendor selling knock-off watches. Barbara stopped me and said, "Look; isn't that the same watch Bob just bought!"

By God, she was right. I couldn't believe it, but here was an exact replica of the watch I'd helped search for throughout two cities. Knowing a little about the prices of knock-off watches, I offered the guy $25.

"Oh sir, this is a genuine Rolex. You must pay me $5,000."

"Bullshit. It's a knock-off and you know it."

I really didn't want the watch, but it turned out that Barbara had other ideas. She took over the negotiations and got the price down from $5,000 to $50. She paid the vendor and handed me the watch, saying, "Happy Birthday, Ron; may this be a reminder of the hours spent helping my crazy husband!" We laughed and headed back to the hotel.

Bonnie had her feet up with a glass of wine in her hand and Bob was still smiling adoringly at his new watch. I sat down next to him and proceeded to stare the same way at my new watch. After a few minutes of silence, Bob noticed what I was doing and did a dramatic double take between the two watches.

"Where the fuck did you get that?" he demanded.

"Barbara just bought it for me for my birthday."

"She did what?" he shouted. "You did what? You didn't buy this asshole my same watch! YOU DIDN'T SPEND $15,000 ON THIS ASSHOLE! Please tell me this is some kind of a sick joke."

"I thought you loved me," I said to Bob.

"I think I'm going to kill both of you!" was his reply.

I looked over at Barbara; with a wink and a nod, we silently agreed that we should tell him the truth before he had a heart attack.

"It's not real, Bob. It's a cheap knock-off."

"I don't believe you," said Bob. "Let me see it. No, it's real. I can tell. It's exactly like mine. Exactly. Barbara, you have to take it back. He can't have my watch, and you can't spend that much money on him. I don't even like him anymore."

It took a while, but we were finally able to convince him that it was just a very good replica of his precious watch. He finally got over being pissed at me when I promised never to wear the watch around him or our mutual friends.

After all the yelling died down, a guy came over to the table and introduced himself as a fellow American; he said he couldn't help having overheard our conversation. He was fascinated that the two watches could look so much alike, and he asked where he could find the street vendor.

About ten minutes later, he returned, wearing the same "limited edition Rolex."

"I found the guy and asked how much. He had upped the price to $10,000! I said, 'Holy shit! My friend just paid $50 for the same watch.' The vendor smiled, winked, and said, 'Okay, $50.'"

No real point to be made there; I just think it's a funny story. If anything, it goes back to Jacobi's advice that it's more difficult to fire a friend than someone the client either doesn't know or like. Bob remained a strong advocate of the agency until his untimely death years later.

While we were attacking Bob's two objectives, I had also been concentrating on learning about hard-core retail advertising from the people on the trip with us. Having talked with all my fellow travelers, I knew the group was made up fairly equally between clients and agency principals. I was the only agency principal who ran something other than a hard-core retail company. The other agency principals weren't shy about characterizing me to their clients as someone who wasted his clients' money on "feel-good" advertising. Although they made their comments with a smile and a wink, many of them, and a good share of their clients, were loud, obnoxious, flashy assholes. And those were their good points. One example was a car dealer who bragged that he had just bought his wife a ten carat diamond ring. "Show them how big your new diamond is," he instructed his wife. After about the fifth time being nagged, she reluctantly pulled out the ring, put it on her finger, and displayed it for the group. Great diamonds radiate light; this diamond sucked light. The guy was right; it was big, but it was also really, really dull and ugly. Kind of like him.

Several of us had congregated in a very nice jewelry store when one of the guys from our group showed up. He came in flashing a big gold chain around his neck. When I say big, I mean like logging chain big.

"Look at the size of this chain! I got it from a guy on the street. He says the retail is five thousand bucks, but I got it for only five hundred!" He was so proud that he took it off to show Bonnie.

My wife was not trying to be cruel, but she handed the chain to the jeweler and asked the value. "About $50," was the answer.

"No, no!" the guy shouted. "The guy told me it was pure 18 carat gold. Feel how heavy it is."

The jeweler smiled sadly and said, "That's because it's pot-metal with a very, very thin gold plate."

"I'll kill the fucker," the now very upset new owner of the gold-plated pot-metal logging chain shouted as he stormed out the door.

Now this is the part that is nearly impossible to believe, but absolutely true. As he stormed out the door, he ran smack into the seller of the piece of shit chain. Damned near knocked the guy to the ground and probably would have had he not had hold of the guy's throat.

"I'm going to kill you! Give me my money back first, you little bastard!"

"Oh, sir!" the little guy croaked. "I'm so fortunate to have found you. I've been searching everywhere. There's been a terrible mistake. I was swindled by a very bad man. I did not know the chain was not pure gold. I was looking for you so I could give you back your money."

Yeah, right.

Back to my objective of using this trip to learn whether there was an opportunity to win some hard-core retail clients and successfully add some positive brand elements to their advertising. These retailers were obviously making money so they must be doing something right. My question to them (without their agency people around) was: Would you be willing to spend a little more to get the kind of work we were doing for Nordstrom and McDonald's? Even though we created work for them that promoted Half-Yearly Sales and Dollar Menus, we also gave reasons to love the brands. To a person, they said, "Yes."

I came away convinced we should start our own retail-only agency. We were going to be game changers. We'd make a shit-pot of money, and in the process, give our people new avenues of growth. We'd go after car dealers, carpet stores, waterbed warehouses. No retailer, no matter how hard-core, would be overlooked. We wouldn't be afraid to talk price, money back guarantees, or close-out specials, but we'd do it with class and style. The clients would be so happy with their increases in sales combined with the likability of their communications that they'd be happy to pay more.

Dave agreed with the decision. We promised not to dilute the original concept of Elgin Syferd but create a new, separate entity. For the time being, we'd own 100 percent of the stock while we searched for one or more people who would come in as partners. We named the retail agency "AdWorks."

Elgin Syferd was at the time occupying about 20,000 square feet on two-and-a-half floors of the National Building on Post Alley in downtown Seattle. We signed a lease for the other half floor and created a separate entry for the new company. We were all set except for employees and clients.

The concept for AdWorks was no secret—especially to the Elgin Syferd employees. I thought as soon as we were ready to staff it, I'd have a line of eager volunteers outside my door looking for new career opportunities. That didn't happen. It soon became apparent that wasn't going to happen without a little encouragement. So I began offering these great new opportunities to employees whom I thought would be perfect for the jobs.

"No thanks."

"I insist."

"Fuck you; I'll quit."

This was not what I expected.

"Look, Ron," said one senior staffer. "It's not just that I don't want to do shitty work, but I joined this company because of your philosophy of not working with or for assholes. I think a company designed to do shitty work is destined to be full of assholes both inside and out."

"Nonsense," I replied. "We're not going to do shitty work. We're going to create great retail advertising. That's how we're going to succeed."

"We're already doing great retail advertising for McDonald's, Nordstrom, and Holland America Line," he countered. "I know that you're going to go after car dealers and the like. You'll never get them to do anything except shitty advertising. Count me out."

I found that to be the sentiment throughout the agency. We'd committed a lot of money and couldn't convince any of our people to come to the dance. I had no alternative but to recruit from the outside. Although one of the prime motivators for creating AdWorks was to create new opportunities for current employees, I figured we'd have to settle for just making a lot of money.

Once the word got out that we were hiring for an Elgin Syferd company, I got a lot of applicants. However, when word got out that it was to be a retail-only company, the applicants fell into one of two categories: people without sufficient advertising skills or experience, or people who had the skills and experience but were either weak, had questionable ethics, had dubious resumes, or were just plain slimy. Most in the latter category reminded me of the agency people who had been on the Hong Kong trip.

Out of desperation, I cast aside most of the cautions we used for hiring at Elgin Syferd. I tried to hire the most promising of those without the hoped-for skills and experience. From the other camp, I hired some whose good I thought overshadowed their bad. I should have shot myself in the head right then and there.

The absolute worst hires were those from the slime ball group. One guy got caught on three separate lies in the same day. I called him into my office and told him there were white hats and black hats in the advertising business. I said that at our agency, we only had room for the white hats. He was insulted at my characterization, denied being a black hat, and proudly proclaimed that, at worst, he was a dark gray hat. I told him to get the fuck out and not to come back.

Even being the birth-father of the concept, I began to lose faith. I started to believe it was a flawed strategy. The more hard-core retailers we met with, the more we realized the fit just wasn't there.

Our connections in the community helped get some meetings with a few upscale retailers. But as soon as word of those meetings got out, the staff at Elgin Syferd would lobby for the business. Playing Solomon, I placed the clients who appeared to be most willing to do extraordinary work and had budgets to match with Elgin Syferd, leaving AdWorks with some of the most undesirable clients imaginable. AdWorks had started off slow, and then it quickly began to slow from there.

I found the perfect candidate to turn the company around. He had a ton of radio sales experience and a dynamic personality. He could go toe-to-toe with the toughest retailer and emerge with a decent product. Then a mogul gave him a radio station of his own to run. Unbelievably, I still love the guy.

A creative guy, with whom I'd worked before, told me he'd turn the company around for a piece of the action. I remembered his ability to sell work irrespective of its merits and hired him on the spot. Unfortunately, he came back from his first new business meeting with an unexpected result. Instead of the client hiring AdWorks, it hired him as its new marketing director. He, of course, didn't feel we were the right agency for him. Asshole.

After several fits and starts, I brought in Ed Augustavo and Kevin Burrus along with most of their staff to try to turn around the nearly dead agency. Because of their combined talent and strength of character, they had been doing what I aspired to—good retail advertising—but on a small scale. They agreed because they thought together we could ramp it up and help make at least some of our dreams come true.

Together, a few of our dreams did come true, but we hit a wall in regards to winning any of the bigger "good" retail clients in the market. In a desperate attempt to grow the company to a significant size, AdWorks began acquiring clients of any size who said they wanted our best thinking, but that was bullshit; they really wanted someone to execute their ideas. We had clients who would drop a thousand bucks on a dinner, but fight us over a two dollar Xerox charge; clients who initially agreed to pay for their media upfront but would end up three months in arrears; and clients whose taste ran to short, loud ties.

I finally admitted after about nine months of futility that my concept had failed. It was tough to admit it, but thankfully, common sense overshadowed my pride. I resigned the shit accounts and turned their past dues over to the toughest collection agency I could find. The collection agent's card had a photo of a man in a coffin with a bullet hole in his head; the caption read: "Let us handle your dead accounts." We absorbed the few decent accounts from AdWorks, along with Ed, Kevin, and some of their people into Elgin Syferd.

There were multiple lessons to be learned from my colossal failure. The first is that a certain amount of greed is good, but it should never be the sole reason for starting a company. The second is that a certain amount of arrogance is okay, but it should never be so great that you start believing you're better than the experts. The third is that just because the work offends your creative sensibilities, it does not mean the intended consumer feels the same. And it's near impossible to become a success doing something that offends you.

46.

CREATING A TRADITION OF GIVING BACK

Both Dave and I happen to be big Christmas people. Although during our first year we were too busy trying to get our feet off the ground to have a party, we really got into the spirit during our second. We put up a decorated tree in the lobby and scheduled an employee party. It had been a good first eighteen months, so in addition to providing food and booze, we decided to surprise our employees by playing Santa to them. We hadn't reached the point of being able to issue meaningful cash bonuses, but we felt we could hand out something more than a Christmas goose. Santa Dave and I spent an afternoon buying a variety of items—a portable TV, a boom box stereo, a case of wine, one night's stay at a local hotel, dinner and wine at a nice restaurant. About a dozen gifts in total.

"He got a TV and I got a fucking blender," complained one. "That's nothing," bitched another. "I got a cheap ass stereo and Keri got a case of good wine. And she doesn't even drink!" No good deed went unpunished that year.

The next year, we gave cash. Screw them. But to make the party more fun, we tried the Secret Santa thing where each person would draw the name of another employee and buy that person a gift for under $25. That year, the party was safe but kind of boring: CDs, candy, gift cards. The good news was no one blamed the shitty gifts on Dave and me.

The following year, a few of our bawdier people decided to make the event less boring by spicing it up with non-PC gifts such as a box of condoms re-labeled "Extra Small" and edible panties. I re-gifted, from my wonderfully weird brother-in-law, a 12" long, five-pound, brass bottle opener in the shape of a penis. I probably wouldn't have been that ballsy, but I had drawn the name of a woman with a great sense of humor. Nancy howled and passed it around to all the ladies. None of the guys would even touch it. "The Tool," as it became named, made its rounds for a couple of years until one woman (to remain un-named) didn't re-gift it. Hmmmm.

Anyway, after a few years, people became bored with trying to embarrass one another so we stopped it. We continued the holiday party but without gifts. *We learned to be brave enough to stop "traditions" before they became onerous.*

Speaking of traditions, we did create one that was never onerous and, in fact, became synonymous with the fun, creative nature of the advertising industry in general and our company specifically.

We met with a representative from United Way who asked whether we would consider supplementing our employee and company contributions by staging a fundraiser. He told us that many companies of our size held successful bake sales, secured pledges for walk/runs, even sold used books. Bake sales? We thought, "No fucking way. That may be okay for an accounting firm, but we're a creative agency. We will find a better way."

Several of our more creative people began exploring ideas not only to raise money but to establish what could become a signature event for the agency. Among the more interesting ideas was a ladies-strip-for-money show (suggested by some guys), a men-strip-for-money show (countered by some women), tightrope walking across a busy freeway by all those supporting the previous two ideas, and even a golf tournament. The consensus was that only the golf idea had merit, but with the caveat that a full-fledged tournament could prove not only to be a pain in the ass to create and manage, but it had the potential to lose more than it made. Before we could completely shut down the primary advocate of the idea, he modified it to a putt-putt challenge at a local miniature golf course. We thought the modification had merit so we sent him off to find out whether it was affordable.

"I think it's a fun idea, Pete," I said the following week, "but based on what you're showing us, there's no way it could generate enough income to offset the costs. We need to find another way to make a significant agency statement. We have to have something that not only raises some good money but will generate some positive noise about us."

A couple of days later, the never-say-die Pete came to my office with the idea of staging a nine-hole golf tournament in the hallways of our office. Before I could object, he went on to argue that we could build our own course using stuff like 2 x 4s, pieces of Astroturf, plastic tubs of sand and water, and lots and lots of beer and wine. "The cornier we make it, the better the drunks will enjoy it. Nothing creates positive buzz like happy drunks!"

"Brilliant!" I exclaimed. "Let's do it!"

For several months leading up to the event, we sawed wood, pounded nails, and painted. We built mazes, ramps leading to the traps and hazards, and festooned them with trinkets and trash.

Meanwhile, the creative team named the event the Charity Golf Classic and developed a logo, a poster, and invitations. Another group became the revenue team and started working on ways to make money. At first blush, the revenue team felt by charging to play the course and up-charging the beer and wine, we could probably generate $2,000 for the charity and have a good time doing it. The birthing process of a big idea was on its way.

Our excited employees began talking up the event with their friends and contacts. One of our media folk was doing just that with a TV rep; while asking the guy to put together a foursome to play the event, he asked whether his station could sponsor a hole. Bingo! The revenue team determined a price-for-hole sponsorship and we invited other media companies to participate. After recalculating the potential revenue, we decided to offer free booze, figuring the more happy drunks the better. The creatives were more than happy to redo the invitations.

The first annual Charity Golf Classic exceeded our expectations. Everyone had a great time—sponsors, participants, employees, and we netted nearly $5,000 for United Way. We felt certain we had a signature event that would do good things for the charity and for the agency.

Literally days after cleaning up the mess and storing the stuff, a team of volunteers started working on the next year's event. One of their first agenda items was to get more sponsors and a deeper commitment from them. For example, we asked our rep from Channel 7 whether the station would consider paying a premium for hole number 7 as well as taking ownership for decorating "their hole." After getting the station to agree in concept, we went to the other stations and told them Channel 7 was paying for naming rights, so, of course, the other four stations signed up as well. The good news was that we had five holes covered; the bad news was that with Channels 11 and 13 committed, we could no longer be a nine-hole tournament.

We didn't have to worry long, however. The word spread and soon we had an outdoor company, a production house, and even our signature clients McDonald's and Holland America Line sign on as sponsors.

Every sponsor wanted its hole to be the most talked about, whether for skill required, uniqueness, or the highest fun factor. Because the sponsors were no more talented at designing and building these things than we were, several hired professionals who actually knew what they were doing. The course became both visibly appealing and player challenging. One hole forced the player to look into a TV monitor to line up the shot to the hole, which was around the corner. An Elvis impersonator entertained at another. Jansport had a fake mountain replete with mannequin climbers. McDonald's had a Golden Arch created out of a thousand yellow balloons at a hole where the players had to putt down an open, curved staircase.

"We don't think it's fair that the employees do all the hard work and you and Dave get to select the charity," said the self-appointed spokesperson for the newly created committee to determine future recipients. How could we argue against that?

Each year, an employee committee screened applicants, interviewed finalists, and selected the recipient agency. The winning agencies ranged from Ronald McDonald House Charities to a single lady who had been using public transportation to deliver diapers to needy families. She was trying to raise money to buy a used van. We gave her $25,000 to buy a new one. One year, the chosen agency was a day-care school for little kids from homeless families. The director asked whether the kids could come to the agency to see the decorated course before play began. Thirty little wide-eyed kids, ranging in age from about four to eight, shyly entered the agency holding each other's hands. They were very quiet until we handed out the Happy Meals donated by McDonald's. By the time they finished eating, they were acting the way little kids are supposed to act. We broke out the clubs and balls and showed them how to hit. They had a blast. It was heartwarming for our staff to witness the transformation from nervousness to giddiness. The following week, we received thirty letters thanking us for the best day of their lives.

The Charity Golf Classic became *the* fun charity event of the year for a wide variety of people. Players included the mayor and council members, prominent business leaders, celebrities, and sports stars. We even had a couple of TV stations do live remotes during their evening news shows. Everyone who attended had fun—even those who didn't golf. Our employees were rewarded for their hard work with an immense sense of pride. And best of all, over the twenty-year life of the event, we were able to donate more than a half million dollars to some very needy children's charities.

Okay, maybe tied for best of all was the fun our own people had during the event. Along with our employees determining the recipient non-profit, they also got to choose the year's theme and apparel. With a modicum of adult supervision, that is. For the first few events, that meant everyone had a T-shirt emblazoned with the year's tag line. That quickly evolved to elaborate costumes appropriate to the year's theme, like Star Wars, the Roaring 20s, and the Old West.

We never encouraged people to drink while attending or working the event. However, we never discouraged it either. There were drink stations scattered throughout the course, and we had runners with trays of free booze with "tips for (the charity) encouraged." Hustling drinks for tips is hard work and the hours were long, so it was no surprise that many of the runners became as numb as some of the players during the course of the evening.

Eventually, the event became so sophisticated that we had digital scoreboards, multiple starts, and people with headsets and microphones to keep the flow of several hundred players on schedule. The year of the Old West theme, three of our better looking females decided to dress as risqué saloon girls. One of the ladies was very new to the agency and may have been having second thoughts about displaying very little costume and lots of skin. It probably didn't help that on a scale of 1 to 10, she was a strong 12, and the guy players were falling over themselves around her. So it was no wonder that she soon sailed past her point of numbness.

One of my all-time favorite employees, Scott Manning, was controlling the flow of the event using a headset whose microphone loudly broadcast his instructions throughout three floors of the agency. At one point fairly late in the afternoon, in a very calm, droll voice, Scott announced, "Emergency alert. Emergency alert. We have a showgirl down on 9. I repeat… we have a showgirl down on 9."

A few minutes later, my wife happened to visit the women's room where she found two of the showgirls holding up the somewhat soiled third. "Bonnie, have you met our new employee, Shannon?"

"Actually, yes," replied Bonnie, "just the other night. Our daughter and son-in-law were in town staying with us. While we were out, they invited some friends over for drinks. When we were being introduced, Shannon crawled out from under the dining room table. No, no, she wasn't like this then; she was under there playing with our granddaughter!"

Shannon will never forget her first two encounters with the boss's wife. By the way, Shannon has gone on to fame and fortune as a key executive officer of a major agency back east. She's definitely making a lot more money, but probably not having as much fun.

Dave and I had set an initial company goal of giving back to the community in as many ways as possible. The Charity Golf Classic was perhaps the most visible but far from the only charity our agency supported.

We encouraged all our employees to get out and get involved. It didn't matter whether it was door-belling for a favorite candidate or serving in the chow line at the Bread of Life Mission. Knowing that not everyone believes the agency business is a higher calling, we instructed employees to pick a cause close to their hearts and become activists. We admonished that as long as their time away from the agency didn't adversely affect another employee or client, they should contribute to the betterment of their community.

The talent and services available from agencies are always in high demand from charitable institutions. Generally, agencies are amenable to pro bono requests because they see them as self-serving opportunities to win creative awards. We were not immune to this reality. However, we had firm ground rules. Our first priority was to those organizations supported by our employees. When a request came over the transom, we would canvas the agency for a champion. If none appeared, we'd pass on the opportunity. Another guideline was from the David Ogilvy story about never agreeing to work for someone who insisted on multiple approvers. With every charity endeavor, we patiently explained about the hazards of leaving direction and approval in the hands of non-marketing professionals—or worse yet, groups of non-professionals. We absolutely refused to start out building a horse only to end-up having a committee turn it into a camel. That policy enabled work that won big at Cannes and in the hearts and minds of the charity's patrons. It's oh so different when there's no money on the line.

Although our primary motivation was to encourage all employees to make our community a better place, we also wanted our senior people to try to do that at the highest levels.

One of my most favorite employees stopped by my office to talk about the subject. "I'd love to sit on big, important boards the way you do Ron," said Tim, "but I'm only thirty-two and would be too intimidated to be an effective contributor."

"First, every legitimate charity is important, Tim. If it weren't, it wouldn't exist. Don't judge importance by the size of the organization or who sits on its board. Instead, look at what it's trying to accomplish. If you are or can be passionate about its mission, become a part of it. Irrespective of the size of the organization or the importance of those who contribute or control the boards, I can tell you from experience they can all use the help of experienced marketing professionals. A person may have a high net worth or a lofty position in a Fortune 500 company, but neither necessarily means the person knows shit about marketing. Tim, you may be relatively young, but that doesn't mean you can't make valuable contributions. Trust me; you may feel intimidated at first, but once you start hearing stupid marketing ideas from important bankers, lawyers, accountants, and prominent dowagers, you'll not be able to stop yourself from contributing. And their organizations will be better for it."

Throughout our long history, we were known as *the* most civic minded agency in the market. Someone once asked whether we were civic minded *strictly* as a new business ploy. I replied that we did it because it was the right thing to do, but if God saw fit to reward us by whispering in certain people's ears, we'd never object.

Doing the right thing for a cultural organization may not seem relevant when pitching a CPG account, but in a tie-breaking situation, it sure doesn't hurt to have already earned the respect of someone at the prospective client.

47.

A NEW DIRECTION

Public Relations is a strategic communications process that builds mutually beneficial relationships between organizations and their publics through a variety of specialties such as investor relations, government relations, special events, and crisis communications. I didn't make up those words; Dave taught them to me. As we grew in size, he also taught me a number of new PR specialties.

One of the surest ways to win a piece of new business is to have people on the team who have a strong passion for the category, brand, or cause. A couple of our PR practitioners had strong personal passions for all things environmental. Because of their passion, the agency started an environmental practice within our PR Group that changed our lives and fortunes.

As soon as the new environmental specialty was announced at the agency, a flood of employees from every discipline was volunteering to become involved. The environmental group grew quickly from a PR specialty to an agency-wide passion.

The group won a few City of Seattle and King County contracts for issues like water conservation and recycling. The work was rewarding and made our socially conscious employees feel good and the commercials and ads won a lot of praise at award shows and in new business presentations. The budgets were small, so we didn't make a lot of money, but we did earn national recognition for our high caliber work in this quickly emerging category.

We were a couple of years into the new category when we received a Request for Proposal (RFP) from the Energy Star Division of the Department of Energy. Our initial assumption was that we were being asked to bid on a local or regional aspect of the contract. After wading through hundreds of pages of small print, we realized the Department of Energy was actually asking our relatively small regional agency to pitch for the entire national campaign. That's when we skipped ahead to the budget page.

"Oh, my God; it says here that it is $50,000,000, spread equally over five years!"

"Okay," I said, "but how much of the $10,000,000 a year is income to us?"

"That's it," was the reply. "That's our fee. All production and out-of-pocket expenses are over and above the fee."

"What's the catch?"

"Well, the only catch we can see is that we have to have an office in Washington D.C. As far as we can tell, the office can be minimally staffed. The department wants its regular contact people to be local. It would mean heavy additional staffing here in Seattle, though."

"Unless either of you want to volunteer to move to D.C., that part of the staffing plan is going to be a problem," I suggested.

They agreed; none of the employees wanted to uproot their families so we put that part of the RFP on hold while we tackled the rest. We felt encouraged about our chances of actually winning the business until we reminded ourselves of the D.C. staffing requirement. Someone suggested that we talk with Candy Cox, one of our favorite freelancers who had a lot of green experience.

We met with Candy the next day and presented the situation. We told her we'd bring her on as a full-time employee, pay for her moving expenses, and subsidize her rent until she could find permanent housing. She said she'd talk it over with her partner, Debra, and get back to us in a couple of days. I told her to think about it overnight and call me in the morning. We needed to roll on this.

Candy called in the morning and said, "We're in!"

An RFP process with any government entity is painful. This one was extremely painfully complicated. But it was worth it. After several months and two presentations, we were awarded the business—$50 million in very profitable fees spread equally over the five years. Candy and Debra moved to D.C. and the agency began its move into even more interesting areas of expertise.

48.

A HEARTBREAKING EXPERIENCE

"Ron, come down to my office," said Sydney Hunsdale into the phone. "Right away, please; we have a big problem." Sydney was the Management Supervisor on the McDonald's business.

"What's up?" I asked, entering her office moments later.

"I just got a voicemail from the head of marketing at McDonald's Corporate saying one of our owners has complained about the work we're doing for Tesoro," she said.

Tesoro was an oil and gas refinery. We'd won an assignment from it a few months earlier. Tesoro was considering going into the retail gas business in a big way. It had purchased a few local stations which it was dramatically updating. Our assignment was to create an image for the retail gas station brand. The carrot was that if the new brand caught traction in Washington State and met certain mileposts, it would expand to other states and take us along.

"I don't get it," I said. "What's the problem?"

"Apparently some of the gas stations have convenience stores that sell hot dogs," she said. "One of our owners claimed that by promoting Tesoro, we're taking sales away from McDonald's."

"Whoa," I barked, "that is complete bullshit. First of all, we haven't even produced a single ad, let alone placed any. And besides, the assignment is to get people to buy gas, not sell food! I didn't even know Tesoro sold food. It's probably a vendor leasing space from them. Which of our owners complained? I need to talk with him. Come to think of it, the fact that an owner complained to Oakbrook rather than talking with us is more troubling than the fact that we may have a conflict. Call Brad back and find out who the fuck called him."

The next day, Sydney reported that the call from an owner was in the form of a voicemail to Brad. The caller never left his name, but the message had been saved and Brad was going to forward it to us that afternoon.

"Ron," Sydney said, "I have the message, but I don't recognize the voice."

I doubled-timed it down to her office. No more than three words into the recording, I yelled, "Son-of-a-bitch, that's not one of our owners. I recognize that voice; that's Dick." I was stunned. Dick was a buddy. He was a close, longtime friend. In fact, I had come very close to buying his agency on two separate occasions. Neither of those times worked out and he eventually sold to one of our primary competitors. We were still close friends, or so I thought.

Sydney hit the play button once again. Immediately after explaining that he was an owner of a McDonald's restaurant in Washington State, the voice on the tape complained that "Your damn agency, DDB Elgin, is taking food out of my family's mouths by promoting this competitor," and he demanded that the corporation "fire these disloyal assholes." I sat in sullen silence for several minutes. I was positive that it was my friend on the tape, but I couldn't accept it. I mean, we're in a very competitive business and most of us are competitive to the extreme, but I was having a tough time imagining this behavior from someone I didn't know, let alone a friend.

I jumped up, ran down the hall, and grabbed Kass. "Come with me; I have something I want you to hear." Kass had worked for Dick prior to joining us.

Literally, three or four words into the tape, Kass said, "Hey, that's Dick. What's this about?"

I had Mark Clarke, our head IT guy, transfer the voicemail to a handheld recorder. I went upstairs to my office and asked Michelle Stevens, my executive assistant, to call Dick and set up a lunch. I didn't tell her the details for two reasons: She was fiercely loyal, and she was also an attorney. I was afraid my feisty assistant might do something that could cause her to lose her license.

As soon as I got home, I played the tape for my wife. She knew Dick very well. Hell, we'd even spent a weekend or two at his country home. She confirmed that the voice was indeed Dick's, and she was devastated that he would betray our friendship in this way.

"Is something going on?" inquired Michelle the next day. "Dick wanted to know why you wanted to have lunch. He said you guys just had dinner a few weeks ago. He seemed kind of weird."

"No, tell him I just wanted to have lunch," I lied.

A few days later, I arrived early at Duke's restaurant. Standing at the bar with an ice tea, I said hello to a few friends from Holland America Line who were having lunch in one of the booths. One of the guys, Peter, looked like he could play middle linebacker for the Seattle Seahawks.

Dick came sashaying into the bar with a very casual, "Hey, what's happening, dude?"

Instead of shaking his hand, I raised the recorder to his ear and said, "I need you to explain something to me." I played the thirty-second message. His expression didn't change a bit as he said, "Can you play that again?"

I was so astounded by his calmness and request that I rewound the tape and played it again. This time when it ended, I looked him in the eye and asked, "Why are you trying to fuck me, Dick?'

"What do you mean?" he asked. "You think that's me on the tape?"

"I know that's you on the tape, Dick," I said, raising my voice. "Now tell me: Why are you trying to fuck me?"

"Do you have a voiceprint proving that's me?" he asked lamely.

"I don't need a fucking voiceprint," I said. "We both know that's you. Now answer my question: Why are you trying to fuck me?"

I guess I was louder than I intended because suddenly Peter was at my side, asking whether everything was okay. With that, Dick spun on his heels and left the restaurant. I stayed for a few minutes to fill in the blanks for my friends from Holland America Line.

When I returned to the agency, I told Michelle the real purpose of the lunch meeting. She was furious. I told her I was done with the fucker. I didn't expect to hear from him, but if he did call, I was permanently unavailable.

He did try to reach me several times. Each time, Michelle calmly and politely informed him that I wasn't interested in talking with him.

I called Brad at McDonald's and explained that the call had not been from an owner but from one of my competitors. Brad had come from the agency business and was appalled that someone would stoop to that level. "I have a great idea," he said. "Why don't you turn that tape into a radio spot and run it in your market? Hell, I'll even pay for the airtime!"

Whether or not he was serious, I loved the idea, but I let my head rule and called the DDB corporate attorney in New York. He loved the idea too, but he cautioned that even though I believed I had irrefutable "proof," anything can end up in litigation . Not wanting to put our company at possible risk, I chose simply to tell the story to anyone and everyone.

A man far wiser than me once said something to the effect that a person must regard his good name as the richest jewel he can ever possess. Reputation is like fire; once kindled it may be easily preserved, but once extinguished, it is an arduous if not impossible task to rekindle it again. The way to gain and maintain a good reputation is always to endeavor to be what you desire to appear. I've always tried to adhere to those thoughts.

49.

A MOST MEMORABLE WIN

My all-time favorite McDonald's owner/operator is a guy by the name of Mike Pegram. He was one of the largest multiple store owners in our co-op and far and away the smartest McDonald's guy I ever knew. Actually, that's not quite accurate. He is one of the smartest guys, period. And while that is always an admirable asset, the reason Bonnie and I love him is that he is also one of the nicest, most kindhearted, and funniest guys around.

Ted Baseler, a former colleague, then a great client as CEO of Ste. Michelle Wine Estates, and one of my closest friends for thirty-plus years, once told me there are three types of people in the world; he calls it the "Basel Metabolic Energy Principle." He says that most people fall into a category he calls Energy Neutrals. These people can be heavily influenced, however, by the next two categories. The absolutely worst people on earth are Energy Negatives. These assholes steal energy; they suck the life out of the Neutrals and can hamper the progress of the next category, Energy Positives. *Although the smallest in number, Energy Positives inject energy into every-*

thing they tackle or encounter. Unfortunately for our world, there are far fewer of these folks. When you find one, latch on. If you can surround yourself with Energy Positive people, it's impossible to fail.

Ted epitomizes an Energy Positive Person. So does Mike.

Mike was born and raised in Princeton, Indiana—just up the road from Louisville, Kentucky. While still a young man, Mike's dad became the owner of the McDonald's franchise in Placerville, California near the Nevada border. Mike went to work for his dad and learned to love the business at an early age. He became a registered applicant and bought his first store while still in his early twenties. The restaurant was in Marysville, Washington.

Mike loved his dad and learned a lot from him. He didn't always follow Jim's advice, but he remembered it. He told me once that one of Jim's favorite sayings was that a person should never spit into the wind, give away a downhill putt, or own something that eats while you sleep. While repeating the story, he would smile and point out that Jim owned a bunch of always hungry Quarter horses.

Mike and I became very close, way beyond a client/agency relationship, and enjoyed many terrific road trips together. He also had great respect and love for Bonnie and our daughter, Alison.

I mention that last fact because one day I got a call from Mike. In his best Indiana/Kentucky accent, he said, "Tell Bonnie to go buy herself a hat." I thought what a cruel thing to say about someone you care for. He'd probably seen her on a bad hair day, but still.

"What do you mean, Mike?" I asked.

"Well, she told me she has always wanted to go to the Kentucky Derby and that's where we're going."

"Really, why?"

"Got me a pony running in the derby. Since you two have never been to a real race, I want you to come down with me a few days early so you see what it's all about. We'll spend some time on the backside, get to know the trainers, jockeys, and meet my horse, Real Quiet."

We did and it was an incredible experience. Everyone loves Mike, and as his friends, we immediately became part of his huge extended family. We met one of his best friends, Hall of Fame trainer Bob Baffert, and several world-class jockeys like Gary Stevens. One morning before breakfast, I went with Mike to the local McDonald's where he bought a couple of hundred dollars of food for the stable guys. He wasn't buying affection; that's just his nature.

We had a terrific time, met many interesting people, learned a bit about thoroughbred racing, and Bonnie even got to feed Real Quiet. If the Kentucky Derby is not on your bucket list, it should be. And if you ever get a chance to meet Mike, jump on it.

Churchill Downs is wonderful in tradition, and on Derby Day, exciting beyond belief. We even tried mint juleps, ugh, and quickly switched to Mike's favorite, Coors Light. (He switched from Bud Light because the cans are skinnier so you can get two more in a cooler.) I learned how easy it is to bet and lose, but I still had a great time.

When it came time for the big race, Mike invited us to go with him to the stables and walk with Real Quiet all the way to the paddock where they saddle the horses. Mike suggested we go back up to our box seats on the finish line for the race while he went down to the rail to be by himself.

When Baffert told Mike a couple of years earlier that he'd bought for him a thoroughbred for $17,000 and showed him a picture of the horse, Mike asked whether the poor thing had cancer or something. In fact, the horse's nickname became "The Fish" because he was big from the side view, but he kind of disappeared when you saw him head-on.

Indian Charlie was the odds-on favorite for the big race, and although Real Quiet wasn't being ignored, most figured he'd finish out of the money.

They call horse racing the most exciting two minutes in sports and they aren't kidding. We were up screaming our heads off from "And they're off!" And then it got really exciting. Real Quiet stayed with the pack, closed on the leaders, passed the lead horse, and WON! Real Quiet won the fucking Kentucky Derby!

We fought the crowd down to the track and into the winners' circle. OUR horse! WE did it! The first real race of our lives and OUR horse won! The rest of the evening was surreal, starting with a formal ceremony at the Churchill Downs Museum and ending at the pizza joint where we'd been the night before. Mike had promised the crew there that if Real Quiet won, we'd come back for a celebratory pizza and he'd autograph some boxes for them. He's just that kind of a guy.

Back at the hotel, we all hugged and said we'd see him back in Seattle. He countered with, "Yeah, and then in two weeks in Baltimore."

"Baltimore?" I asked. "Do we have a McDonald's meeting in Baltimore?"

"No, you dumb shit. That's where the Preakness is run. We're all going to the Preakness in two weeks."

"Thanks for the invite, Mike," I said, "but I have an agency to run. I'd love to do this again, but I just don't have time."

"No, you don't understand Ron. You were here for this win and you're going to be there for the next one." Did you know that horsemen are superstitious? I didn't, but I learned fast.

So two weeks later, we were at the Preakness. The Pimlico racetrack was not quite as grand as Churchill Downs, but the excitement was equally electric. We partied with Mike's family and friends for several days leading up to the race. Real Quiet was no longer overlooked and for good reason. He won again, and we found ourselves in a winner's circle for the second time in our lives. Real Quiet had achieved a feat accomplished by only fifteen other horses in the one-hundred-year history of the Triple Crown.

Our next stop was three weeks later at the Belmont in New York, the final leg of the Triple Crown, which had not been won since Affirmed in 1978. Many have said the Triple

Crown will never again be won. But every year, it's the ultimate goal of most three-year-old contenders, and not just because of the half million dollar first place prize. And not even because of Visa Card's standing offer of $5 million to the winner. It's way more than money.

In a short five weeks, Mike and Real Quiet had become rock stars. They were more than just the betting favorites. Part of it was because Real Quiet hadn't started off as a multi-million dollar horse—he was a working man's horse. A $17,000 working man's horse. But the bigger reason was Mike. Jeans, shirt, cowboy boots, and a sports jacket (when required). Always ready with a smile and a good word, he could win any election anywhere. I saw as many buttons saying "I Like Mike" as I did for Real Quiet. In fact, if Real Quiet could read, I'd bet he'd want one of the "I Like Mike" buttons, too.

It was a hard fought race. Real Quiet took command in the stretch, opening a sizable gap. We were all going crazy. It looked like horse racing was about to have its twelfth Triple Crown Winner and then Victory Gallop started to close the gap. We were going absolutely wild. In fact, there was something like 100,000 fans going crazy. By the time they hit the wire, it was too close to call. The photo finish showed Real Quiet's body in the lead, but Victory Gallop's nose was inches ahead. It was all about whose head was up and whose had bobbed down. Officially, the smallest margin of defeat in the history of the Triple Crown.

We all smiled through our tears and partied like we had won. After all, not many horses had come this far and probably none with the style and grace of Real Quiet and his owner. Toward the evening's end, a reporter came over to where Mike and I were seated and said, "I bet you sure wish you had won that $5 million bonus." Mike immediately jumped up and said, "Why, are we out of beer?"

We have been fortunate enough to be Mike's guests in many winner's circles around the country. His generosity and kindness never cease to amaze me.

With regard to Mike on the business front as a client, he was extremely tough but considerate, which was great for the agency because he treated us as a true marketing partner—not simply a vendor. McDonald's corporate philosophy is to engage its agencies as partners, but there are no specific guidelines. Because of that, over the years we had some great working relationships with the co-op leadership, a few really good ones, and only one shitty one. But none were better than the times when Mike was at the helm.

50.

MORE ON DELEGATION

I have always had strong feelings about what is now known as "work/life balance." I've never disagreed that a person's family should always come first in his heart and mind. What makes me crazy, though, is to see an employee jump up and leave a meeting or assignment just because the clock strikes five o'clock. I get even crazier when sensing during an interview that the candidate is more interested in work hours and vacation time than learning about our culture.

I've debated the issue of work/life balance countless times and have concluded there is no right answer for everyone. The closest I can come is to define home and office not in the literal sense but as a mindset. If a person is physically in the office twelve hours a day, but his mind isn't, his body shouldn't be there either. On the other hand, I've never held back a paycheck from anyone who contributed an honest day's work, irrespective of where he was sitting.

A good example was one of those always-at-work people both physically and mentally. She was the first to arrive and last to leave. Her work was almost always exemplary. She was mostly cheerful. Well, cheerful when you could get her attention away from client calls or the computer screen. She was enormously ambitious and eager to take on additional work. I loved her.

After days, weeks, and months of that kind of schedule, she hit her tipping point. Practically in tears, she told me she was sure her husband was starting to hate her and that their dog sometimes didn't recognize her. Although concerned about her account's profitability, she thought it might be time to hire an assistant account executive to help ease her workload. She had obviously pushed the balance thing too far. Within a couple of weeks, she hired a bright young assistant account executive.

As time went by, I forgot about her work/life balance crisis. However, leaving the office late one evening, I noticed a light still on in her office. When I asked why she was still there, she answered that her client had moved up a deadline and needed the completed project first thing in the morning.

"Why are you here instead of your new person?" I asked.

"It's just quicker to finish this project myself rather than explaining it to her and then having her struggle through it," she explained.

I wanted to criticize her response, but I controlled myself and said, "Please see me in the morning."

She was outside my office when I arrived the next day. She knew I was mad from the night before. "We hired an assistant to lighten your load. Do you not understand the definition of delegation? By not allowing her the opportunity to handle those little things that you were doing last night, you're showing yourself to be a weak manager and robbing your employee of practical experience. You're retarding your growth and stifling hers."

"You don't understand," she pleaded. "I've tried to explain to her exactly how I want it done, but she already screwed it up twice. It takes me longer to redo her shit than to do it myself."

"Then you're either a shitty teacher or you made a shitty hire. You have two weeks to figure out which is the case."

In a panic, she went to her supervisor for guidance.

"Ron's pissed at me because he thinks I'm a shitty delegator," she told him. "I need your help. He gave me two weeks to figure out if our new assistant AE can cut it or if we have to cut her. So I gave her an assignment with some damn good direction. I told her not to bother me unless she had a problem. She never got back to me so I assumed everything was okay."

"Well, wasn't it?" her boss asked.

"I guess so," she said. "I mean there are no factual errors, but it isn't written or even formatted the way I always do it, and the client is used to seeing stuff my way."

"Donna, you hardly ever do anything the way I do, but I've never complained, have I? And the client was used to the way I did things. But the client continues to be happy because irrespective of the difference in style, the content has always been correct. Ron's right; you need to work on your delegation skills."

I'd love to say that she took the advice to heart, learned to become an outstanding delegator, and is now the CEO of a major multinational corporation. Unfortunately, none of that is true. She did improve to a small degree, but when under pressure, she reverts back to her old ways. She'll always be an extremely valuable worker but never a significant leader.

My concern about improper and/or inadequate delegation has haunted me throughout my career. I'm always looking for improvement whether through observation, discussion, or reading. I even fell for one of those courses where you're promised success by participating in a conference call. My plan was to get the majority of our senior people—especially those whom I felt could use help in this area—lined up for the call. I think the cliché about herding cats is the perfect metaphor for getting independent thinking people together. In other words, I failed.

My assistant found the perfect solution to my inability to get twenty people together for a two-hour session at a time dictated by someone on the East Coast; for a couple of hundred dollars extra, we could get a CD of the seminar and conduct it at a time convenient for ourselves rather than a moderator.

When I was in Officer Candidate School, I learned that if you were five minutes early for a meeting, you were on time. If you are on time, you're late. If you are late, you're in deep shit. I mellowed over the years and attributed the lack of attendance or punctuality at meetings to either the creative nature of our free-spirited people or an unavoidable client crisis. One of our managing partners, Tim Pavish, said it was simply rudeness. Tim was all about fairness and efficiency. It made him mad that some people were always on time while others operated on their own time with a wanton disregard for others. His solution was to lock the door at the exact time set for the meeting and to prohibit those in attendance to discuss the content with those who didn't attend. He had great attendance at his meetings. When I used the Tim Rule, attendance at my meetings got a little better but never as good as his. Perhaps it also had something to do with the fact that he was 6' 4" and remarkably fit.

I had a bad feeling from the moment I started the CD. About five minutes into my fairly well-attended meeting, I realized I had really fucked up. The seminar leader had an incredibly boring voice and demeanor. Perhaps in person, she could have carried it off. Maybe she was gorgeous, or at least interesting looking. I kept hoping the content would overcome her delivery, but it didn't.

Her examples were both way too basic for our people and not at all relevant to us. From looking at the faces around the room, I could tell this was a waste of time. I shut off the computer about a quarter of the way through the presentation.

"Okay, what did you learn today?" I asked.

The answers I got ranged from "Not a fucking thing" to "That you wasted our money."

"No, you're wrong," I said. "Purely by luck, I just demonstrated a very valuable lesson in the art and science of delegation. By ordering that tape, I delegated the job of helping you become better managers to someone I didn't know and didn't take the time to understand. I fucked up. It wasn't delegation. It was abrogation. I abrogated my duty.

"Delegation is kind of like the game of baseball. On the surface, baseball is simply a game of throwing, hitting, catching, and running the bases. That's why it can be played and enjoyed by seven year olds. But on a deeper level, the game involves complex strategies and tactics. With regard to delegation, too many managers apply the surface approach, which is exactly what I just did. I handed off an important assignment without a true understanding of the overall strategy and the individual talents of the players.

"If we were like many of our competitors, we'd have clients who couldn't afford good work, didn't appreciate good work, or worse, were too fucking stupid to want good work. If that were the case, I wouldn't need people like you or care if you hired people incapable of doing great work. That isn't the case here. We have great clients who, for the most part, understand, want, and deserve great work. Dave and I have always hired the very best people possible. When we have great players at your level, there is little to no risk in delegating. When you hire people, your first job is personally to demonstrate the level of professionalism expected of them. You must set the standard. Your second job is to show them how to achieve that level by giving them assignments with the admonition that once accepted, it's up to them to sink or swim. You need to help them understand our philosophy of giving them the freedom to fail. Explain that we're not encouraging failure.

So, if they get to the point where they think that's a possibility, they must ask for help. If they don't ask for help and fail or they constantly ask for help in order not to fail, it's your obligation as a manager who understands the art of delegation to admit you've made a bad hire and fire their sorry asses. That's one of the most important aspects of delegation."

51.

A FRIEND'S STORY

I ran into a really good friend, Kevin Burrus, the other day. We had a great time reminiscing about his years with AdWorks and Elgin Syferd.

"Do you remember when you would send notes on your personalized notepad with your simple but recognizable R at the bottom of each?" asked Kevin.

"Yeah, it was the only part of my signature that anyone could read," I said.

"Anyway, while your message could just as easily be good news as bad, a person generally did not want to see a note with an R on it in his company mailbox, if you know what I mean. So one day, after Ed and I had left and restarted Augustavo Burrus, we received a bunch of pictures of beautiful naked models faxed to us from our friend Dan who was still an account manager at Elgin Syferd. After perusing the photos for a few short (okay, long) minutes, we decided to have some fun with Dan. We contacted a friend who was still at the agency and asked him to get us a piece of your personalized notepad paper. We then typed a simple note that read, "Dan, we need to discuss the sordid photos you've been sending out on company machines," and signed it with your big R. We then had our friend slip the note into Dan's mailbox. That night, knowing Dan had picked up the note, we had a good laugh along with a few beers and then decided it was a bit too cruel even for us and that we needed to call the next morning and let him off the hook. To our horror, however, early the next day we got a call from our "prank helper" that Dan had a pre-scheduled meeting with you and was waiting outside your office. We instructed our mutual friend to get word to Dan before he made a fool of himself, begging for forgiveness when you wouldn't have had a clue of what the hell was going on. The good news was Dan was reached and so relieved his job wasn't in jeopardy that he wasn't angry with us. We didn't get any more faxed photos from him, however."

"That's funny," I said. "I wish you had brought me in on it. We could have really tortured him!"

"How about the time you asked me and Ed to design the year's Christmas card?" asked Kevin.

"I remember," I answered. "I always felt bad about that. I was guilty of giving you no direction other than the product needed to express creatively the agency's 'holiday spirit.'"

"That's right! Then you'll remember that our solution was a small box imprinted with the words, 'Are the holidays becoming increasingly commercial?' across the top and when opened, along with a tiny television, a headline read, 'One can only hope so.' We excitedly explained that it would be even more cool if all eighty-five employees endorsed the concept by signing the card. I think the rebellion started in the public relations departments, but it quickly spread to the other suits and even to some of the agency's normal people. We heard vicious rumors, ranging from us needing to be fired to a demand that Ed and I be tarred and feathered for furthering the commercialization of the sacred holiday."

"Yes," I said, "and even though I loved the piece, the only way I could stop them from kicking the shit out of you was to take blame for not giving better direction, declare the work off strategy, and get the executive committee to develop a new, very specific creative brief and open it up for all teams to compete. Except for you and Ed, of course."

"We actually liked the final solution even though it wasn't ours," said Kevin. "It was a large brown grocery bag emblazoned with the Elgin Syferd logo and copy urging it be filled and donated to a local food bank. What we liked best, though, was not getting killed or fired.

"Speaking of which," continued Kevin, "another near death experience started, innocently enough, with a simple memo to all employees from Sydney Hunsdale [media director at the time]. '*We are changing the titles of associates who work in our department*,' the memo read. '*Media assistants will now be referred to as media representatives; media representatives will now be media account managers*,' and so on.

"The memo just seemed a bit too corporate for our company, so I took it upon myself to add a bit of humanity to it. I added a second paragraph stating that some titles were also being changed in the Creative Department, and henceforth, '*Copywriters will now be referred to as: people who truly enjoyed the '60s.'* I then put the revised memo in all employee mailboxes.

"Sydney found out who wrote the revision and was so furious that she demanded I be fired. I was called into Dave Syferd's office, and I was pretty sure I was a goner, especially since Sydney was waiting outside the closed office door. However, in low, serious tones, Dave told me that my memo was really funny and he applauded my effort to add a little fun to the place. Then with a wink, his understated voice increased in volume (loud enough, of course, for Sydney to hear), 'AND IF YOU EVER DO ANYTHING LIKE THIS AGAIN, YOU'RE FIRED!' My job was saved, Syd was happy, and life was good. God, I miss working for you guys."

"I'll bet to this day, Sydney feels she taught you a lesson," I said. "She'll probably kill Dave if she ever hears the real story."

"Ron, someone asked the other day for the one word that best describes you," Kevin said.

"You told him 'asshole', right?" I queried.

"Well, of course, I did! No, all kidding aside, I told him the word I would use would be 'leader.' I've always been impressed with your uncanny ability to inspire those working for you to reach greater heights, and in doing so, make them better than they would have been had they never met you, which helps explain why so many of us have remained loyal to you for our entire careers, wherever those paths have taken us."

"You aren't going to try to kiss me or something, are you, Kevin?"

"Be serious, Ron. For me, personally, this loyalty to you and the company is perhaps best illustrated by a story you probably never heard. I like to call it, 'A Couple of Ad Guys Walk Into a Bar…' It was after a long day of work way back in 1989. Kevin Nolan, an art director at the agency, persuaded me to join him for a few libations at a favorite Seattle watering hole. We were no more than a dozen beers into our evening when a guy at the next table overheard that we worked at Elgin Syferd. For reasons known only to the asshole, he started saying shit like how mediocre our work was, how the agency only cared about being the biggest instead of the best, that Elgin was a prick, and so on. Finally, I decided that I'd had enough. I walked over and asked if he would like to go outside to 'debate' his opinions. It wasn't until he stood up that I realized that he was about 6' 3" and 225. Even though he towered over my 5'10" and 170, I stood my ground. No one, I don't care how big, was going to say shit about my company, our work, or my leader. As I prepared to do battle, Kevin grabbed my sorry ass and hustled me out the door.

"I was never sure why the big guy didn't follow us out and kick both our asses all over Pioneer Square. Could have been the fear of soiling his clothes with the blood from a wimpy copywriter, but the point is that I was willing to fight for you and the agency, even understanding the probable outcome."

"My friend," I said, "I'm sure glad you outgrew your fucking stupidity."

"Actually, me too. But what I never want to grow out of is my desire to be an inspirational leader like you. Thanks for that, Ron."

52.

FORAGING FOR THE TRUTH

I'm human, so I loved the complimentary parts of Kevin's stories, but because of my paranoia, I wondered whether there weren't elements of truth in what the asshole had said years earlier to Kevin in the bar. It bothered me all that night.

I'd read enough management books and been to enough seminars to understand that infallibility doesn't necessarily come with the title of CEO. Setting vision is the CEO's primary job; getting the company to adhere to it is next in importance. But how do I know if I've set our sights too low? Am I communicating our goal consistently and clearly, or am I blaming our lack of success on changed market conditions? Is it not the job of the CEO to anticipate changing market conditions? Am I spending enough time with the big picture or miring myself in the daily grind? Have I quietly stopped learning?

The next morning, I decided to ask my most important audience—my direct reports—how they thought I was doing as their leader. For obvious reasons, I decided not to ask them directly. I'm not quite that stupid. I sent them the following memo:

> I would like for you to give me a performance evaluation. I'm asking you to participate in this exercise because I want to be the best leader of this organization that I can possibly be. I'm very proud of the company we've created over the past twenty-two years, and I intend to turn it over to you as an even better one. I need your honest candor in order to accomplish this, and please believe me that there will be no negative repercussions. To ensure that fact, please feel free to make your answers anonymous. Of course, also feel free to scream my faults directly to my face if you prefer.
>
> Delegation is to empower another to act in your place. The connotation, if not the denotation, of abrogation implies giving up or evading responsibility. There is a fine but crucial line between delegation and how I use the word abrogation. How have I done in this balance?
>
> Manipulation can mean "to manage or utilize skillfully." It can also mean "to control by artful, unfair, or insidious means so as to serve one's purpose." Again, a fine but crucial line between the two. How have I done in this balance?
>
> In today's world, companies must maintain the strongest possible code of ethics. If we were to conduct an audit of our company's ethics environment, how would we fare? How, specifically, would I fare?

How well do you understand the mission and vision that I have for the company?

What am I oblivious to, and what do I need to know to become a better leader?

What is the unique contribution that I make to the company?

What do you need from me that you're not getting?

It's inevitable that someday I will retire, die, or be committed. In your mind, what are the three things that I must begin to accomplish now in preparation for that event?

Is there anything else that you think I could/should be doing to make you and the company better and more successful?

Thanks,

Ron

I was enormously pleased with the response. First, all eight of my direct reports took the time to tell me how much they appreciated the opportunity to roast my ass. They all promised to give each question the thought and consideration it deserved, and they thanked me for allowing them the opportunity. With that kind of reaction, I knew I was going to regret starting the process.

I was wrong. The exercise and similar follow-ups helped me identify and address weaknesses and flaws in myself and the company. I strongly recommend that every leader give it a try.

53.

AN UNTYPICAL DAY IN THE LIFE OF A CEO

"What's it like to be a CEO?" asked a young person during an informational interview.

"Well, it's like this," I answered. "At this company, we pride ourselves on hiring extremely smart and talented people. We allow them the opportunity to fail, which means giving them the freedom to solve their own problems. Sometimes, they encounter a problem they simply can't solve. At every level, our people understand that we don't want the company to fail, so they move the problem up the chain of command in search of a solution. At least a few times a day, one of my senior people will come to me with a hot, steaming turd of a problem and drop it on my lap. President Harry Truman had a sign on his desk that said 'The Buck Stops Here.' I think that was just a politically correct way of saying 'Dump Your Smelliest Shit Here.' That, my young friend, is what it's like to be a CEO."

Obviously, there's much more to being a CEO than what I just described. The three most important elements are setting strategy and vision, building culture, and leading the organization.

I read somewhere years ago that having a vision is easy—all it takes is a few magic mushrooms. But ask someone in that state of mind to describe that vision accurately. Can't be done. A CEO must not only have the vision but be able to communicate it clearly. When that is done effectively, each person is able to understand how his or her individual job helps support that vision. I struggled to maintain our vision in its entirety because of the ever-changing industry dynamics, but I knew it was critical never to waver from our core beliefs.

Difficult as that was, I found that keeping our vision intact was far easier than maintaining our culture. I wrote earlier about how it's possible to hire a bad person by being caught up in that person's stellar resume. Or by misreading an Energy Neutral for an Energy Sucker. Or because of the whacky nature of ad people in general, to allow a truly crazy person to join the ranks. Especially when that bad person has evil intent.

"Ron, there's someone here in the lobby who would like to see you," said Debbie, our receptionist. "She doesn't have an appointment, but I'd appreciate it if you could spend a few minutes with her."

When I entered the lobby, I saw a woman dressed from head to toe in black. She was wearing a black scarf resembling a hijab and a black sack dress that went all the way to the floor. I introduced myself and she did the same.

"How can I help you?" I asked.

"I'm dying of brain cancer," she replied. "I have less than a year to live. All my life I've dreamed of being a copywriter at a famous advertising agency. I've done research and this is the agency where I'd like to spend my remaining days."

Holy shit! How does a person respond to that opening act?

"Why don't you come back to my office with me?" I asked sympathetically. "Can I get you something to drink?"

After she was seated on the couch, I handed her a glass of water. I sat in a chair opposite her. She proceeded to tell me about moving to Seattle from back East because of the area's famed cancer centers. Up to a few months ago, she had been employed as a marketing coordinator at a nuclear plant. I chose not to comment on that.

"But I've always loved the advertising business," she reported. Ever since I was a child, I watched commercials on television and tried to figure out how I could make them better. Copywriting was my dream job, but now at thirty-two years of age, my life is about to end before I can realize that dream. Unless you will help me, that is."

Whoa! How does a person respond to a plea like that?

"I'd love to help you, but we don't have any openings right now."

"I was afraid you'd cast me out," she said while wiping a tear from her eye.

"Well, maybe I could find something for you. How long did you say you had to, uh, live?"

"Just a few more months, maybe a year. Unless, of course, a miracle occurs. And I wouldn't need much money. Only enough to cover some of my medical costs. I could probably get by for ten thousand a month. Until I won't need anything, that is."

The amount was ridiculously high for a beginning writer, but it was to help her stay alive, for God's sake. She gave me her contact information and I said I would talk with our creative director and get back to her by the next day. She gave me a tearful thanks as I walked her to the elevator.

As I walked back to my office, one of our copywriters rushed up to me and said, "Please don't tell me you fell for one of Evil Mary's scams, Ron!"

"What do you mean?" I asked.

"I'll bet it was her famous 'hire me because I'm dying' scam, right?"

"You know her?"

"Not personally, but she worked in a few agencies in LA while I was down there. She's a real nut. And she's pure evil. I hear she was fired from every job after wreaking havoc. She's smart and a great writer, but her idea of getting ahead isn't about doing better work; it's all about torpedoing everyone else. She ingratiates up and shits down. She earned such a bad rep that she had to start using scams to get hired in markets where she wasn't known. Was I right about the 'dying scam' or was it the one where she needed money to complete her transition from being a man?"

I called the "dying woman" the next day and told her we were sorry but we couldn't make it work. She pleaded for quite a while, but after deciding it was not working, ended with "I'll ruin you, you pathetic asshole!"

It took me weeks to get over that experience. Had our copywriter not recognized her, she may have got her nose in the door and done damage to our culture before we could stop it. I'm certain we would have eventually removed the bad apple, but I shudder to think of the turmoil it could have caused. Do we tolerate bad, divisive behavior because a person is dying? Or do we heartlessly fire her? Can you imagine the division within the employee ranks and the resulting damage to the very culture of the organization?

Fortunately, that wasn't a typical day for this CEO.

54.

ARE WE RICH YET?

Back in the beer and chips days when Dave and I first talked about creating an agency, we agreed that our ultimate goal was to get rich. A friend used to talk about the "working well-to-do"—what he meant was folks who were well-to-do as long as they were working. We wanted to be in the position of well-to-do *after* we stopped working. The idea was to run as fast as possible toward the finish line. If we happened to stumble along the way, we'd pick ourselves up, dust ourselves off, and check to see whether we were at the right finish line. If the financial picture showed it was time, we'd sell. If not, we'd start running again until we found the right one.

The loss of Holland America Line was a significant stumble. It had been our largest account by far. Although we were able to pick ourselves back up, it's loss was so crippling that we had no choice but to admit that we hadn't yet found the right finish line.

The shocking significance of the stumble made us realize we were not invincible and the next fall could be fatal. Several of our competitors, both large and small, had fallen by the wayside in the 1980s and '90s. By "fallen," I mean they flat-ass went out of business.

Our agency had been the hot one in the market for seven straight years. We had climbed the ladder nearly to the top, but we understood that even when we got there, we'd still only be a big fish because of the size of our pond. Depending on which report you believed, there were somewhere between 32,000 and 46,000 advertising agencies in the U.S. Although we ranked in the top 3 percent, there was a HUGE gap between agencies of our size and the big dogs.

Dave and I agreed that our options for selling were limited: employee buyout, merger with a similar size firm, or to be purchased by a major player. While we may have paid our people well, we knew there wasn't an employee or even a group who could ban together to make the down payment and still have sufficient capital for continued operations. Quite honestly, with that option, we were concerned about not getting our full price over the term of the buyout. Although we wouldn't completely disregard merging with an agency of our size or similar, it wasn't high on our priority list because of similar concerns about long-term viability. Dave and I also wanted some assurance that when we gave up control, the surviving entity would have the financial wherewithal to pay us off and still take care of our employees. In our opinion, the most logical answer was to sell the company to a large publicly traded agency. I took the lead in exploring all three options but with the heaviest focus on the latter.

Over the years, we'd been approached by at least a half-dozen public companies expressing interest in acquiring us. Those conversations usually went something like: "Are you interested in selling your firm?" To which our answer had always been either "No" or "Not yet."

The first time was in 1981 shortly after Dave and I had announced that we intended to start an agency but before we had an office or any business. I was contacted by the CEO of a fair size Canadian agency. He stroked my ego, telling me that he'd heard good things about us and wanted to meet.

He flew in from Toronto about a week later. We met for breakfast at the Washington Athletic Club. He was a nice-looking, affable guy about sixty years old. We did the normal chitchat and then spent the rest of the time talking about his agency since there was nothing yet to report about ours. His company was about twenty years old, had offices in Toronto, Montreal, and Quebec, and employed nearly 200 people. Although it had some U.S. accounts, most were Canadian-based firms.

After about an hour of eating and our hearing how successful his company was, he asked us, "Well, what do you think?"

"I'm very flattered that you would even consider us, let alone fly across the country to meet in person, but I don't feel we're ready to make any acquisitions—especially of an agency as large as yours."

He knew my tongue was firmly planted in my cheek, but the response also confirmed his belief that he had identified an agency that was going to be successful. He was hoping to buy low and realize a big upside. I thanked him for breakfast and asked that he check back in about ten years with a very large truck full of money.

Now that the answer to us selling had changed from "No" and "Not yet" to a definite "Maybe" or "Probably," I dug out my Rolodex and started dialing for dollars. DDB Needham, Foote Cone Belding, McCann Erickson, Grey, and TBWA responded favorably to my calls. All were excellent agencies with distinctive styles and personalities, and my visits and discussions with them were enjoyable and educational. The experience taught me something that I have shared many times with people seeking advice on selling their agencies. The Canadian agency, by the way, hadn't grown sufficiently to afford a truck with enough money to meet our needs.

My counsel is that ownership needs to look at selling a company the same way people would look at choosing the right spouse. The wrong way is to pick one based on only the size of her tits, or only the broadness of his shoulders, or only the sparkle of her personality, or even only the depth of his intellect. *In the case of picking the right company to sell to, don't look only at its client list, or only at its creative style, and especially only at the multiple of earnings it offers. In order to create a lasting marriage with a spouse or another company, both sides need to consider the entire package. Chances are if a marriage isn't built on a firm enough foundation, it will dissolve over time. The same is true if you sell to the wrong company.*

As a company owner, you get to decide things like whether or not to invest in the future as opposed to posting an annual profit. You get to decide how much of your profits to distribute or hold. You get to choose your clients, style, even the face you want your agency to wear. As a part of a larger entity, you may not be able to make those choices. If you were not in sync prior to "marrying" your business partner, the smallest of disputes can elevate to discussions that can lead to edicts. Edicts can lead to no-win fights when they're with the people who write the checks.

I've seen cases where the fights become so paralyzing that it's impossible for the acquired agency to do good work or make a decent profit. As everyone must realize, it doesn't matter if your negotiated multiple is 2 or 2,000; if your annual profit is zero, your payout will be zero.

It took a few months and a lot of meetings, but I finally made up my mind and recommended to Dave that we enter serious negotiations with DDB Needham and no one else.

"Dave, I honestly believe these guys will be the best long-term partners for us. You liked them as much as I did all the way through the Holland America Line pitch process. The more people I meet and the better I get to know them, the better I feel about selling to them. For example, they put in writing some of the exact core beliefs that we've talked about since our founding."

"Like what?" Dave asked.

"Well, I know it's never been your favorite, but our philosophy about allowing our employees the opportunity to fail."

"I hate that. You make it sound like you want our people to fail."

"You know I don't, Dave, but you do know people learn faster and better when their hands aren't constantly being held. Besides, our folks know if they don't reach out for help while going down for the third time, their ass is grass."

"I still don't like saying we're giving them the opportunity, but what else do we share in common with DDB?"

"Their Mission Statement requires them to encourage creative adventure and freedom of thought. Although you and I've talked about a lot of this from the beginning, Keith has published what he calls 'The Four Freedoms.' It seems like everyone at DDB knows them by heart.

"The first one is The Freedom from Fear. He writes that talent freezes in the grip of fear. The creative mind shuts down, constricting the natural flow of words and ideas. Fear results from decisions arrived at in secret deliberations, the basis for which is not disclosed. People do not fear truth; they fear arbitrary use of power for reasons they don't understand. Fear is paralyzing beyond reason. Management by intimidation has no place in an organization dedicated to nurturing creativity."

"We've always preached that here," commented Dave.

"That's what I'm trying to tell you. Listen to how he states their Freedom to Fail philosophy. He says it is in the nature of creative talent to venture beyond the known, to poke into the unheard of, to pick its way through scary places, untrod by conventional minds. Because there are no assurances, these idea-searching patrols will succeed; the seekers must be granted the latitude to fail in order to sustain their willingness to pursue again. It's the job of management first to point talented people in the right direction and then to judge their work. But if the approach to that work is responsible and intelligent, people must never be criticized for daring to fail."

"I love that," said Dave. "Shit, if you had described it like that from the beginning, I would have never objected."

"I'm no Keith Reinhard, Dave."

"That's for damn sure. What's the next one?"

"He calls it The Freedom from Chaos. He says that talent flounders in an atmosphere of management indecision, vacillation, arrogance, and uncertainty. It requires benign discipline. The talented mind may seem erratic, but it welcomes an understanding of responsibilities that is clear, yet roomy enough to permit the floating dream. Such responsibilities must be freely agreed to and well understood by all hands before talent takes its place in our organization. Once committed, continuing instructions from management must be consistent with that understanding."

"I'm not saying you have any talent, Ron," said Dave, "but a lot of that sounds like the reasons you left Cole & Weber. What's the fourth freedom?"

"Simply, The Freedom to Be. He writes that each individual has the right to be treated with dignity, to be supported in his or her ambitions for higher achievement, and to be provided with a place where a career can grow in the direction of one's own choosing. But beyond providing for professional growth, talent must be permitted to enjoy a life in which there is also time for laughter, and music, and love, and celebration, and the space to enjoy them."

"Are you sure he didn't pirate those thoughts from us?"

"I'm positive, Dave, but now do you feel better about selling to them?"

"I do; let's see where the next step takes us."

55.

THE NEGOTIATIONS

In preparation for our first financial discussion with DDB Needham Worldwide, I had our various entities send to me their P&L's and balance sheets. I combined the relevant numbers from Hornall Anderson Design Works, CF2GS (nee Christiansen & Fritsch), and Elgin Syferd/Drake, along with those from Elgin Syferd, and called Jerry Germain, DDB Needham Worldwide CFO, for guidance in preparing a consolidated balance sheet.

"No need to do that, Ron," replied Jerry. "We're not buying those other companies."

"What the hell are you talking about? Of course you're buying all our companies."

"No, we're not. I thought you understood that. Omnicom is our holding company; they own us and won't let DDB Needham buy any below-the-line companies. We're only able to buy your ad agency."

"If anyone had ever said anything about that to me," I said, "it went right over my head. These are not 'below-the-line-companies' to us. You guys must not understand how important the disciplines those companies represent are to our core company, Elgin Syferd. You've all said from the outset that you wanted to buy us for three reasons: the quality of our work, our people, and our client list. Those three are intricately intertwined. We're not a traditional advertising agency. Through interaction with our other companies, we provide clients with world class design and direct marketing capabilities. Didn't anyone back there stop to think about what makes us so different from all your other offices?"

"Ron, no one said you couldn't provide your clients with those services. Omnicom would prefer that the services you mentioned were outsourced to sister companies like Interbrand and Rapp Collins, but if you want to continue doing them in-house, fine. But as I said, Omnicom will not let us buy anything but ad agencies. And it's their money."

"What about our office in Boise?"

"Ron, if it wasn't for the quality and diversity of your work, your people, your client list, and the fact that you guys make a lot of money, there is no way in hell we would want to be in a place as remote as Seattle. Does that answer your question about Montana?"

"Boise is in Idaho."

"I know where Boise is, so did locating it in Montana make my point?"

"Well, what do we do with our ownership positions in the other companies?"

"I don't give a shit. Do whatever you want. All I'm saying is that we aren't buying anything except your ad agency."

After I talked it over with Dave, we decided to fight the issue. My written argument began with a quote from none other than the head honcho himself:

> "The future of our business must not be limited to thirty-second TV; to succeed at becoming the biggest and best builder of brands, we must be idea centric and media neutral."
>
> — Keith Reinhard

I followed that with a quote from our own Vice Chairman, Jan Edmondson: *"If we don't get ourselves out of the advertising-only box, it will become our coffin."*

I pleaded that we had always done it differently in Seattle. We had created a multi-disciplinary, separate-but-equal, completely integrated communications company. We had staffed it with smart, passionate people from each of the several communications disciplines, and in order to retain that staff, we gave them equality and the autonomy of their own profit center.

I told them this would make the sale a tough decision for us because it would be extremely difficult to function in our market strictly as an advertising agency or even as an ad/PR shop. The multiplicity of our offerings had not only become integral to the way we thought and operated, but it was one of our key market differentiators and very important to our existing clients.

I was confident that my argument would make a difference.

"I told you, Ron," Jerry responded, "I don't give a shit. We can't buy anything but your ad agency. The only exception we'll make is because Syferd is half-owner of Elgin Syferd, we'll grandfather your PR business."

Our partners at the three companies were understandably surprised at the turn of events. John Hornall and Jack Anderson were actually relieved because they weren't looking forward to having a global entity owning half of their company. There were mixed emotions at CF2GS. Two were looking forward to a big payday; two were excited to be a part of a global entity; one was like Germain and didn't give a shit. With regard to Elgin Syferd/Drake, Bill Drake looked at it as a non-event as long as Dave and I remained his partners.

Although mildly upset that our payout wouldn't be based on consolidated earnings, we were more concerned about how we would be able to continue providing all the services necessary to help make our clients successful. Let me be more specific. How would we be able to continue providing those services without outsourcing the work away from our people and the bottom line?

56.

ANOTHER BUMP IN THE ROAD

"Ron, we gotta talk," said Dave.

Whenever Dave said those words in that tone, I knew it was trouble.

"While you were in New York last week, some of our people expressed a concern about the sale, and this one has nothing to do with our other companies."

During the early years when money was scarce, Dave and I had granted shares instead of bonuses or raises to a half-dozen key staffers. If memory serves, the total represented only about 2 percent of the outstanding shares, but they were owners and, more importantly, they were our partners.

"I presume you're talking about the minority shareholders. What's their problem?" I asked.

"It's not just them; I've become concerned as well. We're worried about a couple of things. First, can we be sure that when DDB takes over, it's not going to fire all our key people and replace them with DDB employees? Second, what's to prevent New York from coming in and telling us how to do our jobs? You know that we're different from the other DDB offices. What if they try to make us conform to the way they work? The 'minority shareholders' as you put it, want us to call off the deal. I convinced them that you would go back to New York and get them employment contracts and a written pledge that they won't try to tell us how to do our jobs."

"Dave, this is fucked. You've met these guys; you know they're not assholes."

"I'm not saying they're assholes, Ron; we just need some assurance that the world doesn't get tipped upside down the day after they take over."

"I still think this is fucked, but it's apparent you've made up your minds. As embarrassing as this may be, I'll go talk to them."

I made an appointment through Keith's executive assistant for the following week. I tried to make it as casual as possible by saying I was going to be in town and would like to stop by for a few minutes to confirm a couple of details.

When it came time for the meeting, I was nervous. Walking into Keith's office, I knew my nervousness stemmed primarily from embarrassment.

"Keith, I'm embarrassed."

"You're not here to tell me the deal is off, are you?"

"No, no! At least I hope the deal will still be on after this conversation. My embarrassment is because I couldn't talk Dave and our minority partners out of a couple of concerns. They're concerned that as soon as DDB buys us, you're going to replace our key people and turn the rest of us into Stepford Wives."

Keith just sat there for a moment, staring at me. I had this terrible feeling that Dave was right and I had just caught them red-handed. Then he started laughing.

"Ron, they must think we have a big warehouse somewhere here on Long Island filled to the brim with brilliant people in need of a place to work! That is so funny. Do they think we grow them on trees? Harvest them and store them until we can find them a home? I love the naivety!

"One of the principal reasons we want to buy your company is because of your people. Irrespective of what they may think, good people do not grow on trees. One of the other reasons is because of the work those people are doing for your clients. Of course, we love your client list, but we realize clients come and go. You have a wonderful record of employee longevity and brilliant advertising. I give you my word, as long as you continue doing good work and making decent money, you'll not even hear from us unless you initiate the conversation. Then we'll always be there for you."

I immediately called Dave.

"Dave, I'm happy to report that we have nothing to worry about!"

"We have contracts for everyone?"

"No, even better. We have Keith's word."

So we moved forward with the deal.

On the advice of our accountant, we sold Elgin Syferd's 50 percent ownership of Elgin Syferd/Drake to Dave and me for $50,000. No money changed hands; we simply had to get the ownership of the entity off our books. The number was an arbitrary one suggested by our accountant. At the formal signing of the documents, I happened to notice that $50,000 had been deducted from the down payment due to us from DDB.

“What’s this $50,000 deduction?” I asked.

“That’s the money you and Dave owe the company for the sale of the Boise office.”

“Bullshit,” I said. “That’s complete bullshit. That was our company to start with, not yours. We’re not paying you for our company.”

“You don’t understand,” responded their lead accountant. “That transaction is required by GAP [General Accounting Procedures].”

“I don’t give a shit if it’s required by you and every clothing store in the entire world, we’re not going to pay you for our own fucking company!”

“I’m sorry, Ron,” interrupted Jerry, “but rules are rules.”

“Then fuck you,” I said. “We’re calling off the deal. There’s no way we’re selling this company to an outfit so chicken shit that it tries to fuck its partner even before the papers are signed. Pack it up, Dave; we’re out of here.”

“You can’t be serious,” complained Jerry. “You’d walk away from this multi-million dollar deal over a lousy fifty grand?”

“Yes. Are you willing to do the same?”

Dick Girvin, CEO of DDB Needham Retail, jumped in and said, "Strike the $50,000 from the contract. Seattle will be on my P&L. I'll take the heat from Omnicom."

The deal was done. Everyone signed the papers, shook hands, and we sent our new partners off to the airport.

"Nice bluff," said our attorney.

"It wasn't a bluff, Bob," I answered. "I was dead ass serious. It wasn't about the money. If we let them get away with bullying before they legally own the company, can you imagine the respect with which we'd be treated in the future?"

Every few months, for as long as Keith remained CEO, he would call and ask how DDB's most neglected president was doing. I'm sure I was far from being the most neglected and also sure that he used that line on many presidents around the world. But I'll tell you, it sure the hell made me feel good personally and confident about his commitment to us.

A few weeks after the deal was consummated, Keith returned to Seattle, but this time our company was his company. We used his visit as an opportunity proudly to introduce him to our employees and clients.

I'm sure Keith had been born gracious and somehow grew to be even more so over time. "Thank you so much for agreeing to be part of our family," he told Dave and me. "I realize this can be as much or as little as a five-year commitment on your part. Have either of you given thought to the future after your earn-out period?"

Dave spoke first. "The day after our payout is complete, I'm out of here. Five years from now, I plan to open a bookstore without a front door in some remote location like on a mountaintop in Sun Valley."

"Good for you, Dave; you'll have earned it," said a sincere Keith. "How about you, Ron?"

"Does DDB Needham have a retirement age?"

"No, it doesn't, Ron; why do you ask?"

"Without trying to sound too much like a suck-up, I love what I do. If I continue to love what I do while being a part of DDB Needham, I'd like to be found dead at my desk at age 100 or so."

"Welcome to the long-haul, Ron. You're going to love it!"

Before any of the scheduled formal events, I took Keith on a tour of our newly expanded office space. Since co-founding Hornall Anderson Design Works, our two companies had always shared office space. In the beginning, an imaginary line separated us. As both companies grew, each office became increasingly distinct, but they continued to be adjacent to one another. For the past several years, we even had separate entries but with connecting interior doors. As we were about to walk by one of those doors, I decided to give Keith a tour of Hornall Anderson's ultra-cool offices.

Our offices were cool too, but where we had some traditional touches, Hornall Anderson's were over-the-top industrial modern. For example, most agencies like to display their award statues, plaques, and what-have-you on bookshelves and the like. Display just about anything except the paper awards, that is. HADW had won so many awards that it had long since run out of room for the hardware so it devoted an entire twenty-foot long wall to paper award certificates hung at different lengths from the ceiling. The really interesting thing was that the company had received so many it created a layered effect several inches thick.

After a very brief description of what HADW was and what it did, Keith said with a huge grin, "You mean I own this, too?"

"No, Keith," I said. "We own it. I tried to make it part of DDB's purchase, but your corporate policy said you could only buy the ad agency."

"Dammit," he replied. "I fought against that when we formed Omnicom. I wish I had this back then to use as an argument. I think I could have won."

Before we leave Hornall Anderson, I have a couple of more stories. At one point, our two offices were separated by a thirty-foot long, three-foot wide corridor. The ceiling was at least twenty feet high, and on one wall, from ten feet up to the top, was an area indented about two feet deep.

"Who owns this hallway?" Jack asked me one day.

"I have no idea, Jack. Why do you ask?"

"Well, we're running out of space again, and I've been thinking that if we're paying rent for this hallway, I could certainly use it."

"How could you possibly use this space? If you put desks or even chairs here, it would become impassable."

"I've been thinking a lot about this. You see that indention up there?"

"So?"

"We could install shelves for work spaces about fifteen feet up."

"How could anyone use them?"

"Simple! We could install pulleys to hang the workers at just the right height. Hoist them in the morning and lower them occasionally for breaks and lunch."

Fortunately for his workers, the parsimonious Jack needed even more space than his idea afforded so they moved all their people to a new space on the other side of ours.

The second "space" story has to do with the design of HADW's new office. Back then, we both used the same talented architects but to different ends. This was the ultra-modern industrial space I mentioned in connection with Keith's visit.

"I'm loving working with Anderson on their space," said Scott, the architect.

"I'm sure it's going to be great," I replied. "What's going to be its single most outstanding feature?"

"Without a doubt, the main conference room. It will be situated adjacent to the lobby area. What makes it so unique is that on one side will be an actual functional garage door with glass panels. At a touch of the remote control, the garage door raises, doubling the size of the room!"

"Do me a favor, Scott. Let Jack know that you told me about the door. Tell him that I plan to get a duplicate remote control to use randomly from over here."

"Would you really do that?"

"Probably not, but I know Jack will think I would."

He obviously did. Nothing was ever said about it, but Jack opted for the much safer manual operation.

57.

SOME OF THE DDB NEEDHAM CHARACTERS

One of the DDB guys integral to our sale to DDB Needham was a Mr. Magoo-type character by the name of Martin Michael. Martin had successfully started, ran, and sold an agency to DDB. If memory serves, he sold the same agency a couple of different times.

Martin was legally blind. His glasses were Coke-bottle thick, but I swear, he could better see what needed to be seen than any normal sighted person. He was Mr. Magoo-esque in other ways, too. He was short, round, and perpetually in motion. He was as energetic as he was smart. I really liked Martin and respected his knowledge of our business and the business of our business.

His title was Vice-Chairman of DDB Needham Retail. For reasons we still didn't quite understand, that entity was the legal owner of Elgin Syferd. I know we asked the question, but quite honestly, we never really paid attention to the answer. As long as big bucks Omnicom was responsible for our earn-out payments, we didn't give a shit about the structure above us.

The CEO of DDB Needham Retail was a different story. His specialty was the retail business. He had a pretty good understanding of how to make money. His taste when it came to the advertising product was marginal at best. I always got the impression that his philosophy was to give the client whatever it wanted, but if the client asked for his opinion, he would give the client what he thought it wanted. Let's just say that he would have fit in very well with the ad agency people I met on the trip to Asia.

DDB Needham Retail had its head office in Sacramento, as well as offices in San Francisco, Los Angeles, Denver, and now, Seattle. Interesting to note, DDB Needham also had full service offices in San Francisco and Los Angeles. Martin explained in those two markets the difference was the DDB offices did brand advertising and the DDB Retail offices did "retail" advertising. It didn't take me long to realize that "retail" was for the most part an euphemism for mediocre to bad advertising and clients.

"Okay, Martin, explain again why Seattle is part of Retail," I said.

"I've been trying," he responded, "you're hearing me, but you're not listening. Your company is unique. One of the reasons we pursued you so doggedly and paid you so well is that you do brilliant, award-winning, brand-building work for your corporate clients, but you also understand and produce equally effective work for your retail clients. You are going to become the model for the DDB Needham Retail offices."

"I don't get it, Martin. In Seattle, we only have one client list. For some of our clients, we do strictly brand messaging; for others, we do a blend of brand and what you refer to as "retail." We fit more in the DDB Needham camp than the DDB Needham Retail one."

"But DDB Needham Retail owns Seattle."

"Sell us."

"We don't want to. Our goal is to duplicate what you have in Seattle all across the country. We'd like to see a network of ten, maybe twenty Retail shops."

"That makes no fucking sense. Why duplicate expenses? Why not simply teach the people in the regular DDB Needham offices how to do good retail?"

"We've tried. They refuse."

"Then create a group of specialists as a stand-alone entity within their offices."

"We've tried that, but it hasn't worked for at least two reasons. First, we have a terrible time hiring because these 'specialists' are treated like shit by the 'real' advertising people. Equally important, when we do win a good retailer and start doing good work, we constantly have to fight our own company from stealing the business."

"I've been to this rodeo before."

"What do you mean?" asked Martin.

"Well, we tried a retail-only shop in Seattle a few years ago."

"You never told me that."

"You never asked. Besides, I try not to go around bragging about my failures."

"What happened to it?"

"It went out of business."

"Why?"

"For the exact reasons you just mentioned."

"Ouch. We may be in trouble."

• • • •

Another of the DDB Needham characters who deserves a few paragraphs was the president of DDB Needham West. Let me first attempt to draw a word picture of the man.

Raconteur: a person who is skilled in relating stories and anecdotes interestingly; a person who excels in telling stories with skill and wit often by improvisation or embellishment.

To use that word alone to describe Alan O. Pando would definitely short-shrift the man. You'd also want to add descriptors such as debonair (Webster: suave, urbane, affable, and genial) and bon vivant (Webster: a person having cultivated, refined, and sociable tastes).

In addition, Alan was a damn good ad guy. He earned his chops in the New York office of DDB running accounts like American Airlines before leaving to become president of Della Femina, Travisano & Partners. He was wooed back to DDB to be president of the West and, as such, was the big dog for the traditional as well as retail offices in L.A., San Francisco,

Sacramento, Denver, Honolulu, and Mexico City. And now Seattle.

After my discussion and admission of failure to Martin, I decided that I needed to talk with the big guy. At my first opportunity, I flew down to L.A. to learn from Alan his vision of the role Seattle would be playing in DDB Needham, Retail or otherwise.

"Let me explain what we have in mind, Ron," Alan told me. "We don't think the differences between retail and brand advertising will last forever, but we are sure that DDB Needham Retail is not being managed properly in the meantime. It's not bad; it's just kind of average in everything from its client list to its work to its margins. We like what you and Dave have done up there in Seattle, so we would like you to become president of the Retail division now and take over as CEO as soon as we can get the current guy to retire."

"You mean having all the Retail offices report to me?"

"Yes."

This was not at all what I had expected. First, Alan was obviously aware that the current model was not only flawed but going away. Second, there might be a personal revenue opportunity here for Dave and me.

"I'm flattered, Alan, but I don't know how I could do that without hurting the Seattle office and our earn-out. If I take my eye off that ball, our profits could drop and our payout will be less."

"We thought about that and are willing to pay the Seattle office a significant salary for your efforts, which will drop directly to the bottom line and be increased by your multiple. I've heard how greedy you are, and I can't believe you'd let anything get in the way of your earnings. The salary added to those earnings will help add a whole new wing to the house you're building."

"Throw in a performance bonus and you have a deal."

"No."

"Okay, as I said, you have a deal!"

Dave loved the deal. He especially loved the part about me being out of the office for at least a week every month.

DDB Needham Retail Worldwide was like our failed AdWorks on steroids. It was deja-vu times five. Once again, I was in charge of a company half full of people who shouldn't even be alive and the other half a combination of semi- to really talented employees, most of which were hoping to use the experience to get a real job in advertising. Actually, that was even true for the leaders of the offices.

• • • •

I have never been called a prude. In fact, outsiders have often wondered aloud why I've never been accused of sexual harassment. I honestly believe that any affection I have ever shown to an employee—both male and female—is heartfelt and never inappropriate. Or maybe I've just been lucky. In any event, thanks to one of Omnicom's law firms, Davis and

Gilbert, who gave us annual seminars on the subject, I at least understood the definition of inappropriate.

Shortly after being appointed CEO of Retail, I was informed of a sexual harassment complaint against a senior executive in one of "my" new offices.

I reported the incident to my boss and was instructed to work with corporate counsel in New York, which recommended a letter of reprimand. While I was personally offended by the guy's treatment of a subordinate, I agreed to the punishment. Sometimes even scumbags deserve second chances.

Since I visited all offices at least once a month, the guy was unaware of the main reason for me showing up. I greeted the receptionist and had her announce me. While we were walking to his office, he casually patted a female employee on her ass. To my astonishment, he then said to a different woman, "How's it going today, sweetie pie?"

As I closed the door, I said, "Dude, you just committed two sexual harassment offenses in less than ten seconds."

"Relax," he said. "That's how we roll here."

I calmly explained that we no longer rolled that way or any other way that was inappropriate. Fortunately for both of us, he chose to resign before getting any further complaints.

The head guy of another office wore so much cologne I couldn't stand meeting in his office. There's a saying that a person's cologne or perfume should never enter a room first. This guy abused it so badly that he didn't even have to be in the same building to be offensive. One of his staffers told me he did it intentionally so no one would bring him problems. Another said it was to cover the stink of the work he supported.

Another old saying is that the fish stinks from the head. In the offices where that didn't apply, there was enough stink from the body of the beast.

• • • •

I struggled to make a difference. The work continued to be mediocre, employee morale was non-existent, and the company continued to lose money. No matter which metric I used, I was failing miserably.

Failure was not something I was used to and I didn't handle it well. My performance in the Seattle office was being affected. I decided that the extra money wasn't worth the grief. I made an appointment with Pando and jumped on a plane to Los Angeles.

"Alan, this Retail thing just isn't working. I've been busting my ass to make a difference, but it seems the harder I try, the worse it gets. I'm at a loss."

"Well, Ron, you accepted the challenge and the money that goes with it. I'll give you one more year to stop the financial bleeding. I don't really care how you do it; just stop it from losing money."

I wasn't sure whether Alan was intentionally giving me a way out of my predicament, but I didn't want to take a chance, so I thanked him and left. Believing in the adage that it's better to beg for forgiveness than ask for permission, I flew home formulating a plan. Seattle was making significant money, but not enough to make up for the combined losses of the other offices in the Retail network. I'd failed to make the other offices profitable, but I knew that by getting rid of some or all of them, Retail's gross revenue would shrink dramatically but our profit percentage would skyrocket. I had always fought against the idea of making more money by downsizing an organization, but when your existence depends on drastic measures, it's best at least to explore them.

Pando was once again way ahead of me. In fact, if I remember correctly, he began the conversation by telling me that I had failed and he was removing me as CEO of Retail. He then said he had decided to get rid of the retail concept entirely. I'm not always the best employee and I do have an enormous ego, but I do remember praising him for both of his brilliant ideas. Hearing no objections from me, several accounts were moved from the Denver office to Chicago and our CFO bought his way out of a nearly expired lease. The employees were given the option of moving to Chicago with the accounts. None took the offer. We resigned the rest of the accounts, but in each case, we suggested to our former employees that they go after the business with our blessings. The former leadership from Sacramento and some of its employees took over the remaining clients of that office. The San Francisco office had a few good size accounts. Three of the most talented employees started their own agency and paid a royalty to take some of the business with them. Some of the accounts and people from L.A. Retail were folded into the

L.A. office. In all, most of the accounts and employees found homes, and I went back to Seattle with a big smile on my face. By the end of the year, after paying severance and the balance of the lease payments, Retail went from a balance sheet showing a -8 percent EBITDA (Revenue – Expenses) to a +28 percent. All of it coming from the Seattle office.

I was neither lucky enough nor good enough to make a success of either AdWorks or DDB Needham Retail. I credit myself, however, with being smart enough to resist the temptation of ever again stretching beyond my level of expertise.

• • • •

One of my closest friends is Frank Palmer, legendary head of DDB Canada. From humble beginnings in Vancouver, Frank created Canada's most creatively acclaimed marketing communications agency, and in the process, changed the face of Canadian advertising. In recognition of his outstanding contributions to the advertising industry, Frank has been inducted into the Canadian Marketing Hall of Legends by the American Marketing Association and is a recipient of the Association of Canadian Advertisers' prestigious Gold Medal Award. It's not only his ability as an exceptional business leader that made Frank unique. He is also a philanthropist at heart and a true believer in corporate social responsibility. In fact, he is a Founder of the National Advertising Benevolent Society (NABS) in Canada, and he has provided his expertise and influence to numerous industry and charitable organizations.

But anyone who knows Frank (or has been on the receiving end of one of his famous practical jokes) knows he is a strong advocate for what he calls "fun shui," a.k.a. having fun at work. My buddy Frank has had fun shui several times at my expense. Probably the most embarrassing for me happened at a DDB North America board meeting dinner in New York City. Let me set the scene for you. The private party room upstairs at the very famous La Grenouille features a wood-burning fireplace, Juliette balconies, high ceilings, and meals starting at $195 plus booze. The room was once the home of the painter Bernard Lamotte, who along with his friend Antoine de Saint Exupéry (author of *Le Petit Prince*), hosted many parties with Greta Garbo, Jean Gabin, and Charlie Chaplin. I was fairly new to the company and still in awe of my bosses and most of my peers. In this setting, I felt like the kid sitting in front of Lee Jacobi with dirty hands.

The room was elegant but cozy for ten. At one end of the small room was a very petite restroom. Just before the first course was about to be served, I needed to visit said room. After urinating and washing my hands, I turned the doorknob and pushed the door. It didn't open. I pushed it harder. It still didn't open. I could clearly hear the conversation in the other room. I tried turning the knob harder, twisting it from one side to the other. I'm not claustrophobic, but I started to feel panicky. My source of panic was a growing embarrassment about the amount of time away from the dining table *in the shitter*! Why else does a person spend more than two or three minutes in a john? This was getting ridiculous. I was twisting and pushing and panicking. Finally, after about five minutes that felt like five hours, I gave a mighty shove and stumbled into a dining room filled with laughter and big Frank standing by the door with a huge grin. The asshole had been using his considerable weight and leverage to imprison me. Being the butt of his joke was just as embarrassing as me believing the gang thought I was in there sitting on my butt.

Here are a couple of other examples taken from Frank's biography, which is currently being written:

> No sooner does the unassuming customer find a spare seat in a crowded coffee bar than he notices a stuffed envelope on the counter near his elbow. The envelope, which is unsealed, is labeled "Rattlesnake Eggs," and it belongs to the person next to him: a tall, bald-headed man with the build of an ex prize-fighter and a taste for stylish black garb.
>
> "Rattlesnake eggs?" the customer asks, and his neighbour wearily cocks an eyebrow.
>
> "Yeah. An idea I had for the food service industry."
>
> "Food service? Like restaurants?"
>
> The bald man sighs. "Don't laugh. Snake eggs are a delicacy in some countries. But not here, unfortunately."
>
> As he sips his cappuccino, the customer's eyes are fixated on the envelope. How can eggs be so small as to fit into that? Probably dehydrated, he concludes. But how can they possibly taste good?

After a long pause, during which time his neighbour stares wistfully into the distance, he asks, "Could I take a look? I've never seen rattlesnake eggs before."

The bald man shrugs. "If you want."

Placing his cappuccino on the counter, the customer picks up the envelope: it weighs almost nothing. He gently lifts the flap, and suddenly a sharp rattle pierces the air; he and cappuccino leap skyward.

After a perilous struggle to regain his composure and wipe coffee from his eyes, the customer realizes the envelope contains a tightly-wound rubber band attached to a noisemaker.

The gag is so corny, so high-school-ish, that it's downright funny, and he and the bald man erupt in laughter. Onlookers either shake their heads or look away: for them, the only thing that matters is it's pouring outside, with a chance of snow.

The prankster and his victim are well aware of the lousy weather, but for a few dizzy moments it feels like summer for them.

Several weeks later, I'm visiting the downtown Vancouver headquarters of DDB Canada, of which Palmer is chairman and CEO. It may not be the biggest ad agency office in terms of physical size, but the reception area is modern, sleek and spotless. The finishes and lighting are high-end, and Kirsty, the young woman behind the tall counter, greets visitors with a dazzling smile.

Unfortunately on the day of my visit, she's having difficulty with the flat screen mounted on the wall beside her. It's supposed to be fixed to a single channel, but occasionally—maybe it's because of the heavy rain outside—the channel keeps changing. Kirsty aims a clicker at the flat screen and relocates the correct channel, but the channel changes again.

By the time Palmer materializes (he has an unnerving habit of doing so, and even on concrete flooring his footsteps are silent), Kirsty is clicking at the television like a movie cop firing bullets at a mad killer. "What in hell's going on here?" he asks.

"I'm sorry, but this TV….." Kirsty stifles an expletive, and to her further consternation the channels start flipping like the pages of a book.

Palmer turns to me and produces a key fob from his pocket. "You see, this device can manipulate flat screens from a distance, as long as you aim it at the television…."

Keith Bremer, our brilliant Worldwide CFO/COO, is nearly as demented as the famous prankster himself. When Frank was out of the country on an extended vacation, Keith hired a team to remodel his office. Well, not exactly *his* office. The remodeling team removed the only door to his office, filled it with sheet rock, and painted it to match the rest of the wall. To find out Frank's reaction, you'll have to buy his biography. I guarantee it will be worth your while.

58.

HEAVEN BOUND

A little over a year after Elgin Syferd/DDB Needham had won the Energy Star Division of the EPA, I got a call from Candy Cox, managing director of our Washington D.C. office.

"Boss, I hate my fucking job."

Horrible thoughts raced through my mind. We had just celebrated our first anniversary with the Energy Star client, leaving four more years on a very profitable $50 million contract. Candy was extremely important to the account and, therefore, to the remaining $40 million.

"Candy, what have I done wrong? Where did I let you down? I'm here on my knees; what can I do to make you not hate us?"

"No, no, no. You don't understand. I love our company. It's the client I hate. Well, that's not even totally accurate. I like a lot of the people over there, but I hate the everyday bureaucracy. We've been working on the account for more than a year and we haven't executed a single program. Even when they love something, it doesn't get done because everyone has authority to say, 'No,' but I can't find anyone who can say 'Yes.' They're all like, 'Oh, my God, what if I approve something and it fails?' I simply can't handle not getting anything done. It's driving me batty."

"I don't know what to say, Candy. Is there anything I can do?"

"I was hoping you'd ask, boss. This client doesn't need me over there every day holding its hand. I'm sure it would be just as happy if I just sent one of my staff members. In fact, they'd probably be happier not having me bug them about getting shit done. But then, without anything to do, I'd probably end up hating my job out of boredom. So my question is: Can I pitch other businesses to put some variety back into my life?"

"Candy, if that's what it will take to make you happy, please feel free to pitch any and everything to your heart's content! If you win something, that's even better!"

Six months later, I got another call from Candy. "Boss, we have an opportunity to pitch a really big, high profile account, but I thought I better get your permission first."

"Why in the world would you think you had to get my permission to pitch a really big, high profile account? Is it something illegal?"

"Absolutely not. In fact, it's something about which I feel very strongly. Have you heard of NARAL?"

"Of course, the National Abortion and Reproductive Rights Action League."

"Good job, Ron! Based on our credentials and a written proposal, it has narrowed the field to Y&R, Chicago, and us.

It invited us to make a pitch in person in two weeks at its office, but I thought I'd better ask you first because there will be some costs involved. Can we do it?"

"Absolutely, Candy! Don't worry about the expense; just tell me how we can support you from the Seattle office."

"Don't you need to check with your bosses in New York? Aren't you afraid of what they'll say?"

"Candy, I'm more afraid of what my wife would say if she knew we turned down the opportunity to help make a difference in the lives of women."

Two weeks later, a very excited Candy let me know that we had won the business. A few weeks later, she called to ask whether I had told anyone in New York about the new client.

"No, I haven't had a chance to share the good news with them. Why do you ask?"

"I was just interviewed by *The New York Times*. They're going to run a story about NARAL hiring its first big multinational agency. I think it might be best if your bosses hear that news first from you. NARAL is pretty controversial, you know."

I knew she was right. That was probably why, subconsciously, I had delayed sharing the news with them in the first place. The problem was I had never discussed politics or issues with my bosses, so I had no idea where they stood on this issue. Keith Reinhard seemed to be a very liberated guy. But he also had six kids. So was he pro-choice or pro-life? Was I going to be congratulated and appreciated for this win or simply fired?

Fearing the worst, I chose not to go directly to Reinhard. Instead, I called Keith Bremer, DDB Worldwide CFO. "Keith, is Reinhard pro-choice or pro-life?"

"I don't know. I'll go ask him."

"Wait, Keith, wait!" Too late, I was yelling into empty space. Shit. This was not how I had planned it. Actually, I didn't have a plan, but I was hoping to develop one based on what Bremer said. Shit.

A few minutes later, he returned to the phone and said, "Okay, I have the answer, but before I tell you, I want to know why the fuck you're asking the question. I know you; there's got to be something fishy going on."

Dammit, this was not going the way I had hoped, but Bremer was way too smart for me to bullshit him or even to obfuscate the issue. "I'm sure you know what NARAL is. Well, we won the national account out of our D.C. office, and there's going to be a big story about it in the morning *New York Times*. Am I going to be fired or something worse?"

"You're one lucky fuck, Elgin. Keith is very pro-choice. Personally, I'd love to see something bad happen to you for springing shit like this on us, but since you said it was a big piece of business, I'll let it go. You better be sure it's profitable, though."

With those encouraging words, I lived to see another day.

The Issues & Advocacy practice grew both in size and as a source of immense pride to our employees. The group did some remarkable work for women's health issues, gay rights, and environmental concerns to name just a few of the causes that were embraced. The principle reason for the success was the brilliant people we had working on the accounts, but their secret sauce was positioning us at the intersection of Madison Avenue and Issues Street. Many of the larger D.C.-based public relations firms had more people and more experience in many of the required areas, but they lacked the strategic planning capabilities, the media science, and the art of persuasive humor and seduction found only at the best advertising agencies. On the other hand, we never competed against another advertising agency that could apply any of its core skills or art to the good fights, the struggles being waged for the environment, human rights, personal freedom, and responsibility.

"Boss, I really want to thank you."

"For what, Candy?"

"I want to thank you for providing me a way to stay in advertising and still go to Heaven."

A few years later, Laurie, our creative director walked into my office with a sad look on her face. Reluctantly, I asked whether she was going to quit.

"No, no, and don't take this wrong because I love when my work helps sell hamburgers and cruise beds, but being able to do work that helps make our world a better place has changed my life. Thank you for giving me that opportunity."

As she turned to walk out of my office, I couldn't help notice the tears in her eyes. It made me feel good that I had some employees who didn't live exclusively for honors or for pay. It moved me to know that much of their interest was not just in taking and holding, but in doing and giving.

59.

THREE OF MY HEROES

I've been fortunate enough to be associated with three advertising legends: David Ogilvy, Bill Bernbach, and Keith Reinhard. I studied Ogilvy in college and became even more of a fan as a young ad guy at Cole & Weber after it was sold to Ogilvy & Mather. Although I never had a chance to meet David, I learned a lot from his disciples and "Magic Lantern" series. All Ogilvy employees were required to watch slide and film presentations of David's Magic Lantern, which revealed all the principles, techniques, and takeaways the agency had discovered through its advertising campaigns. I'm not sure whether any of that is still mandatory, but it should be.

Ogilvy firmly believed that the function of advertising is to sell, and that successful advertising for any product is based on information about its consumer. He claimed his copy was written to sell products, and he followed these basic rules of advertising: research and position the product, develop a brand image, and have a big idea. He advocated passionately for striking photographs, lengthy, pellucid headlines, and lengthier, fact-crammed text blocks beneath. "Every advertisement is part of the long-term investment in the personality of the brand," he espoused. One of my favorites is from 1957: "At sixty miles an hour, the loudest noise in this new Rolls-Royce comes from the electric clock." David claimed that on a "peppercorn budget sales went up dramatically because of the wit and wisdom of that ad." Another favorite was the ad series that ran for twenty-five years, featuring a guy with an eye-patch selling Hathaway shirts.

My favorite story about David Ogilvy has to do with one of his new business presentations. I don't know whether the story is fact or fiction, and it doesn't really matter. His reputed action became one of the basic principles of our business philosophy.

As the story goes, while his agency was still quite young, it was invited to pitch a tourism account. When it was the agency's turn, the team was shown into a large room with a raised dais on which sat a long table and ten stern-faced people. After exchanging introductions, the Minister of Tourism opened the meeting by explaining that the agency would be given forty-five minutes to state its case. At the end of the allotted time, the minister would ring a little bell. He asked whether Ogilvy had any questions.

"I have but one question," said Ogilvy. "Who will have approval authority for the work we do on your behalf?"

The Minister of Tourism looked first to his left, then to his right; then looking Ogilvy in the eye, he said, "Why, these ten gentlemen you see sitting before you."

"Please be kind enough to ring the little bell now, Minister," said Ogilvy as he and his team gathered their materials and politely exited the room.

I also like the fact that David was able to make enough in the agency business that he bought a castle in France with thirty-seven bedrooms and six dungeons as his retirement villa.

• • • •

Another industry giant who had significant influence on my career was Bill Bernbach. It was virtually impossible to be an agency person in the '70s and '80s and not know about Bill and Doyle Dane Bernbach. Even today, he is remembered by many as the Father of Modern Day Advertising.

Bernbach was born in the Bronx in 1911, attended New York University, and graduated in 1932 with a major in English and minors in philosophy, business administration, and music. The Great Depression made it nearly impossible to find employment, but through a family connection, he got a job in the mailroom of a distillery. His skill with words, combined with his natural ambition, shone through in his first year with an ad he wrote, which got him a promotion to the ad department. Although his goal was to work at an ad agency, much of America at the time was anti-Semitic. Many Jews found it difficult to enter the mainstream advertising community, since clients often refused to have them working on their accounts. After several years on the client side and two years in the service during World War II, Bernbach joined Grey Advertising and ultimately became its creative director.

In 1949, Bernbach, along with eleven of his fellow Jewish staffers, opened Doyle Dane Bernbach. It took the famed agency ten years before being recognized for creating advertising that embodied the creative revolution of the 1960s.

Bernbach never considered breeding, ethnicity, or race; he only wanted talent. The agency's first clients were all Jewish: Levy's, Orbach's, El Al, and VW. The work was brilliant and appealed to the masses. One of the reasons was his revolutionary idea to pair art directors with copywriters. Up to that time, they were segregated by departments and disciplines. At DDB, art directors contributed headlines and copywriters began thinking visually, combining to create a superior output. The competition to work on accounts and develop even better ads and campaigns pushed the bar to never-before-reached levels. Bernbach became, without question, the most important and influential figure in the history of modern advertising. He literally changed the face of advertising, and almost every agency today relies on the ideas and structure that he provided throughout his career. He died in 1982, one year after Elgin Syferd began. Years later, Bob Kuperman, one of his earliest partners, gave me a rectangular frame containing several handwritten pages of notes by Bill. My favorite:

Client: I feel compelled to make a suggestion for that ad.

Me: You must resist that temptation.

Damn, I wish I could have met him.

• • • •

Another industry giant, and the one who had the most influence on me, was Keith Reinhard. Historians may never regard Keith as highly as David and Bill, but I do. Obviously, I'm influenced by the fact that not only did I know him, but he was my boss and a friend. Those factors aside, I believe him to be one of our industry's greatest visionaries.

Keith grew up in rural Indiana, loving advertising and wanting to be on the art side of the agency business. He ended up instead as one of the most awarded copywriters of his time. But Keith was destined for much more than writing ads. At Needham Harper & Steers he led the pitch to win the McDonald's account. His campaign and the line he wrote, "You Deserve a Break Today," redefined the eating-out category. Some of the McDonaldland characters were his inspirations. He also penned "Like a Good Neighbor" for State Farm, led the Anheuser-Busch win in the early '80s, and helped guide Super Bowl winning spots for Bud and Bud Light year after year.

Keith once gave me advice concerning the hiring of a creative director: *"In most cases, the more creative the person, the worse they are as businesspeople. The opposite also seems to be true."* While I've found this to be generally true, it definitely wasn't the case for this multi-talented, multi-faceted man. As CEO of Needham Harper & Steers, he went on to become one of the founders of Omnicom, one of the world's largest holding companies of advertising agencies and marketing services firms. If you want the particulars of Omnicom, go look them up. I'll not belabor the details further than to tell you that part of the deal was the merging of Doyle Dane Bernbach with Needham Harper & Steers resulting in DDB Needham Worldwide with Keith as the founding CEO.

I've heard that even though Keith's roots were with Needham, he wanted the name of the merged entity to be DDB. If he had won that battle, it would have made one part of our post-merger a little less cumbersome, which I'll mention a little later.

Although both the DDB and Needham agencies were well-known globally, the combined entity was not. In fact, the first several years after the 1986 merger was a struggle of cultures. Keith referred to the new company as a "confederacy of piracies."

In any event, the brand Elgin Syferd had far more equity in our market than DDB Needham Worldwide when we sold to them in 1989. Keith left the decision of what to call ourselves up to us. We decided that slow and steady would be the best strategy. The "new firm" was introduced to the world on November 12 of that year as:

Elgin Syferd

A DDB Needham Worldwide Company

A year or so later, we took the next evolutionary step. DDB Needham Worldwide was still not top of mind for most folks, but the brand had been emerging nationally thanks to some breakthrough work for Bud Light. The next step in our evolution was to stop whispering the last part of our name so we became:

Elgin Syferd/DDB Needham Worldwide

The combined name may have looked cumbersome in print, but it was even worse when spoken. That was never more realized than when our wonderful receptionist of twenty-plus years, Debbie Patton, came into my office laughing, saying our new name was so cumbersome it came out with the familiar: "Elgin Syferd" then, with a slight hesitation continued with, "DeeDee Beneedum." Since then, several people had been responding with, "Hello, DeeDee. May I speak with…?" Eventually, the company dropped "Needham," which helped a bit. No one called her DeeDeeBee.

After Dave retired at the end of 1994, we became:

Elgin DDB

And Debbie was happy once again.

DDB Worldwide had 204 offices in ninety-eight countries. To be honest, at that time I didn't know there were that many countries in the entire world. Many of these offices, like our own, had been purchased by either DDB or Needham Harper Steers. Like ours, the vast majority of those offices kept all or part of their original identity as their "first names." A few of the examples in addition to ourselves were Palmer/Jarvis DDB (Canada), BMP DDB (London), Tandem DDB (Spain), Olympic DDB (Greece), DM9 DDB (Sao Paulo). So these offices were known not only in their own countries but globally because of award shows and stories in trade journals as Palmer/Jarvis, BMP, Tandem, Olympic, DM9, and Elgin, to name just a very few examples. The common belief within our company was that dual branding was a good thing; you know, like the McDonald's famous philosophy of "Think global, act local."

About every eighteen months, DDB held a worldwide management conference. Most of the 200 offices were represented with anywhere from one to a half-dozen of their top management people. If you've attended big conferences, you know that only about 10 percent of the value earned comes from pronouncements from the pulpit; the rest comes from employees networking with other employees. Although attendance at the conference was not mandatory, since the conferences were convened at places such as Bermuda, Monte Carlo, and Marbella, it was always a packed house.

At one particular meeting, part of Keith's sermon from the mount touched on DDB's recent lack of success in winning a lead position on several of the larger global brands. I remember him saying, "Actually, I understand why many global companies question placing their brands in the hands of a company that can't even clearly articulate its own brand. When global companies hire McCann, for example, they are comfortable believing that McCann knows enough about branding to use the same identity at every one of its offices worldwide. As you know, agencies traditionally go by their first names. Because of our unique history and culture, we come in at least fifty flavors around the world. If we are truly to become a global force, our first name must be DDB wherever we have a presence." With that, Keith paused. Complete silence enveloped the mammoth auditorium. He slowly looked at the audience from left to right and back to the center.

What he had just said made complete sense to me. Since we had sold to DDB, the global company had been winning more and more business and sweeping the award shows. In other words, the DDB brand was becoming well-known not just to the trade but to the world. I was proud to tell a new business prospect that "We at DDB" are responsible for the brilliant advertising seen daily for Bud Light, Budweiser, Volkswagen, State Farm, and many more. I was starting to take more professional pride in our last name than my own.

Without really thinking much about it, I found myself standing and shouting out, "Keith, I hear you. I'm going to drop the Elgin from our name as soon as we get back to the office!"

Keith smiled and said, "Thank you, Ron," as silence once again enveloped the room.

I thought every president of every DDB office with a different first name would leap to his feet with the same pledge. Nothing, nada, zilch. I was the only one standing.

Later, I got a lot of "suck ass" comments from my buddies with different first names, but I didn't care because I believed it was the right thing to do. I did come to realize, however, that it had been easier for me because it was my name I had volunteered to drop. Most presidents had inherited the names of their agencies and didn't feel comfortable making the decision on their own at that moment.

After a year with no other office volunteering to change its name, finally an edict was issued. I thought at the time about a quote from D.H. Lawrence:

> I don't like your miserable lonely single "front name." It is so limited, so meager; it has no versatility; it is weighted down with the sense of responsibility; it is worn threadbare with much use; it is as bad as having only one jacket and one hat; it is like having only one relation, one blood relation, in the world. Never set a child afloat on the flat sea of life with only one sail to catch the wind.

In other words, a "family" name is so much more inclusive for a company. I know I'm a traditionalist, but I seriously doubt the long-term value in trendy or goofy made-up names. Naming a daughter Chardonnay may seem a cool thing for the parents toasting a newborn, but it may not be right when she's older and running for the Senate. Try as I may, I can think of only a few big-time agencies with little-time names.

60.

NEVER SAY DIE

"Ron, this is Dick Rogers. The New York office just received an inquiry from a new business prospect. I don't have the specifics, but it's something called Exclusive Resorts. Ever hear of them?"

"No. Where are they headquartered?"

"Denver. They're looking for a national agency. Cleve says they have at least a million bucks to spend. He said they were looking for a shop that could do both advertising and direct. He got the impression that all we had to do to get the business was to show up and ask for it. Both the New York and Chicago offices are now fighting to go after it. I'm thinking that because of your upscale cruise experience as well as your great knowledge of direct response, Seattle deserves the call. Interested?"

"Absolutely! We're all over it, Dick! Thanks!"

Turns out, Exclusive Resorts wasn't exactly a hotel/resort. Instead, it was one of the world's foremost private clubs for luxury vacations. An orchestrator of once in a lifetime experiences all around the globe, it claimed to combine stunning luxury villas, customized journeys to far-off places, immersive cultural experiences, and access to elite private clubs into a single seamless membership. And all for only an initial investment of about a half-million dollars each! Kind of like a very exclusive golf club membership. We figured if the idea was good enough for Steve Case of AOL/Time Warner fame to be a significant investor (he eventually bought the whole company), it was good enough for us.

Our first contact with the company was a delightful young woman with not a lot of experience but tons of personality. She was not off-put with the idea of Seattle handling her business and, in fact, liked the idea that we were the closest DDB office. She was very open and provided good background material.

"We're so excited to be able to work with you. When do you suggest our team come to Denver to get started?" I asked.

After a few uncomfortable moments of silence, she said, "Yes, we're excited as well that you'd like to be one of the five agencies in our finals next month. You're welcome to bring as many team members as you'd like to the briefing next Tuesday—at your expense, of course."

Shit. If it seems too good to be true, you can be pretty damn sure it probably is.

After a little more probing, we discovered Exclusive Resorts had scheduled briefings over two days, and we were the last. In a new business competition, being last is neither good nor bad. I've always been ambivalent about when you present or meet with a prospective client during a competition. Some say it's best to be first because you then set the standard. Others say the last is best because it enables you to outshine the previous competitors. It's all bullshit, of course. If you're the best, you can be in the middle and still win. If you're not the best, you're going to lose irrespective of positioning.

Five people from our agency showed up for the briefing. One person could have easily gathered the information, but agencies believe in overkill when it comes to showing the prospect that they care. We came away with only a scant amount more of company intelligence than we had gathered on our own, but with a whole lot more enthusiasm for winning the business based on the terrific people we met. That along with greed fueled our efforts for the next few weeks.

The original team of five packed up our multimedia presentation and headed to Denver for the shootout. We had scoped out the presentation room on our previous visit and had coordinated our equipment needs with the hotel staff over the phone.

When we arrived, the hotel staff assured us our materials would be placed in the presentation room along with the electronic equipment and the room would be ready first thing in the morning. With that, we went out for a quick bite, an early sleep, and a promise to meet at 7 a.m. for a final rehearsal. The pitch was scheduled for 9 a.m.

"What the hell is this?" I asked no one in particular. "This room is occupied, and it's not Exclusive Resorts' name on the door."

After a bit of nervous scrambling, we found a hotel person who told us that our presentation had been moved to a different room, which turned out to be the mammoth Grand fucking Ballroom!

"This can't be," I shouted at the hotel event coordinator. "There won't be more than twenty people total and this room is big enough for 200!"

"Actually, we can seat 250," she proudly replied.

"The way you have it set up, everyone will have to have a microphone or bullhorn to talk with one another!"

"We can provide those," she proudly replied.

We immediately set about reconfiguring the room. Everything was moved to a corner. We couldn't do anything about the ceiling height, but we made the rest as cozy as possible. At the same time that we got everything rearranged, members of the client team started arriving. Fortunately, we were already well-rehearsed.

The presentation went well, despite the circumstances. We were told to expect a decision within a week. Our flight wasn't until later that afternoon, so we checked out and headed to the airport to drink a late breakfast.

The call came a week later, and it wasn't good. The CMO said all the right things to make a loser feel as though he were a hairsbreadth from winning. They had awarded the business to a direct response firm with offices in New York and Los Angeles. I knew the agency and knew the client had made a bad choice. Not because of the agency per se, but because of the concentration of its offering which was light on strategy and heavy on tactical execution.

Rather than badmouth or argue, I told him how much we enjoyed getting to know Exclusive Resorts and its product, and I asked whether I could stay in touch. He seemed relieved that I didn't react like an asshole and encouraged me to do so.

It took me a couple of weeks to get over being an asshole about their stupid decision before calling to find out how things were going with Exclusive Resorts' new relationship.

"Well, it's early yet," he replied. "I'm sure it's going to be fine."

Those words were music to my ears. Not "great" or even "good" but "fine." That plus "It's early yet" was all I needed to hear. I was on the phone with him every few days for the next two weeks. Listening, sympathizing, being a friend.

Finally, I said, "Michael, you hired the wrong agency. They're approaching the problem all wrong. They may be great at direct response tactics, but they need to start at the beginning, not at the execution stage. You need someone to help articulate the brand. You need to cut them loose and hire us. At the bare minimum, you need to hire us at least to help put you on the right path."

"Thanks for the offer, Ron, but I still think we can make it work."

I called the next week with the same request.

I called the following week with the same request. This time he was even less positive about their relationship. I asked whether he was free for dinner the following evening. He was. I jumped on a flight to Denver the next day.

Barely into our first course, I said, "Michael, you're being too nice. You've given your new agency plenty of time, but they're still not getting it. You know in your gut I'm right. Make it right. Either let us handle the branding part of this assignment for them or fire their asses and give the whole account to us."

By the end of the dinner, he agreed to sever the relationship with the agency that had beaten us less than two months earlier. We shook hands and he drove me to the airport. Elgin DDB became its agency of record the following week. Within a few weeks after that, together we had created a brilliant position, a new logo, and marketing materials that helped Exclusive Resorts begin acquiring more qualified leads at a fraction of what it had been paying.

We had a great run with Exclusive Resorts. The people with whom we worked were smart and fun. The company was also one of the most appreciative clients ever. Without our knowledge, for our one-year anniversary, it created and placed full page ads in *Advertising Age* and *Adweek*, praising our work and its valued relationship with us. It's possible that other clients with other agencies may have done something similar, but none of us had ever heard of it. Hell, even if it had been done for lots of others, it still made us feel like a million bucks.

The lesson reinforced my belief that it pays not to be a sore loser. And to understand that when a client says the competition was close, sometimes the client actually means it. If you truly are passionate for a piece of business, don't forget that not all marriages last.

Most importantly, remember that you are never defeated until you give up trying.

61.

THE HOUSE

My wife and I had a house built on an acre of land with 150 feet of Puget Sound waterfront. Bonnie called it, "The house Ron's ego built." I countered with, "I could never squeeze my ego into only 10,000 feet."

In all seriousness, growing up in a tiny place in a housing project and walking past my schoolmates' "mansions"—probably two to three thousand-foot ramblers—gave me a lifelong passion for a big house of my own. I admit, ego played a big part, but having such a house was also me telling me that I had made a dream come true.

The architects called the main level "the public space" because we designed the Great Room for entertaining. The room is about 2,000 square feet, with four sets of French doors, leading to a large terrace overlooking the Sound. I delighted in hosting countless cultural, charitable, and civic events for thousands of people over the years. To give you some examples: a sit down dinner for 150 of one client's customers; routinely hosted cocktail parties for 300-plus people; an intimate event for fifty people, who donated $5,000 per couple to the Seattle Repertory Theater to have wine and hors d'oeuvres with Meryl Streep and Wendy Wasserstein—they were both absolutely delightful, by the way.

What's the value of dreams if you don't share them? Or, as Bonnie admonishes, "flaunt them"?

I've already told you that Dave and I were big believers in the Christmas parties. With this house, it became possible to have a party for the whole agency. When I announced at a company meeting that the upcoming holiday party was going to be at our house rather than the office, the employees were so excited that they voted to make it a semi-formal event. I was excited because I thought perhaps they might drink less when they dressed up. I should have known better.

The party was amazing. About 150 employees and significant others were thoroughly enjoying the beer, wine, cocktails, and catered food. Several hours into the festivities, however, one of my senior people approached me and in hushed tones told me that one of our art directors was banging his girlfriend on a counter in one of the downstairs bathrooms.

"What did you just say?" asked a visibly annoyed Bonnie. My wife has remarkable hearing.

"Sorry, Bonnie; I didn't see you standing way over there," the employee stammered. "Well, I walked into one of the unlocked bathrooms downstairs and found Paul and his girlfriend having sex on the counter. I excused myself and left."

"Ron, I'm going to kill you," hissed Bonnie, "right after you burn down this entire house."

She neither killed me on the spot nor forced me to torch the house later. She did have me spend several hours the next day with Lysol and bleach. It was months before Bonnie would even walk into that bathroom.

What happened to Paul? Well, even though he was a very talented guy (with great taste in women), after a few expense account mishaps and three wage garnishments, we decided it would be best if he moved on. Bonnie said he couldn't move far enough.

When it came time for the next holiday party, Bonnie was hesitant, but since Paul had been the only one to have screwed the pooch so to speak, she agreed to give it another chance.

As before, it was a dress up party, and everyone looked and acted great. Or so we thought throughout the evening. During all large functions, Bonnie would routinely lock off the bedroom suite on the third level, which prohibited anyone from invading our most private of rooms. She wasn't taking into account, however, the creativity and mischievousness of our people.

On the third floor, we also have a study, gym, laundry, dressing rooms, and a kitchenette. There's also a wrap-around terrace with doors and windows to many of the rooms. One or more of our creative pranksters figured out how to get into our locked bedroom through an unlocked terrace window.

"Oh, my God!" Bonnie shrieked upon entering the locked bedroom after the guests had departed. "Someone got in here and had sex in our bed!"

It was very late. I'd had enough drinks, and I didn't have enough sense, so I started laughing.

"What the hell are you laughing at?" Bonnie demanded. "I don't think it's a bit funny that some of your perverted employees broke into our bedroom and had sex in our bed!"

"Honey, I'm sure no one had sex in our bed. One of my people just saw a challenge and wanted me to know they creatively overcame it."

"Well, you can sleep in this bed, but I'm not. And I want a new bed and everything that goes with it before I'm coming back into this room! And no more parties in our house for your weird fucking employees!"

And that's the story of why we had only two Christmas parties at our new house.

62.

PROFIT PLAN BEATINGS

Each October, all of DDB's offices had to prepare, submit, and present their annual plans. The domestic offices presented theirs at the global headquarters in New York City. Even though the company leaders were uniformly good guys and relatively casual, these meetings were stressful for the presenters. It was kind of like wanting to shine for your parents.

The written plan mandated things like how your office ranked in the market with respect to size, reputation, and number of creative awards, and if you didn't score in the top three, you had to be specific as to how you were going to get there. If your shop was already in the top three, you had to detail how and when you were going to become number one. The report asked you to list: key employees and what was being done to further their careers; the strength and weaknesses of our main competitors; potential acquisitions for us; problems and opportunities with existing accounts; a new business plan; creative examples; and financial forecasts. All that had to be squeezed into fourteen pages, but the company expected an in-person elaboration at the two- to three-hour meeting. I always viewed this exercise as a lot of hard work but never a chore. In fact, I recommend everyone go through a similar process for their own companies.

As I mentioned, the plan had to be presented in person. In the early years, management allowed each agency to script its own presentation as long as all areas were addressed and enough time was allowed for questions. On management's side of the table sat the company's CEO, CFO, executive creative director, and a few North American executives. In addition to myself, I alternated our top people in order to give as many as possible exposure and still stay within our limit of three to four.

I liked starting the meeting with examples of our creative product for a couple of reasons. First, we were doing kick-ass work and I was very proud. Second, most of those in the room were ad people who loved looking at great ads. It was a good mood-setter. After that, there was always good discussion about how to improve in the various areas. The last area was the financial forecast. Even though our performance had always met or exceeded the previous year, there was always a polite request to do better. A few weeks later, we'd receive our financial target, which, as expected, would be higher than we had forecast.

As the years wore on, the world's financial picture changed and the agency business changed with it. Gone was the commission system, replaced with various fee structures. Also cast aside was the ability of the marketing departments to authorize compensation agreements. Enter the dreaded procurement people. Sadly, our industry went along with it. Of course, agencies could have resisted, but that would have resulted in even faster deaths. We allowed a commoditization of our industry, which for the most part continues today.

Stockholders were screaming for higher dividends and share value, so the holding companies were yelling at their operating units for higher profits. Agencies and clients were in constant conflict over profitability, and of course, he who controls the purse strings usually rules the day. But that didn't stop DDB from demanding higher returns from us in order to protect its bosses from those damn stockholders. It was a vicious cycle that took its toll.

So the frequency of our meetings increased along with the increasing dollar demands. The holding companies became so nervous they began requiring twice a year reports, then quarterly. It finally got so bad that at the end of each quarter, we had to submit weekly updates. At the end of the year, there were sometimes daily phone reports.

These financial demands changed the nature of our Annual Plan Meetings as well. They were renamed "Profit Plan Meetings," but most of us called them "Profit Plan Beatings." In any case, management formalized the structure around the 3 P's—People, Product, and Profit. The concept is valid. Hire, train, and retain the best people. Allow them to create the best product. Profit will be the inevitable result. I gave management an A for effort, and perhaps in a utopian environment, it would have worked.

The emphasis and, therefore, the structure of the Profit Plan Beatings evolved. No longer did we have time to dazzle our bosses with the work. The beatings now started and ended with financial discussions. The senior executives responsible for the company's creative product and people development were superfluous to the beatings. Now we needed only calculator heads. However, because the calculator heads were nice guys and at least pretended to like me, I was allowed to begin with my positive outlook for the upcoming year. They listened with feigned attention until I stopped babbling and turned the meeting over to our CFO. Then the meeting officially started and the beatings began.

63.

PRO-BONO WORK

Some of the best work done by any agency is its pro-bono work for non-profit organizations. It's much easier to create an emotional bond when advocating a cure for cancer in kids than one promoting a hemorrhoid ointment. Not only that, most charitable organizations are so grateful for the free help that they are usually more willing to be risk-takers. Perhaps it's because they don't have to justify the cost (none) to their bean counters.

Some of our best work over the years was for Big Brothers ("It'll make a man out of him and a boy out of you"), Pacific Northwest Ballet ("Guts and Grace"), and many others, but my all-time favorite was the body of work we created for the Martin Luther King, Jr. day.

Frank Blethen, publisher of *The Seattle Times*, decided not enough was being done to promote the true meaning of the holiday. Research showed that a majority of people thought of it either as an apology to African Americans for years of oppression or a day off for them rather than a celebration of equality for all. Frank enlisted our help in strategic development and creative execution, promising space in his papers and help in getting other media outlets to donate on and around January 17th. *The Seattle Times* was a wonderful partner for ten years, but that was the pre-determined time limit of its commitment. Research showed that our combined effort had made a difference in public attitude, but there was still work to be done, so we continued the campaign on our own. We became both the client and the agency. Our work grew from merely really good to brilliant. Cannes Gold, brilliant.

Every campaign was my new favorite, but there were two that I vividly recall. The first was a radio spot featuring a woman in a rather droll voice telling a story about a guy who walks into a diner and orders a turkey sandwich and a cup of coffee at the counter. The guy sitting next to him pours sugar on his head and spits in his coffee while the rest of the customers cheer. The police arrive and arrest the man with sugar on his head for disturbing the peace. There was never a mention of the arrested man's race, religion, or sexual orientation. The man was simply different from the other customers. The other was a compilation of old footage featuring Dr. King's speeches and marches. The incredibly moving script was penned by one of our best writers, Pamela Mason-Davies. The spot brought tears to eyes and gold to our award collection.

We halted the campaign after an additional eight years, eighteen years in total, not because the work of Dr. King was done, or we ran out of ideas, or we had stopped liking awards. We stopped because we couldn't afford to spend our diminishing resources on non-revenue producing ventures. Quite simply, we had to work smarter, harder, and longer to make our numbers. As much as we wanted to use our talents to better the world, we simply didn't have the time or energy to do both. I learned to envy the few big public agencies that can do pro-bono work and still make their required numbers and the privately owned little and mid-size guys who get to set their own numbers.

64.

KEITH THE FUTURIST

Keith Reinhard is as much an icon to many of the McDonald's corporate people and franchise owners as he is to those of us in the ad biz. Keith was responsible for the iconic line "You Deserve a Break Today," the jingle "Two all-beef patties…," several of the McDonaldland characters, and much more. He readily agreed to speak at one of our McDonald's co-op meetings shortly after selling our company. After the meeting, we had time to visit a few of the restaurants to spread the love.

During the drive, Keith and I talked about the state of our industry.

"Ron, hundreds, maybe thousands of years from now, historians will look back at the seventeenth to twenty-first centuries as an aberration in the way humans buy and sell products and services from one another. From the dawn of time, when a caveman wanted to trade a hunk of meat for a bushel of greens, he would negotiate face-to-face. If we think of advertising as a way of negotiating but on a larger scale, we might say advertising began when a man brought his crops to market and shouted his wares. He was effectively delivering a "commercial" or attempting to increase his chances to make his sale by broadcasting to more than one person at a time. Long before printing was invented, traders would make signs on walls to call attention to their products. And merchants hung out signs with pictures of boots, or gloves, or whatever they sold, as a way of "advertising" their businesses. The town crier was also used to advertise in olden times.

"But advertising as we know it, however, really began with the invention of printing. With the coming of the newspaper, advertising developed from just being an announcement about something to being an argument and suggestion to entice people to buy the product. But the evolution of reaching more people also had the effect of less actual interaction between the seller and buyer. Next came magazines, then radio and television; sellers were delivering their messages to millions of potential buyers at once. But there was no interaction. It was one-way communication. No ability to negotiate. No direct way immediately to determine the strengths and weaknesses of the offer as it pertains to the buyers' interests. This is an aberration of human nature. It's inevitable that someday humans will return to face-to-face buying and selling."

"Wow. That's an incredible theory, Keith. How will that be possible?" I asked.

"I haven't the slightest idea, Ron," replied the greatest communications visionary I know.

Of course, this discussion took place before Al Gore invented the Internet. With today's technology in place, it's possible to see that by sometime tomorrow or the next day, Keith's prediction will become reality and advertisers will be able to negotiate a face-to-face sale the way the cavemen did.

65.

TIME TO PULL THE PLUG

"I'm not sure if you realize how selfish you are," said Bonnie.

"What are you talking about?" I replied.

"We nearly lost our only daughter to cancer and you continue to tell people you're going to die at your desk at a hundred years old."

"I'm sorry; I don't understand."

"You sure don't. I think you must have some sort of impulsive-compulsive disorder. When I can get you to take time to visit our daughter, her husband, and our only granddaughter, you're all in—you're a very loving, attentive grandfather. The problem is I can't get you to take time off. You're more married to your job than you are to your family. And you continue to say that's going to continue until you die. Don't you see how selfish that is?"

"Honey, it's true that I love my job. It's one of the biggest reasons besides luck that I've become successful. But it pales by comparison to my love for my family."

"Then prove it."

"How?"

"Retire."

"When?"

"Today."

"I can't just walk away from my people and what I've spent my whole career creating. How about if I start a transition now so we can retire in five years?"

"Okay," she said with almost a smile.

Shit, I should have said ten.

A few days later, I called my boss, Ken Kaess. I'd known Ken since selling to DDB. We became close friends when he was head of the L.A. office. When Reinhard neared retirement, he wisely moved Ken to head the New York office in order to mentor him as his own replacement. Ken was a great ad guy and one of the most charismatic leaders I'd ever met. I loved the guy.

"Ken, Bonnie says I have to retire."

"Okay, when?"

"She says in five years."

"Okay, call me in five years and we'll talk about it."

As I said, I loved the guy. I made the mistake, however, of telling Bonnie his exact words. Hey, I was proud that he didn't want to acknowledge me retiring. Pride can make people say and do stupid things.

"When are you going to announce your five-year plan to your staff?" she craftily inquired.

Bitch.

"I'll do it soon. I don't want to upset my staff or clients. I'll figure the right time."

"Oh, no, you don't. I know you. This will become a rolling five years. You're the one who said you needed a five-year transition. We're retiring five years from today. You need to start the transition by making the announcement to your staff and clients immediately."

"I can't just blurt something like that."

"Trust me, Ron; you're important but not *that* important. The world will be able to get along without you—especially in five years."

Our company has never been too formal. We try to be professional. Well, most of the time. But as soon as any of us tries to be too formal, the true culture guardians slap the shit out of the offender. Even our weekly management committee meetings were professional but not formal.

At the end of that week's meeting, I said, "I have a formal announcement I have to make."

A chorus of "Yeah, sure" and "What's so important that it has to be a formal announcement?" rang out.

"Seriously," I said. "I'm coming out of the closet."

The room was filled with looks of bewilderment, disbelief, and confusion.

"Bonnie has convinced me that I'm a closet retiree and I need to come clean with you about it."

Another chorus of "Yeah, sure" and "Bullshit" filled the room.

"No, it's true. We've decided that it's unfair to my family and to you for me to stick around for another thirty-five years, so I'm going to retire in five years."

This time, the chorus was singing tunes like "You were honestly considering thirty-five years? That's nuts" and "Five years? We can live with that." The real question on their minds was who was going to replace me.

We had evolved to a structure that wasn't perfect but seemed to be functioning fairly well. I was president and CEO, and reporting to me were seven managing partners. Not all had that exact title, but all seven functioned as such. We had a COO, CFO, executive creative director, and managing partners of advertising, public relations, issues & advocacy, and direct marketing. My job was to select the future CEO from that group.

If Syferd and Edmondson hadn't already retired from the company, either would have been a logical candidate. But they were both gone and there was no clear choice. All were outstanding leaders at the top of their games in their particular areas of expertise. Additionally, each was a strong contributor to our culture. I agonized over the decision for several weeks.

Although each of the seven candidates expressed a desire to be considered, I knew that some didn't really want the job.

A couple of them were looking at retiring around the same time as me, if not shortly after. I thought one or two might be so discipline specific as possibly to be unable to handle the balance our agency had finally achieved. I felt that one or two might be pushing their limits managing a company of two hundred. However, when comparing strengths, they were all pretty damn comparable.

Perhaps I was overly influenced by my background in advertising account management or the fact that the majority of income was derived from that group. Perhaps it was his diverse background before joining DDB or that he was the newest shiny object, but I selected the managing director of advertising, Chris Lloyd, to succeed me.

I called both Ken Kaess and Dick Rogers and told them of my decision. Ken laughed it off and said that it didn't matter whom I chose because he knew I'd never retire. Dick said that before I announced anything, he wanted to have dinner with Chris and me. Although I felt this was to be my decision and mine alone, realistically, I knew it shouldn't be. Besides, I loved Dick, and any chance to spend time with him was great for me.

A couple of weeks later, under the cover of darkness, Dick came to town. I picked him up at the airport and we met Chris at a private club called The Ruins. It was mid-week and the dark library room was mostly deserted. We had a pleasant conversation about a variety of topics, a fine dinner, and two bottles of wine from my cellar. I took Dick to his hotel and promised to pick him up early the next day for his flight back to Chicago. It was still dark the next morning when he climbed into my car.

"He's not the right guy, Ron."

"What do you mean, Dick? I thought you liked him."

"I do like him; I just don't think he's the right guy to carry on your legacy."

"So does that mean I can't name him president?"

"No, no. You can make him president. But when you went to the john, I told him he could put his hand on the wheel, but you would have control and would continue driving until you left the scene entirely."

My ego liked hearing that, but even then, little warning bells were ringing in my head. But I had the blessing from corporate to make the move.

As you'd expect, the only managing partner truly thrilled with my decision was Chris. On the surface, the other officers appeared at least to accept it.

Shortly after the announcement, I had Chris join me for our first "transition" meeting. On a whiteboard, I wrote on the left side the current date, below that "Ron, all powerful," and below that "Chris, wants to be." I then drew a five-year line to the right side of the board where I wrote "Chris, all powerful" and below that "Ron, used to be."

"Chris," I then said, "I'm sure you think you're ready now to take over my job, and you may be right. The problem is I'm not mentally or emotionally ready to give it up. I conceived, birthed, and raised this company. All of its employees, past and present, are my children or brothers and sisters. It's going to take every day of those five years for me to learn to walk away from it and them."

This proclamation proved to be even harder than I had imagined.

It started with the resignation of some of our most valued employees. None of them cited my decision regarding Chris as the reason for their departure, but when we lost people who had been with the company for ten, fifteen, even twenty years, it became painfully obvious. We were losing the people who had helped shape our culture. More importantly, people who were key to maintaining our culture.

Within the first year, we lost three of the managing partners, followed shortly by two more. Although these people had been consistently courted by other agencies throughout their careers with me, each had always rejected the offers. It was personally heartbreaking to see them leave, but I had to admit that professionally they were making the right decisions. At our company, there was only one job higher than theirs, and I had closed that door to them. But on the good side, each had accepted very prestigious and better-paying positions elsewhere. I was happy for them, but as I said, it broke my heart.

By the end of the second year, we started losing more long-term, mid-management employees. Although the exit interviews varied in most specifics, the one constant negative was that the place just wasn't the same.

Chris is very smart and extremely ambitious. I was trying to let him grow, but he was hampered by my tendency not to let go. I was a fucking mess.

"Ron," he finally told me, "I think it would be best if you no longer came to the management meetings."

"What the hell are you talking about, Chris?"

"Well, first of all, you always sit at the end of the table. That's where I need to sit. Second, I should be chairing the meetings instead of sitting in the audience. How am I going to learn to take over if you don't give me a chance?"

He had a point. Actually, he had a couple of points. We were a couple of years into the transition, and Chris had grown in responsibility but not in authority.

"Okay, how about a compromise. I'll still attend the meetings, but you'll sit at the head of the table and I'll acknowledge the fact that you're chairing them."

"It's a start," he said.

A few weeks later, he came into my office and said, "It's not working."

"What's not working?" I asked.

"You being in the management meetings. No matter what I say or do, everyone in the room looks first to you to see whether it has your approval. I can't begin to run the company if you don't allow it."

I knew he was right. I also knew I was right when I had predicted that it would be easier for Chris to take over than it would be for me to give up control. Instinctively, I also knew that Chris didn't want to inherit and run "Ron's agency." He wanted to change it enough that everyone would know that it was now his creation.

"Okay, we'll compromise," I said. "I'll stop attending the meetings, but you will discuss with me the agenda items beforehand. We'll hash it out here in private. That way I won't openly fuck you over by rescinding your decisions after the fact."

The company was changing in more ways than transition at the top. The economy was slumping. Clients were cutting back on budgets. There were more dogs in the fight for new business. Profits were shrinking. Raises were scarce. Bonuses disappeared. Morale was flagging.

"Chris, you need to get the team to crank up its new business efforts. The old adage 'If you're not growing, you're dying' is alive here. Our accounts are all shrinking, and some are even drying up or leaving at an unparalleled rate. I can't even remember the last big pitch. What is going on?"

"What do you mean?"

"Tell me about your new business efforts," I said. "What's in the pipeline? What disruptive measures are you taking? Who are targeting? What the hell's going on?"

"We're not currently talking to anyone, and we won't be until we figure out who we are."

"What the hell do you mean 'figure out who we are'? We know damn well who we are. We've been the same for the last twenty-seven years!"

"That's the problem, Ron."

Ouch. Perhaps he was right and the world had moved past our model.

"Okay, well hurry up and figure out who we should be before there's nothing left to save!"

The economy continued to shrivel. Our revenue continued to decline. Now it became our turn to say goodbye to employees. Morale was in the shitter.

"Chris, you have to stop trying to find the perfect answer to who we should be before it's too late. Pick a path and go with it. We have to start building back our revenue. We're fucking dying!"

"Ron, you don't understand how difficult this is. We want to shed the tired old model of just doing ads or PR programs. Or, even what used to be called "integration." We want to offer solutions to business problems. In fact, we've decided that we only want to work with clients who will give us their business problem and their budget and let us provide the solution."

"Well, that explains why we lost the pitch last week. The client wanted a direct marketing agency to help solve its direct marketing problem. I heard we went in with a broad, multi-discipline answer. The company narrowed the field to three DM agencies."

"That's my point exactly, Ron," Chris replied. "That company has a much bigger problem than can be solved by direct marketing alone."

"I don't disagree that in most cases business problems are best solved using a variety of communications disciplines, but I fear your approach will not win friends or business."

"How would you have done it, Ron?"

"The way we've done it forever! The way you keep pissing on. For the client seeking a direct solution, I would have jumped up and said, 'We're the best direct response agency in the fucking universe!' I would have gone in with our best direct people and best direct cases and won the business. Then I would have helped our direct people confirm the client's decision with work that worked within that specific discipline.

"Only after winning the client's trust and loyalty would I attempt to offer assistance in other areas. We built this agency with parts that can stand alone against any competitor as well as working together as one. I know there are clients out there who not only need but realize they want one-stop-shopping, but they're few and far between. A foot in the door is the way to go with the rest of them. Even if the relationship never goes beyond the use of one or two of our disciplines, it's our duty to provide the best possible solutions within those constraints."

"The world is changing, Ron, and we need to change with it."

"I still think you're wrong, but for Christ's sake, publish your manifesto or whatever you need to do and start bringing some new business in the door!"

"We're trying, but it's difficult because everyone has his own opinion on how it should be done."

"Chris, I know your style is to be a consensus leader, but it isn't working here. Lanterman is famous for saying that democracy is a fine form of government, but it takes too fucking long. He says benevolent dictatorship is the way to go. The older I get, the more I agree with his thinking. We have too many strong-willed and strongly opinionated people. You need to take charge."

"I am in charge, but I also value their opinions."

"Yes, you need to value their opinions, but you must also lead." I walked to the window of my office and pointed to the sports arenas to the south and the Space Needle to the north. "Follow this metaphor: right now, some people are saying, you'll find the solution you seek somewhere near the Space Needle, and others are saying it's in the opposite direction down by the stadiums. So here you sit paralyzed in the middle. The job of a leader is to make gut decisions based on the best information available. Get up and start them on a march in the direction about which you feel best. Some may piss and moan at first, but chances are they'll be happy at least to be moving. You can expect to make slight course corrections along the way, but the main thing is with each step, you're that much closer to your goal. Once in awhile, you may lead the company in the wrong direction, but you'll never know if you never do. And believe me, that is better than being stuck in the middle."

Our business continued to slide and the Profit Plan Beatings became ever more brutal. After one particularly bad one, Dick Rogers pulled me aside and said, "It's not working, Ron. You have to take back complete control of the company."

"I can't do that, Dick. If I do, Chris will leave. We're already thin on management, and if he leaves, I don't know what we'd do."

"How about postponing your retirement for a year or so? You could get the company back on track, and if Chris decides to leave, it will give us time to get a new leader in place."

"Dick, you know it was never my decision alone to retire. But now I have one foot out the door and Bonnie's pulling on the other. I don't have the balls to ask for more time. Why don't I give you her number so you can ask?" That ended that conversation.

Chris understood the seriousness of the situation and doubled his efforts to define the agency, marshal the forces, and move us forward. Unfortunately, our negative momentum and the terrible economy plagued us. I started to get weekly calls from Dick and now from Mark O'Brien, the CFO for North America, asking whether I had taken over control. Knowing the repercussions of that action, my standard reply was, "I'm sorry; you've dialed the wrong number. Let me give you Bonnie's number."

"Ron, this is Rogers. Give me Bonnie's number."

Whoa. These guys were now very serious. I told him I'd talk to Bonnie that evening and get back to him in the morning.

"Honey, the guys are putting a full court press on me to delay retirement for a couple of years. I keep telling them I can't do that because of my commitment to you. I'm only telling you now because Dick is threatening to call and ask you himself."

"I think you should tell him that you'll do it."

"What? I thought you wanted me to retire. Almost four years ago you called me a selfish asshole. We agreed on a five-year plan. What changed your mind?"

"If you'll recall, I said that you were being selfish and only thinking of yourself when you were telling everyone that you wanted to die at your desk at one hundred. I wanted us to be able to spend more time with our growing family in California. I had visions of an idyllic retirement."

"How has that changed? Why do you no longer care if we put off that idyllic retirement for another two years or so? I don't understand."

"Because over the past couple of years, you've turned into an even bigger asshole. What's happening to the agency is tearing you apart. You've always said that when you left the agency, you wanted people to ask, 'How can you possibly leave now? The company's never done better work, made more money, or had higher morale.' You said you'd smile and reply, 'That's the perfect time.' None of what you wanted is true right now, and it's turned you into someone with whom I have no desire to go dancing off into the sunset. Take back control of the agency; get it back to the way it used to be. Most importantly, learn to live with whatever happens so you can become at least a semblance of the guy I married instead of this asshole you've become."

Wow.

"Okay, Dick. You don't have to call Bonnie. You don't need to hear the reasons, but she's agreed for me to stay for a couple of more years."

My decision to postpone retirement again was met with relief by most but not by all. Chris moved on.

I don't know whether it was inflated ego, eternal optimism, or stupidity, but I actually believed I could turn around the sinking ship. And perhaps if I had the original team back plus the ability to boost the national, regional, and local economies, I could have been successful. But I didn't and I couldn't.

At the next Profit Plan Beating, I bemoaned the fact that with Chris gone, the only senior management person left was our CFO, Brenda Massey. Brenda was brilliant and a great, helpful partner, but that still left me directly in charge of account management, creative, production, traffic, digital, PR, new biz, and several of our major accounts. In all, I had about a dozen too many direct reports.

Keith Bremer, our brilliant Worldwide COO/CFO, who is eminently capable of simultaneously managing about two hundred direct reports, showed no sympathy. "Look at it this way, Ron; you're driving a car on the interstate, and because of your lack of attention, it runs out of oil, water, transmission fluid, and grease, and therefore, it needs a complete overhaul, including replacing all the major parts. There's no time to pull over and stop for repairs. Your fucking job is to keep your foot on the gas, keep one hand on the steering wheel, and use the other to fix that broken piece of shit. And, by the way, you're going too slow—speed the fuck up!"

With that helpful guidance, we were able to stabilize our revenues and even modestly grow our profitability, but I could see this was a job for a shining knight on a gallant steed rather than a battle-scarred goat riding a turtle. So I set out to find the knight. But this time, I asked the help of our intergalactic agency.

As I said before, DDB has about two hundred offices around the world. In size, the Seattle office ranked in the top third. With the help of the corporate office, we put out the word that DDB Seattle was looking for my replacement. We were looking for the top person in a mid-size agency or a number two in a larger shop. Our agency still had a good reputation, and we were, after all, located in the coolest city in America.

We received interest from people as close as California and as far away as South Africa. I'll put these people in two broad categories: those interested in the position but not qualified, and those qualified but who became uninterested.

The first category of people is self-explanatory; the second is more complicated. I'll give you a couple of examples.

"Ron, I was given your name by Mark O'Brian at Corporate. He told me you were planning to retire soon and are looking for your replacement. I've heard good things about the work you do and may be interested in moving my family to the U.S. Could you send me samples of your current work—especially your newest TV spots?"

"Thanks. Mark told me good things about you and to expect your call. I'm surprised we didn't meet at one of the worldwide meetings. As to a reel of our current spots, we haven't done any TV work for at least a couple of years. The work is stellar but dated."

"How can you be an ad agency without a current reel?"

"Actually, we've never been just an ad agency, and for the past several years, most of our work was being done in below-the-line areas."

Similar conversations were held with at least a half-dozen candidates. Of course, more than just advertising is being done at other DDB offices, but when I started talking about our successes in public relations, direct marketing, issues & advocacy work, they all lost interest.

On the other hand, when I said the other category of candidates wasn't qualified, it was generally because of their lack of experience in the other communications disciplines. Most could probably learn, but none were ready to step in and lead.

After several months of futility, Mark called and said they had resolved the quandary.

"Great. Are you coming out to run the shop?"

"Don't be an asshole, Ron. We've decided that the Seattle office needs to be more like the rest of our domestic offices."

"I don't understand."

"The office needs to concentrate on the basics. You need to get rid of the PR and direct people and their clients. Anything that isn't mostly advertising. We have several qualified people who will be able to step right in and run the shop without having to contend with all your 'below the line' disciplines."

"How am I supposed to do that?"

"You'll figure something out."

66.

THE END OF MY STORY

"Mark, I can't simply get rid of my PR, direct, and issues people and their clients. We're talking family members and close friends, both at the agency and client-side. If you have no objections, I'd like to work with the clients to find homes for them in other shops."

"How would that help your people?"

"Simple. The other shops will have to agree to hire the people who work on the business they're inheriting. The promise to the clients is they'll be able to continue working with the same team as before the transition."

"Sounds like a great solution. You have my blessing."

"Thanks. Now I'll tell you the probable downside. This agency was created under the premise that most clients' problems and opportunities can be best addressed by using a variety of communications disciplines. Our clients now take that way of working for granted. We do have employees who are specialists, but they are so used to working in the same building, sometimes on the same floor with specialists from other disciplines, that I fear they're not going to want to work in a more limited environment."

"It's a gamble we're going to have to take, Ron."

In the long run, DDB's decision to buy Elgin Syferd was a gamble that paid them back many times over both financially and through the contribution our work did to enhance their brand further. Without me at the helm setting a new vision and strategy that I could believe in and support, the gamble to change our direction proved to be fatal. During the final months of operation, we helped every one of our clients find new homes. Most importantly, although we suffered through several layoffs in the years leading up to closure, in the end, we were able to find homes for all the remaining employees. And it finally enabled me to retire from the company I had lived with from womb to tomb

A month before closing our shop, a guy who had recently started his own agency confessed to me that he was several months into it and was still having sleepless nights. Before heading to work in the morning, he was nearly physically ill with nervousness and worry. He asked how long it would take before he had his life back.

"Well, let's see," I replied. "I recall throwing up every morning for at least a year. I gradually got it down to once a week or so. Then it was only when we lost business, a pitch, or a good employee. Of course, it was an automatic when a campaign didn't meet its objectives. Once in awhile, it happened when I thought a client might be looking around for another agency or when we didn't make our financial projections. Come to think of it, I guess throwing up is just part of owning your own agency. As to getting back to a normal sleep pattern, forget it."

"That's incredibly depressing," he said. "Didn't that make you want to shoot yourself or at least get out of the business years ago?"

"Actually, depression comes from having a low level of serotonin in the brain. You can relieve severe symptoms by taking anti-depressant drugs to mellow you out and maintain balance. The problem with maintaining balance is that it means you also reduce the level of your highs as well as the lows. I learned to live with the depths of depression because *this business provided me with highs so incredible I needed those lows for balance*."

On December 31, 2011, I officially retired from the company I had helped birth and raise from infancy until it was only a memory that I'll always cherish with pride. Today, there are very few agencies in the Pacific Northwest that aren't either owned by, run by, or employing our graduates. I consider that to be a worthy legacy.

Reflecting on the tens of thousands of decisions made in my career, I readily admit that some were undoubtedly wrong for the business. I consider those to be learning experiences from which I was able to make better future decisions. But if God gave me the opportunity to live my life over, there are many decisions I'd change in a heartbeat—those that adversely affected my family. For example, I would have attended our daughter's high school graduation rather than being in

Germany to help win a piece of business for that office. I would have celebrated that important wedding anniversary with the Beautiful Bonnie rather than attending a finance meeting in New York City. I would have taken more family vacations and not left in the middle of some. In hindsight, I understand why so many times Bonnie considered me an asshole.

My incredibly successful business career may never have been as successful without my passion, drive, and total commitment. And to be honest, my terrific forty-five-year marriage may not have been quite so terrific without my business success. I'll never know now whether a change on either side of the equation would have been meaningful.

I do know that I still plan to work until I'm 100, but it will no longer be at a desk in front of employees. I'll always be a Huckster; it's in my DNA. So for my next thirty years, I'll be Huckstering exclusively with the fun, smart, interesting people I love—and when time allows, people like that other than Bonnie, Alison, Brett, Logan, Hutton and Ripley.

A perfect ending could be a great meal, a bottle of truly fine Cabernet, and Bonnie telling me that I wasn't such a bad asshole after all.

ABOUT THE AUTHOR

Huckster is a humorous account of Ron Elgin's forty-year career in the intensely challenging, extraordinarily competitive and sometimes insanely whacky advertising agency business. A friend once told him "the very idea of you becoming a success isn't just funny, it's fucking hilarious!" That comment inspired him to share his delightfully entertaining history from gas station attendant to mud-hopper to college kid to Army officer to co-founding an agency that grew to a quarter billion dollars in billings with clients such as Holland America Line, McDonald's, Jansport, Ste. Michelle Wine Estates, and Nordstrom.

His philosophy of not working with or for assholes, coupled with hiring people better than himself and a strong belief that the harder you work, the luckier you get, not only put his agency in the national limelight but, at the same time, enabled him to help lead a number of other successful companies as well as non-profit enterprises. His four decades of business successes, failures, and experiences will instruct, educate, inform, and keep you laughing for hours.

Ron's primary residence is in Seattle where he lives with his beautiful, extremely bright and extremely patient wife of forty-five years, Bonnie. As their bones get older, they're spending more and more time in Laguna Beach with "the world's most wonderful daughter," Alison; and equally wonderful son-in-law, Brett; granddaughter, Logan; and grandsons, Hutton and Ripley.

ACKNOWLEDGMENTS

I'm not going to write a paragraph on every employee who was a significant contributor to the agency; there were just too many and this section would be longer than the book itself. However, there were several who took the time to put their memories on paper for me and others who spent time reminding me face-to-face of our experiences together. This book is significantly better because of their contributions. Here are the biggest contributors in no particular order: Jack Anderson, CEO Hornall Anderson; Tom Phillips, Microsoft executive; Frank Palmer, CEO DDB Canada; Scott Battishill, founder Curator; Dan Miller, VP Curator; Account Director Wunderman, Bill Fritsch, CEO Digital Kitchen; Kevin Nolan, founder Craters of the Moon; Sydney Hunsdale, CFO EMEA—VivaKi; Scott Manning, partner Moroch; Vandy Kindred, writer-extraordinaire; Kevin Burrus, partner Augustavo Burrus; Bill Drake, owner Drake Cooper. A special mention to my good friend Michael Nalley, owner of the very creative agency Wax and photographer extraordinaire, who not only conceived the cover layout and shot the photos but also talked me out of my original stupid title and into *Huckster*. Sorry if I left you out. If I did, feel free to leave me out of your book.